BOOKS BY DOROTHY CLARKE WILSON

THE BROTHER
THE HERDSMAN
PRINCE OF EGYPT
HOUSE OF EARTH
JEZEBEL
THE GIFTS
DR. IDA
TAKE MY HANDS

DOROTHY CLARKE WILSON

take my hands

THE REMARKABLE STORY OF DR. MARY VERGHESE

McGRAW-HILL BOOK COMPANY, INC.
New York Toronto London

TAKE MY HANDS

Library of Congress Catalog Card Number: 62-22228

70747
Eighth Printing

The author makes grateful acknowledgment to:

Dr. Paul Brand, for his cooperation and support throughout the project, Miss J. M Sharp and Mr. A. G. Jefcoate of the British Friends of Vellore, who inspired the idea of writing the book;

Dr. John Carman, Director of the Vellore Christian Medical College and Hospital, and his wife Naomi, for reading the manuscript and offering valuable criticisms;

Dr. Hugh Johnson, for his account of the episode that begins the book, and for other helpful material;

Dr. Chandrahasan Johnson, for his account of the accident;

Dr. Howard Rusk, for permission to quote material from certain of his articles and speeches;

Innumerable friends of Dr. Mary Verghese who supplied details, anecdotes, and personal recollections, including the following: Dr. Aleyamma Bhaktavizyam, Dr. and Mrs. Mammen Cherian, Dr. Carol Jameson, Dr. Grace Koshi, Miss Helen North, Dr. N. Palani, Drs B M and Ramani Pulimood, Mr. Sadagopan, Dr. Ida B. Scudder, Miss Effie C. Wallace; and finally to Dr. Mary herself, as well as to the members of her family, for sharing with all of us the intimate details of her unusual experience.

I

In the hospital of the Vellore Christian Medical College, in South India, one October day in 1958, Dr. Hugh Johnson, an American plastic surgeon, donned a mask with a sense of keen expectancy. He was about to observe an unusual operation by an unusually competent young surgeon.

"You must see Doctor Mary operate," he had been told by an enthusiastic colleague. "She's more than a good surgeon. She's an artist."

Entering an operating room, Dr. Johnson, who had come to the college for a term of service on a Fulbright grant, regarded with interest the slender figure seated at the low table under the floodlight.

There was nothing unusual in the fact that the surgeon was a woman, for in this institution, founded by Dr. Ida Scudder a half century earlier, half of the students and a much higher percentage of the graduates were women. Nor was it strange that the surgeon should be seated at her work, for operations on the hand demand exacting precision.

"This is the Doctor Johnson we've been hearing so much about," said a nurse, introducing the visitor. "Doctor Johnson, meet Doctor Mary Verghese."

As the American doctor came closer, a pair of merry dark eyes lifted in a flash of welcome, hinting of attractive girlish features hidden under the surgical mask, then lowered with renewed intentness. Dr. Johnson watched the fingers resume their delicate task of transplanting tendons that would restore function to a hand deformed by leprosy.

The operation itself, unheard of a few years before, still held the interest of novelty. It had been devised and perfected by a young Englishman, Dr. Paul Brand, here in this very medical center.

"I've heard a lot about you, Doctor Verghese," said Dr. Johnson with friendly interest.

The dark eyes lifted again, slightly wary. "What have you heard?"

"That you're an expert at this particular job you're doing."

"Good!" The eyes brimmed with warmth. "I hope it is true. If it is, then you have heard everything about me that is worth knowing."

The fingers continued to perform their miracle on the twisted and useless hand, detaching the tendon of a wrist muscle from its insertion, then suturing to it a free tendon graft taken from the patient's forearm and splitting it into four slips. The slips were then passed through the tunnels of the hand and sutured to the tendons on the back of each finger. One day, after healing and therapy, the hand would be able to move again at the knuckles, to handle objects, even to manipulate tools.

Occasionally the surgeon spoke reassuringly in Tamil to the patient, who was fully conscious. The American regarded the man with unusual professional curiosity, for in his area of interest psychological factors were often more important than physical in determining medical procedures. What emotions lay hidden behind the stolid features? Hope? The resignation which so often accompanies suffering in India? Resentment at the contrast between the young surgeon's supple fingers and his own claw, between her smooth skin and his disease-ravaged face? The patient's eyes, fixed with doglike intentness on the masked face, seemed to hold no resentment, only a rather surprising humility.

As the intricate operation progressed, the American was more and more impressed. Once he remarked, "They tell me Doctor Ida was noted for her patience and painstaking skill in surgery. She had a way with human tissues, someone said. It was as if she could almost re-create them. You must be like her."

"Thank you." The briefly lifted eyes were radiant. "That is the highest tribute you could pay any woman graduate of Vellore—telling her she is like Doctor Ida. Even though it isn't so," the surgeon added with a twinkle.

The operation was finished, the hand neatly encased in a plaster cast. Dr. Johnson rose and stood waiting for Mary Verghese to rise also and walk with him from the operating room. Instead, an attendant entered and, grasping the handles of the chair in which she had been sitting, wheeled her from the room. The American stared after them, aghast. He had not even noticed that she had been sitting in a wheel chair! He was glad that his mask hid the embarrassment which must have shown in his face.

He was even more grateful for its protection a moment later when he entered the adjoining room. Dr. Mary was already scrubbing for her next operation.

"This case coming up may be of special interest to you," she told him with matter-of-fact briskness. "It's a free tendon graft for the thumb, but the paralysis has also caused wasting of the first dorsal interosseus muscle. I wish I had your skill for filling in the depression."

"Then why not let me help?" he returned promptly. "I haven't my instruments here, but I can get them from College Hill. I can easily be back by the time you've finished on the thumb."

Dr. Mary agreed with alacrity. "Would you? It would mean so much to this boy! Appearances are so important to a patient who still bears the marks of arrested leprosy!"

"I'm sure a dermis graft can be done for it," continued Dr. Johnson, relieved to be able to cover his reaction with professional glibness. "It's the same type of graft we do for depressions on the cheek."

Dr. Mary lifted her expressive eyes to his. The warmth in their depths seemed suddenly ignited by a spark of—could it be mischief? She slipped off her mask.

"For a cheek like this?" she asked.

The American surgeon barely stifled an exclamation. Instead of the smooth girlish features he had anticipated, he saw a grievously scarred cheek, deeply depressed.

"Well—no," he managed. "I'm afraid that's too deep for a dermis graft. That needs a bone graft. "But why—?" He floundered. "You have good surgeons here—"

"Why haven't I had it attended to before this?" She finished the question for him. "I just haven't seemed to find the time. I've been too busy."

When she had been wheeled away, Dr. Johnson turned to an attendant.

"Why didn't somebody tell me?" he demanded.

"Tell you what, sir?"

"About Doctor Mary Her—her—"

"Oh!" Light broke. "You mean her accident."

"How did it happen?" Removing his mask, the doctor wiped his perspiring face. He was still shaken.

"A bus, sir. It overturned, full of students and residents. Doctor Mary suffered the worst injuries. It's really amazing how well she manages, for a paraplegic."

"A paraplegic! You mean she's—?"

"Yes, sir. Paralyzed from the waist down."

The doctor was almost without words. "It's strange nobody told me."

The attendant himself looked puzzled. "I guess we just didn't think of it, sir. You see, no one of us here in the hospital thinks of Doctor Mary as anything but a jolly good surgeon."

And that, thought Dr. Johnson later, was the most remarkable fact of all. What sort of young woman was this who could make people feel that the loss of a pretty face and the use of half a body was unimportant?

The story of Dr. Mary Verghese is the answer to this question.

2

When did her story really begin? With her decision to become a doctor? With her birth on May 27, 1925, in the native state of Cochin, now a part of Kerala, South India? Were you to ask the question of Mary herself, she would probably tell you that it began at least sixteen hundred, probably nearer two thousand, years before she was born. For there is a tradition that Saint Thomas, one of the twelve apostles, introduced Christianity to her Indian ancestors soon after the middle of the first century. Whether or not this is actually true, it is a matter of record that there has been an organized Christian community along the Malabar coast since at least the fourth century of the Christian era. Because of its affiliation from early history with the Church of Antioch, this community has been known through the centuries as the Syrian Christian Church.

To the child Mary, as to all Syrian Christians of India, the visit of Saint Thomas was more than tradition. It was fact, as unquestioned a verity of her small world as the giant coconut palms, the Indian Ocean with its sprawling blue lagoons and lazy backwaters, the dust, the heat, the drenching monsoons, the lavish abundance of green foliage, the spotless white saris and *dhotis* worn by her neighbors, and the big black umbrellas they carried. She learned to savor the story's spice and flavor almost as early as she did those of shrimps and mangoes and coconuts and curries.

It was usually *Amma,* Mother, who told it, for though *Appan,* Father, was the more religious of the two, he was far better at keeping books and supervising coconut groves than at storytelling. In Mary's time it was often her brother Joseph, the book lover, pet-named *Babi,* her senior by less than two years, who set the narrative stream in motion.

"Tell us a story, Amma? Tell us about Saint Thomas?"

Amma needed no second invitation. John, the oldest and most mischievous of her three sons, had long ago discovered that interest in the apostle's adventures could even divert Amma's attention from the *irkili,* or coconut rib, used as an instrument of discipline. Babi had less occasion to practice such strategy, because Amma had grown more patient and lenient with the years.

"Saint Thomas." She repeated the name with both zest and reverence, her devotion to the fabled saint equaled only by her love of storytelling. The tale flowed from her lips in the musical Malayalam language.

"Once, nineteen hundred years ago, there was a great king in India named Gondophares. He wanted to build a big palace for himself, the biggest and most beautiful palace in all the world. So he engaged a merchant, by name Abbaneese, to bring him an expert from the land called Palestine. Abbaneese met Saint Thomas in the streets of Jerusalem.

" 'I hear you are a builder,' he said to the apostle.

" 'It is true that my Master was a carpenter,' replied Saint Thomas.

" 'Can you build a palace, the finest in all the world?'

" 'I can build houses fit for God to dwell in,' said the apostle. 'What palace could be finer than that?'

"Abbaneese was overjoyed. 'What, indeed!' he exclaimed. 'You must come with me.'

"So he brought Saint Thomas to King Gondophares in India."

Though not as fond of stories as her brother Babi, Mary absorbed every detail of the unfolding legend—how the king had explained to Saint Thomas the details of the palace to be constructed and given him a large amount of money for building it; how the apostle had spent all the money for the poor and all his time in preaching the gospel of Jesus; how when the king heard that his money had been wasted, he was wild with anger and had the saint brought before him.

" 'Where is my palace?' he demanded.

" 'I have built you a palace,' replied Saint Thomas. 'The finest in all existence.'

" 'Where is it? I want to see it.'

" 'You cannot see it now,' the saint explained. 'Your palace is in heaven.'

"The king put the apostle in prison and decided to hang him. But one night the king dreamed a dream, and in his dream he saw a wonderful palace prepared for him in heaven. The next morning he released Saint Thomas, and later the king and all his family became Christians."

After that, Amma continued, the apostle came to Malabar and made many converts. He built seven churches, one of them at Parur, just across the harbor from their own village of Cherai. Later he traveled to the Madras area on the eastern coast, and here the Brahmins became so enraged at his success that they determined to kill him.

"Ayoh, kashtam! What a pity!" At this point the story became so suspenseful that even the older boys, John and George, bored by its frequent repetition, pricked up their ears. "South of the city of Madras there is a rocky hill called the Little Mount. Here the holy one sometimes went for several days, living in a cave and going to the top of the mount to pray. And here in the cave his enemies found him, stealing up behind him while he knelt in prayer and thrusting a lance into his body."

"But they didn't kill him that time, did they?" inquired Babi breathlessly.

"You know they didn't," scoffed George in disgust, more interested in contests with his live younger brother than in the fate of the dead saint. "You've heard the story dozens of times: how he ran to another cave on the big St. Thomas' Mount and how his enemies chased him and he climbed out of a hole in the top of the cave and got away—"

"Keep still, can't you!" erupted the outraged Babi. "You *mandan,* stupid! You don't know how to tell a story."

"Oh! So I'm *mandan,* am I?" blustered George. "Do you want to know what you are? You're a *kizhangan,* idiot. You're—"

"*Nirthu!* Stop!" It was second sister Annamma, not Amma, who usually called a halt to her two youngest brothers' incessant quarreling. Though Mary's senior by only eight years, she was fast developing habits of stern supervision, not to say bossiness. "Quiet, both of you!"

"*Athay,* yes, he went to the Great Mount," continued Amma, once more lost in the story. "And it was there that his enemies finally found him. Kneeling on a great stone, he was, when a Brahmin came and transfixed his body with a lance. It was on the twenty-first of December, they say, in the sixtieth year of our Lord. The stone where he knelt is now the central altar of the great Cathedral. If you go to Madras you can see it."

"Did you ever go?" inquired Babi eagerly.

"*Illa,* no," regretted Amma. "Never have I been beyond the mountains. But it is the dream of my life to go."

"Some day I will take you," promised Babi.

"You will not," protested George hotly. "I will take her. It is my right, being older."

Babi's handsome face flushed. "Not much older. What's a year?"

"Nearly two years," corrected George, adding with his usual outspoken, sometimes brutal, candor, "Besides, you're sickly, not strong like me. It is probably a wild place, Madras, and you could not protect her so well."

Babi lunged toward him. "So I'm sickly, am I? I'll show you!"

"Nirthu!" Amma practised no leniency when blows appeared imminent. "Shall I get the *irkili*? Out of this house, both of you! Out, I say!"

They complied, George slamming with noisy disgust, Babi stalking with injured dignity, for he was a stubborn and sensitive child. Once, when banished by Amma in this manner, he had gone out and stood by the gate for hours, moodily nursing his anger, refusing to come in even for dinner. Of the two, Mary thought she preferred George to Babi. He was hot tempered and outspoken, but at least you knew where you stood with him. With Babi you could never be quite sure.

Besides, Mary could not at this stage forgive her youngest brother for an incident reported as taking place soon after her birth. The jealous Babi had deeply resented her appropriation of his junior status. One day when a fisherwoman had come to the house peddling her wares, Babi had tried to drive an unusual bargain.

"Leave us all the fish," he had suggested furtively. "Then put my new sister in your bag and take her home with you."

Of course John, her oldest brother, was really Mary's favorite. And why not? Did he not always take her part when he felt that their parents were partial to sister Martha, pet-named *Kunjamma,* the small one? Two years younger than Mary and much less shy, Kunjamma was the darling of the family and especially of her brother Babi, who by the time she arrived had apparently graduated from the role of protected to that of protector.

In these early years three elements constituted Mary's small world: HOME, FAMILY, CHURCH.

HOME was the big sprawling two-story house wtih its walls of whitewashed cement, its red-tiled roofs, its verandahs, its barred windows with their wooden shutters to keep out the noonday heat. It was the courtyard surrounding the house and leading to the front gate, its low wall of tiles a mass of red and orange crotons, its smooth cement surface covered with white sea sand that glistened like jeweled toe-rings when you burrowed into it with your bare feet. Once each year, during the September rice harvest, the sand was swept off so the rice could be spread out to dry. Every day for two or three weeks there was great excitement in watching the new grain poured out in shining cascades and spread around each morning, taken up and stored in the paddy shed each night.

HOME was also the acre-and-a-half compound filled with mango, jackfruit, tamarind, and plantain trees, but mostly with coconut palms, their long scaly brown trunks topped with spreading fronds like huge green umbrellas. Mary had her own mango tree just south of the front courtyard and her chamba tree to the west of it, planted and watered with her own hands and nursed in jealous competition with similar projects of her brothers and sisters. HOME was the outdoor pool in which Mary insisted on such long baths that the family dubbed her "Duck."

And HOME was also the sweetness of ripe custard apples and of the "tender" coconuts thrown down by the pickers at harvest time, the puckering sourness of green tamarinds. It was the smells of simmering curries and chutneys so hot that the very anticipation of their flavors would make your throat smart deliciously. It was wind clattering like rain in the tops of dry palms and rain pounding like sea breakers on the roof tiles. It was an *ayah*—nursemaid—to take care of your needs when you were small and servants to provide for them when you grew older. It was clean clothes and healthy noise and affection and a full stomach.

"Because of Babi we can't have shrimp today," John would complain, disgusted with the apparent favoritism that catered to his younger brother's food dislikes. But neither John nor any other of the children of P. V. Verghese ever complained because there was not enough to eat.

No, HOME was not hunger, though there was often hunger not far outside the walls of the snug compound. Sometimes during the monsoon months Mary would hear Amma telling Maria, the cook, to make up baskets of food for some of the coconut pickers whose families did not have enough to eat.

It was not poverty, either, though Mary had only to step out the gate and walk down the path to see the thatched hovels of the poor crowding every available space, their women in ragged saris, their naked children playing in the dust. Some of them were tenants of her father or other neighboring landowners. Others were mere squatters, their makeshift huts clinging to bits of unoccupied soil, depending for their meager livelihood on the seasonal work in coconut groves and rice fields. Most were lower-caste Hindus, some Pulayas, the plowmen, some Kanakkas, those who with their ancestors from time immemorial had climbed the coconut trees to pluck the fruit; but the majority belonged to a caste called Ezhava, which had no special occupation.

And, thanks to wider spaces and superior education and cleanliness, HOME was not prey to the sicknesses that overspread the tropical country like the flooding waters of the monsoons: malaria, smallpox, leprosy, elephantiasis. Only occasionally did disease approach the compound gate, as in the form of the beggar Joseph.

Never would Mary forget her first experience with Joseph.

"Praise to the Lord! Praise to the Lord!"

She was playing in the courtyard when she heard the high piercing cry, repeated over and over and growing steadily louder. Curious, she ran to the open gate.

A strange-looking figure was coming down the path, otherwise deserted, which was odd, for there were usually a dozen or more people in sight—idlers, romping children, women with babies on their hips.

The man—that is, it looked like a man, though Mary could not be sure—moved with a queer, stiff sort of gait. As he came closer, she saw that both his feet were heavily bandaged. His hands also were wound all about with dirty cloths, and the protruding fingers did not look like fingers at all. They were unshapely stumps. It was his face however, that looked strangest of all. He had no eyebrows. His skin hung loosely over his cheekbones, and there was a queer flatness where his nose should have been. Fascinated, the child watched him come closer.

"*Adukkallai!* Don't go near!" A hand suddenly seized her arm and pulled her roughly back through the gate. "Come away—quick!"

It was Theresia, called "Muthi" by the children, the *ayah* who looked after Mary and her younger sister Kunjamma. Mary was half frightened, half indignant.

"*Nirthu!* Let go of me, Muthi. You hurt."

"Then do as I tell you. Come away from the gate."

"But why? I want to see that man—"

"Better for you not to see. *Pakavum,* dangerous!"

"But why? Can't you hear what he's saying? 'Praise to the Lord!' "

To Mary's intense displeasure Theresia dragged her forcibly into the house. "It's the beggar Joseph," Theresia reported to her mistress. "He's out by the gate."

"I know. I heard him," said Amma. Though her voice was calm, there was the same glint of fear in her eyes as in Theresia's. "I've asked Maria to take him some food and a few annas. If he has money, perhaps he can go for treatment at the hospital in Ayyampilly."

"May I go with Maria?" asked Mary, still more curious than frightened.

"No," said Amma. "Until the beggar leaves, you are to go no farther than the verandah."

Mary ran through the house to the kitchen end of the verandah and watched Maria move slowly across the yard, holding a dilapidated basket. The closer she came to the gate the more reluctantly she moved. Finally with one swift motion she darted forward and set down the basket in the space between the gateposts, then darted back again.

"There you are!" she cried. "Come and get it if you're still there. And you can keep the basket."

A shadow fell across the space, and Mary saw one of the bandaged hands reach out and slide under the basket's handle.

"Praise to the Lord! Praise to the Lord!"

The shrill voice grew fainter and fainter until she could hear it no longer. And then slowly the path came to life again. A man ambled past carrying a huge bale of coconut leaves. A group of women walked by, chattering, heads loaded high with water pots. Children shouted and scampered.

Afterward Amma explained to Mary why Theresia and Maria and the others had been afraid. Joseph was a leper. Leprosy was a terrible disease which people were afraid of catching. No person who had it must ever be touched.

Mary nodded soberly. A chill went up and down her spine. She had heard about lepers in Bible stories at Sunday School. No wonder Theresia had cried, "*Pakavum!*" The very word *leper* suggested something evil, like "sin" and "outer darkness" and "gnashing of teeth." She had known there were lepers long ago in a faraway land called

Palestine, but to discover that there were some of them right here in her own modern land of India was frightening!

"Praise to the Lord! Praise to the Lord!"

She was to hear the cry often throughout her childhood and youth, followed by her mother's saying quickly, "There's Joseph! We must hurry and give him something!" And sometimes it would be Mary instead of Maria who would carry the basket to the gate, darting forward to place it on the ground, then drawing quickly back again. But unlike Maria, she would linger to watch Joseph thrust his bandaged hand awkwardly under the handle, then walk stiffly away down the path.

3

If HOME was the outer shell enclosing Mary's small world, then FAMILY was the living organism snugly filling it.

Appan, of course, was the head of FAMILY, as his male ancestors had been for centuries before him. In spite of his scant five feet six, he seemed to the child Mary an awesome and aloof giant, for he paid little attention to his offspring in their early years.

"My children have a father," Amma would complain good-humoredly, "only after they are five years old."

Once they entered school Appan took an intense and personal interest in every one of his children. Perhaps his inability to finish his own education made him more determined to provide fully for theirs. He had been in college in Trichinopoly when his father had died. His two brothers had been too young to assume responsibility. Two of his three sisters had still been dependents. Discouraged, he had had to leave college and come home to manage the coconut groves. Over the years he had maintained the family's moderate prosperity and become a respected leader in both church and community, often called on unofficially to mediate disputes among his neighbors.

Presiding at a distance over Mary's small but satisfactory world, leading in morning and evening prayers, sitting at the head of table at eight o'clock dinner, he seemed more than Appan, Father. Strong, slightly stern features, with heavy brows and deep-set eyes, accentuated his natural role of parental authority. Curling white hair and mustache, spotless white cotton garments—white *dhoti* and shirt, white shawl draped across both shoulders—endowed him with an almost superhuman aura. It was hard to believe that his pet name was *Kunjooru,* the "small" Verghese!

Names were queer things anyway, thought the child Mary. Her own name for second sister Annamma was *Kochaduthi,* "Second of the two older sisters," while she called first sister Aleyamma *Valiaduthi,* "Big sister," though she was really the smaller of the two. Then there was Babi. Joseph was not really the baby of the family at all, for both she and Kunjamma were younger, but *Babi* he still was. (Yes, and Babi he would still be called twenty-five years later, when he had become a construction engineer!) Even Amma had hard work remembering her third son's real name. One time he came home from primary school saying proudly, "Teacher told head master today, 'Joseph is the best student in the class'!"

Amma looked at him disapprovingly. "Then where are you?" she demanded.

The family name was Puthisseril, but it would appear nowhere except in the first initials of all members of the family. Hence, brother John was P. V. (Puthisseril Verghese) John. His son would be P. J. (Puthisseril John) Verghese, because the eldest son was always named after his grandfather. John's second son would be P. J. something else, probably a biblical name, though not necessarily. The name "Verghese" meant "Saint George."

Girls followed the same custom until they married. Mary's name was really P. V. (Puthisseril Verghese) Mary. Unlike most Syrian Christian girls' names, hers did not end in "amma," which was a general female suffix. But she did not mind. She rather liked being different.

Amma's family name was Mazuvancheriparambath, so perhaps it was a good custom, confining its common usage to mere initials!

FAMILY was an expansive organism, like some of the shellfish which kept building themselves larger and larger shell chambers to live in. Mary knew at an early age that it included far more than her father and mother and brothers and sisters. There was Uncle Matthew, Appan's brother, the only one in the family who drank tea instead of coffee. When he came to visit they made quantities of tea, enough so he could follow his usual custom of a cup each hour. Then there was Appan's first cousin Abraham, who was always poking fun at Mary's shyness.

"That daughter of yours," he boomed one day to Amma. "I heard a rumor in the village that she's both deaf and dumb. Is it true?"

Flushing, Mary took refuge in the bulging fan at the back of Amma's white *dhoti*. But her mother refused to spare her. "Ask her some questions, and you'll find out," she retorted. "Ask her if she wants to go to my uncle's house."

"Do you want to go to your mother's uncle's house?" demanded Cousin Abraham.

"*Seri* yes," Mary murmured.

"Now ask her why," prompted Amma.

"Why?" parroted Cousin Abraham.

"To see *Uppappan*," replied Mary with dignity

So great was her fondness for Uppappan, Great Uncle, that for his sake she forgot her shyness.

Valiamma, Big Mother, was a part of FAMILY too, with all her six children. Valiamma was Amma's aunt. She lived in Parur, the big town on the mainland across the backwaters from Cherai, and to visit her they had to ride in a *vallam*, one of the wooden boats covered with a canopy of woven reeds. Mary liked visiting Valiamma. She was a motherly person, like Amma, and her house, also in a big plot of coconut trees, smelled of mango preserves and shrimp chutneys.

Though all the six children were older than Mary, the girl cousins, Kunjannam and Aleyamma, were near her age. Valiamma's sons were as noisy and energetic as her own brothers, so there was plenty of fun and excitement.

With such journeys the child's small world expanded. Its bounds were no longer the village of Cherai on the island of Vypeen. There were other villages on the island's fifteen-mile length: Ayyampilly to the south, where the hospital was; Pallipuram, two miles to the north, where they went each year to a big church festival and market, bringing back exciting treasures of silks, brasses, sweets, and glass bangles.

With some discoveries her world shrank instead of expanded. To her dismay she learned that most of the island's 80,000 population were Hindus; that only a fifth were Christians and most of them were Roman Catholics. Only a small fraction were Jacobite Syrian Christians like herself Mary found all the many customs and beliefs bewildering.

"It's Onam tomorrow!" she announced one day in August.

"Not for us." Second sister Annamma frowned disapprovingly. "That's a heathen festival."

Mary's face fell. "But Lakshmi says it's to honor a great king named Bali and the god Vishnu—"

"Nirthu!" Even first sister Aleyamma looked horrified. "Vishnu is a Hindu god. You should not even speak his name."

"We have Christmas and Easter for our festivals," explained third sister Thankamma with a superior air.

"They aren't so exciting as Onam," grumbled John, careful not to let his mother and sisters hear. "In some villages at Onam they have big boxing tournaments. No matter how much they bleed, the fighters never give in. And they get wonderful prizes."

John was the athletic member of the family. It was he who insisted that all the younger children do gymnastics regularly. Sometimes he made them stand on their heads for long periods with their legs resting against the wall.

"Don't worry," Amma comforted Mary. "We shall have excitement at Onam also. Remember how we give gifts—clothes and rice and coconuts—to all the workers? And the head man in each caste which works for Appan will come to receive the gifts and in return will bring us big bunches of bananas."

"And our turn will come at Christmas," Aleyamma reminded her. "Remember what fun we have making the stars?"

"Bananas!" scoffed George under his breath. "Stars! While the Hindus have boxing and painted elephants!"

Mary did not agree with her brothers. She thought Christmas was very exciting. Two or three days before, the children started making huge stars out of colored paper stretched over bamboo, several working together and competing to see which group made the best. A little kerosene lamp or candle was placed inside each one, and then Cherukandan, one of the caste which did the climbing during the harvest, hung them in the coconut trees in front of the house. Up the trunk he went, bare feet clinging to the bark, not even using the usual loop of fiber to hold his feet together. There the lighted stars hung, bright colors glowing, when the boy carolers came from the church on Christmas Eve. Afterward there would be fireworks in the courtyard—Roman candles, fiery whirling wheels, sparklers.

Christmas Day was even more thrilling. Getting up before daylight, the family would walk silently along the zigzag path to the church, while stars shone through the lacy fronds over their heads. In the church yard there would be a huge bonfire. After prayers and ceremonies around the fire, a service was held inside the church from four to six o'clock. Then, at home, the long Advent fast was broken. There were delicious holiday foods: *appams* with meat stew; *vatteppams,* a steamed pudding made of sugar, flour, coconut, and toddy; Christmas cake. The servants' and employees' families came to eat the Christmas meal, sitting on mats along the verandahs. Amma helped the servants cook the food, and the children helped Amma serve it. Oh, Christmas and Easter were exciting times! Even Good Friday, most solemn of all holy days, when the whole day was spent in church and there was much kneeling, Mary did not find distasteful.

In fact, next to HOME and FAMILY, CHURCH was the most pervasive reality of her life. She liked the half-mile walk each Sunday morning along the path skirting the coconut plots, where there was no need of umbrellas because the interlacing foliage kept off the sun. She liked the feeling of good clean clothes against her skin, and the sound of the church bell: one bell meaning that there was plenty of time, two that they had better hurry, and three that there was no time at all, for the service was about to begin. She loved the church with its freshly whitewashed walls and its carvings of old gray stone, its three sections seeming to rise tier on tier: first the arched vestibule, then the nave, finally the chancel under the highest roof of all. Yes, and she even enjoyed the two-hour service when the congregation stood most of the time, because Sunday was the day of resurrection, and there should be no prostrating or kneeling as on weekdays. Only during the intercessory prayer and the sermon was it permitted to sit, cross-legged, on the bare cement floor.

The service was a colorful drama. Joseph Achan, the priest, was an impressive chief actor, with his white curling beard, round black cap, and long robes. There was much walking to and fro among the three high altars, much swinging of censers and burning of incense. The grand stage containing the central altar with its wooden cross and elaborate carvings even had a curtain, a beautifully embroidered Persian tapestry screen, which was drawn at the climax of the drama, the mysterious partaking of the Holy Qurbana, or Communion, by the priest.

Once, when a baby, Mary had been an actor in the drama. Seated in the water of the stone baptismal font, she had been held firmly while the priest laid one hand on her head and with the other poured water over her head and shoulders. Then she had been anointed with the *moron*—holy unguent. And often, after confession and absolution, members of the congregation became actors when they partook of the Holy Qurbana. Joseph Achan stood on the altar steps with the shining silver holding the round thin loaves of bread baked right there in the church building. As the people came through the gate of the altar railing, he broke off small bits of bread, previously dipped in wine, and, descending, placed them on the tongues of the communicants.

Mary also came through the gate and knelt, year after year, an awe-struck child, a dutifully reverent schoolgirl, a thoughtfully maturing young woman. But, though CHURCH was an all-pervasive influence in her growing years, religion meant little more than a drama to be observed, prayers to be repeated, a catechism and stories to be learned, an ancient ritual to be followed. The bit of bread and wine was a sweet tang on her tongue, a brief burning in her throat, a slight yet tangible factor in the growth processes of her young body. But it furnished little nourishment for an adventurous and deeply sensitive young spirit.

4

It was SCHOOL that burst the bounds of Mary's small world. When on that June day of her first term she passed through the gate of the family compound and turned right instead of left on the familiar path, it was more than the main island highway that she entered. It was the highroad to worlds that had no bounds—the fascinating worlds of history, of biography, of travel, of philosophy, and especially of science.

The road was wide and sandy and crowded with people carrying baskets and water pots and books and loads of fresh coconuts or leaves and big black umbrellas, for here the trees were wide apart and did not protect from the sun and rain. It ran through a paradise of lush green coconut plots with glimpses of brimming squares of blue and green rice fields bordering the intense blue of the Arabian Sea. Mary traveled the mile to school in the morning with her sisters, Annamma and Thankamma, who were in high school, but she immediately asserted her independence by coming home at night with her new friends, Mariamma and Marthamma.

Her flair for independence showed in other ways also. There were two divisions in her first-year class. The teacher of one, Subadra Amma, was very strict and hence unpopular. It was Mary's good fortune to draw the more lenient Dakshayani Amma, whose class, due doubtless to her popularity, was so large as to be unwieldy.

"Is there anyone here who would be willing to change to the other division?" asked Dakshayani.

No response. The pupils sat motionless at their desks in the crowded classroom. Suddenly Mary put up her hand.

"You will go, my dear?" The teacher beamed in relief.

Mary looked straight ahead, ignoring the shocked stares of her classmates. "If my sisters say it is all right," she replied calmly.

She did not suffer with the change. Subadra Amma, knowing it was her choice, welcomed her with unusual cordiality. When Mary's sisters came at noon from the high school next door to take her to lunch with them, they frequently found her lunching with her teacher.

"Teacher's pet!" scoffed Babi in disgust when such incidents were reported at home during the evening meal.

"*Illa*, no. It is good, not bad," approved Appan. "My daughter is not afraid of running alone instead of with the herd." His long fingers carefully kneaded a portion of rice and curry as his gaze traveled down the table to his seventh offspring. "But see that this special favor becomes not an excuse for neglecting your studies, my child."

Now Mary also had moved into the orbit of Appan's intense paternal interest. He inspected her report cards with concern, his approval always slightly tempered with restraint.

"*Nallathu!* It is good! But let us never be satisfied, daughter. Let us always strive to exceed our own achievements."

She was now included in Appan's strict daily regimen for his children, which prescribed an hour of study each morning after prayers and before breakfast. But the moment Appan left the house or became involved in business with visitors in the reception room off the verandah, John, always the ringleader in mischief, would spring into action.

"He's gone! You stand on guard, Mary. Tell us if he's coming. And leave your books open, all of you. Come on, George and Babi. Let's see which one of you can walk the most steps on your hands. I'll count. *Onnu, rendu, munnu. . . .*"

Then would follow an interval of lively diversion until Mary, or another guard posted, would warn that the visitors had left or Appan was entering the gate, whereupon all would rush back to their desks.

When Appan went on business to Ernakulam, the big city across the backwaters, the children always considered they were having a holiday.

Amma was inclined to wink at the boys' mischief except on occasions when they imperiled the household or their own safety, as when she lifted her eyes one day in horror to see them walking the wires stretched for the drying of clothes between the coconut trees. That day instead of the tender coconuts they were after, they got the *irkili*.

Amma was concerned that they should leave for school with bodies rather than minds well fortified with nourishment. While the study hour was Appan's stern province, it was Amma who presided with equal vigor over the breakfast that followed: milk, fruit, *appams,* and often hearty helpings of *puttu,* a dish of flour and coconut, steamed and eaten with plantains. At noon she dispatched to the school an equally nourishing lunch of rice and curry, which arrived, via a servant's head, steaming hot in its tiered nest of metal vessels. And when the children returned in the afternoon there were more lunches—fruit, sweetmeats, bananas, or sometimes Mary's favorite *kinnathappam,* a steamed pudding made of flour, sugar, and coconut milk—to fortify them until the eight o'clock family dinner of rice and curry.

In spite of this apparent sufficiency Mary frequently received a scolding from Amma for her persistent habit of eating between meals!

If brother John was the playful terrier in the family's strict regimen, the overly conscientious Annamma was its watchdog.

"What time is it?" she would demand of the younger children when they sneaked downstairs at night from the upstairs study room. Then, if it happened to be eight and a half plus ten, she would make it sound even later than it was by saying, "Come back here, children, and get into bed. Don't you know it's five minutes to eight and three quarters?"

But Mary had one bond with Annamma. First sister Aleyamma was never very strong of body. Third sister Thankamma had an attack of fever when she entered her teens. And fifth sister Kunjamma was from infancy a delicate child. Of the five sisters, only Annamma and Mary were blessed with an abundance of strength and good health.

"You Annamma, you Mary," Amma would always call if there was some heavy object to be lifted or some hard task to perform. "*Ividae va,* come here! I need your help."

And Mary's healthily expanding mind kept pace with her growing body. Unlike John, she found the morning study hour no burden. When Mary learned to read she discovered a new world of boundless delight. It was a world of fact, however, rather than of imagination. Fairy tales and romances held small allure. Mary's heroes were mountain climbers, explorers of the faraway, the unknown. Sea shells were no longer toys for playing *ithal,* the childhood game of shells; they were the mysteries of unfathomed oceans and far countries. It became more exciting to hunt for the answers to math problems than to play hide and seek among the little brick cow sheds and storehouses scattered about the compound.

During her four primary years Mary attended the English Girls' School, so called because English was taught from the time a child entered it. In spite of its name there were four boys in her class, and they were a popular minority because of their proficiency in organizing games, chiefly simple country diversions involving much hopping, skipping, and jumping. Aside from this superior genius, their sex held dubious appeal for Mary.

After two years Mary's younger sister Martha—Kunjamma—joined her in school, as irrepressibly talkative in classroom and on playground as Mary was withdrawn and silent. But Mary adored Kunjamma too much to envy her self-assurance and popularity.

Mary was about seven when the household was thrown into sudden turmoil. First sister Aleyamma was going to be married! The groom was a young doctor from Ayyampilly, with whose family the marriage had been arranged, a third party making the preliminary proposals, then the parents of the young people meeting and coming to an agreement.

Mary watched the preparations with mingled excitement and foreboding. It was fun having new clothes and watching the goldsmith who came to the house to make the gold necklaces, bracelets, and earrings which Appan was giving his oldest daughter as part of her dowry. But Mary had a keen sense of impending loss. What was happening to the safe, comfortable shell of FAMILY? It seemed to be cracking right before her eyes!

The excitement finally prevailed. When on the day before the wedding friends and relatives swarmed into the compound bringing gifts and consuming the mountains of specially cooked food, Mary hovered in the background, dark eyes shining, no less happy than the chattering Kunjamma. She listened to the sweet voice of Cousin Saramma, Aunt Maria's daughter, who always sang at weddings—and not without a trace of envy, for she herself was unable to carry a tune.

The next day, at the church service in Ayyampilly, Mary listened to the long solemn ritual which did not change Aleyamma's name, for she was becoming the wife of another Verghese, a common name among Syrian Christians. But it changed Aleyamma, nonetheless. In wonder Mary stared at the familiar face, suddenly so unfamiliar in its frame of white, gold-bordered sari. How could Valiaduthi look so —so *serene* when she was leaving Appan and Amma, going to live with this handsome young stranger whom she did not even know?

But her sister's marriage, Mary found to her relief, merely bulged the shell of FAMILY instead of cracking it. For Aleyamma's home with her doctor husband in Cochin Town, reached by steamboat across the backwaters, became a fascinating place to visit during vacations, with all the allurements of a big seashore city—movies, beaches for swimming, crowded and colorful bazaars And presently there was Joy, Aleyamma's son, just ten years younger than Mary as Aleyamma was ten years older, a chubby curly-haired baby on whom Appan and Amma lavished an excess of affection they had never dared show their own children.

Moving up to middle school over in the high school building, Mary changed from a child's straight frock to the long full skirt and tunic blouse of girlhood. She let her short hair grow into dark glossy braids, never again to be cut. And she had her earlobes pierced for the earrings of gold which Appan bought her in Cochin Town. Now when she danced the folk dance called *kolattam* at the school anniversary festival, her wide skirts billowed, and the slender wands she carried wove and spiraled in rhythm with her tossing braids. It did not really matter to her that the music teacher asked her not to sing for the folk dancing, because she could not do it properly.

Though she found few of her school tasks unpleasant, some of her teachers were hard taskmasters. One, Mr. Rao, was as stern and strict as Subadra Amma, but fortunately his subject was mathematics, which Mary liked better than all others. Tasks at home, however, were a different story. She could remember her multiplication tables through the nineteens and twenties, yet forget that she had been sent to the shop to buy a spool of thread. Asked to bring Appan a cold drink of water from the *kuja,* the porous long-necked clay water jar, she would disappear into the coconut grove and be gone for hours.

"I declare," exclaimed Amma, "if you didn't get good marks in your examinations, I would think you had no brains at all!"

But she did get good marks. In fact, all of Appan's children did. With some of them, especially John, it required stern supervision and artful persuasion, for the fun-loving *Valiangala,* Big Brother, preferred tennis or volleyball any day to the discipline of a school system whose chief end was grooming for the bitter competition of state examinations. But, thanks to Appan's goading, he emerged from high school with the highest mark in his class and went on to join his sister Annamma at the Maharajah's College in Ernakulam. With only half the effort the handsomer but less popular Babi duplicated his brother's record in scholarship and also became a college student. The gay tales of college life, especially Annamma's, enlivened the dinner hours in vacation times, and Mary absorbed them with intense interest, impatient to be a part of their widening world.

By now she was in high school herself, the change after three years of middle school having been accomplished with a minimum of upheaval, for both were conducted in the same building, a long rectangular structure of whitewashed brick and red tiles. Graduation into high school was largely a matter of entering different doors.

The institution was called Union High School because it had been started by three different religious communities—Jacobites, Roman Catholics, and Hindus—who had cooperated to receive a grant from the government. Though it was a coeducational school, boys and girls were divided, occupying seats on opposite sides of the rooms. As in other parts of India, custom permitted no social mingling of the sexes in adolescence. Although football, volleyball, and tennis were provided for the boys, the girls had little organized recreation.

Mary felt no deprivation. Always strong and healthy, she found outlets for her abundant physical energy in walking the mile to school and back, running about the compound, and practicing brother John's prescribed gymnastics until she could stand on her head with feet against the wall for minutes at a time.

And there was no dearth of exercise for her keen intellect. Having passed her middle school examinations with marks high enough to please even Appan, she eagerly began her high school courses, especially those related to science. Her questioning mind applied the same principles of reason to all areas of living as to chemistry and mathematics. She had endless arguments with John, who persisted in clinging to some of the common village superstitions.

"No!" he told her sharply when he was starting for college and she accompanied him to the gate eating a banana. "Throw that away or take it back into the house. Don't you know it's bad luck to start a journey when somebody is eating?"

Mary was more annoyed than amused, for she knew he was not joking.

"You Valiangala!" she scolded her big brother. "You should be ashamed. And you studying to be an engineer! Don't they teach you the laws of cause and effect in college?"

"Athay!" John replied defensively. "But I'd rather be on the safe side, just in case there's something in all these stories they tell. Karthikayan says he knew a man who left home when somebody was eating and he died before the day was over."

"An uneducated servant!" scoffed Mary. "You'd take his word above that of your college professors? Why don't you try generating electricity with black magic?"

But John stubbornly refused to leave until she had finished the banana, and Mary just as stubbornly took her time about it, even though both knew he was likely to miss the steamboat.

The lively reports of college life about the dinner table would have kindled her ambition—if it were not already at white heat.

"I'd like to be an engineer," she mused once when John had been grumbling about the difficulty of one of his scientific courses. "It would be wonderful, building—changing the world—creating—"

John burst into a howl of laughter. "Hear that? Hear what Little Sister says? She'd like to be an engineer!"

"She was joking, of course," said third sister Thankamma soberly. "Who ever heard of a woman engineer?"

Appan did not laugh. "A woman can do constructive things," he told Mary gently, "even if she cannot become an engineer."

"What?" asked Mary bluntly, both hurt and angry.

"She can teach," said Appan. "She can be a lawyer. Occasionally one even finds woman doctors. Several have come from this very village."

"I don't want to teach," said Mary stubbornly. "I don't want to be a lawyer. I don't—" She stopped. Was it the tang of her favorite shrimp chutney that seemed suddenly to set her pulses tingling?

"Want me to tell you what you'll do?" teased John with affectionate indulgence. "It's easy. You'll go to college, of course, like the rest of us. And then—"

Mary held her breath. "Then—" she echoed.

"You'll get married."

"No!" Mary gasped. "I will not!"

"How do you know you won't?"

Mary could not answer. She felt suddenly uncertain and helpless. Was it true? Would she be like Aleyamma, who had learned little since her marriage except how to embroider? Like Annamma, whose marriage to a stranger named George was even now being arranged? She did not want to be married, at least not for a long, long time. She wanted to keep on learning things, to discover, to explore, to travel to far places, to create. And more than all else, she wanted to be dependent on no one, certainly on no strange man. She wanted to walk by herself along the adventurous road of learning and doing, on her own two strong and sturdy limbs.

5

Even for a student like Mary the high school examinations loomed formidably. Not that she feared she would not pass—she wanted desperately to excel, not for herself so much as to please Appan. Two of his sons, John and Babi, had won the school's Kunjavara Prize, given each year to the student ranking highest in the state examinations. Mary determined to show Appan that a daughter could be as capable of scholarly achievement as a son.

She had always done well in the annual tests, covering each year's subjects, but these final comprehensive examinations over the whole three years' work were different. Failure would be almost the equivalent of public disgrace. Success would be a matter of pride for the community as well as for the family.

Mary studied for the ordeal with a fierce intensity. There was no need of Appan's pre-breakfast regimenting. Amma worried because she passed by the most tempting after-school lunches, barely tasting her favorite *kinnathappam*.

"Of what use being a scholar," she scolded, "if you have not the strength to lift a book?"

Mary won the prize. Part of it was a book, the autobiography of a northern Indian who was becoming more and more famous, even as far south as Cochin. His name was Jawaharlal Nehru.

"*Nallathu*, good!" pronounced Appan with satisfaction. For Mary the one word was more of a reward than the prize itself.

To her disappointment she could not go immediately to college, for it was a university rule that only a student fourteen and a half years of age or older could matriculate. Mary was in reality fifteen, but for some reason the date of her birth had been incorrectly registered. It was necessary that she stay at home for a year.

Though she fretted at the delay, she tried to make good use of the interval. Previously she had never been allowed to spend time in the kitchen because her parents had felt that it would interfere with her studies. Now she helped Amma supervise Gouri and Karthikayan, as they did the cooking, and she prepared market lists for Pappachan, who, in addition to being supervisor of the coconut groves, did the family shopping, for it was not the custom for women in this part of India to move freely in the bazaars. She even took lessons in embroidery from Aleyamma, who after her marriage had studied needlework in a school in Madras, but she never became as proficient in the art as Kunjamma, who spent much of her leisure time embroidering counterpanes and cushions.

To Amma's delight, Mary now lost her childish lankiness and became almost plump, looking so mature in the new saris which took the place of long skirts and blouses that Kunjamma, much shorter and two years younger, seemed a child beside her.

Amma's pleasure was tinctured with regret that Mary wore a sari rather than what she, Amma, considered to be the proper Christian woman's dress.

Mary tried to be patient, pointing out that it was no longer the style for young Syrian Christians to wear the *dhoti* with a bulky fan at the back, a white blouse and a half sari, wrapped once around. She would feel as much out of place as in a Cochin Hindu woman's fanless *dhoti* and colored blouse.

"I know," sighed Amma. "Times change. But it is not good. Syrian Christian women have worn white for centuries."

Reading Nehru's autobiography, listening to her brothers' guarded comments on world conditions, Mary became aware of other changes in the making far more momentous than women's style of dress. It was 1940 now, and Europe was at war. The fires of nationalism were sweeping India, not only in the provinces directly under British colonial control but also in the more than five hundred native states like Cochin and Travancore. Members of the nationalist Congress Party, many of them young men like Mary's brothers, had gone to jail by the thousands in Gandhi's campaigns of civil disobedience. Though the campaigns had won certain concessions from Britain in the new Constitution of 1935, India was still a long way from independence. Now the nationalists had been further shocked and aroused by the British action in declaring India a belligerent in the war without her consent.

"It isn't that we don't condemn German aggression," explained Babi earnestly in reply to Mary's puzzled questions. "We do. But we want to make our own decisions. Let Britain give us our independence, or even promise it to us as soon as the war is over. They'll find we're willing enough to defend both our freedom and theirs. But until they do. . . ."

"Take care," advised Appan with a sternness he did not often show. "You are in college to get an education, not to become involved in political problems that are not your concern."

"My country's freedom is my concern," retorted Babi hotly. "Don't you want India to be free?"

"Yes, of course," replied Appan. "But these things come slowly. Leave them to older and wiser minds than yours. You have a brilliant future. You can serve your country best by going to college, not to prison."

Babi did not argue, but Mary saw his eyes darken and his lips compress. After that he and George spoke of such things only when Appan was out of earshot.

At last the year was over, and Mary moved out of the constricted island world to Ernakulam, the capital of Cochin State, where the Maharajah's College was. Though only twelve miles from Cherai, Ernakulam seemed almost another world. A seaport city since the completion of its harbor development only the year before, it was a rapidly growing commercial and residential center, the hub of the most densely populated area of India. Along its wide, picturesque main street moved a bewildering array of human life and vehicles, all strange to Vypeen: busses, automobiles, hand-drawn carts and rickshas; paled faced foreigners in shorts and sun helmets; Indians in *dhotis* and shirts, in Western trousers and turbans, in saffron robes, in the ash-strewn half nakedness of Hindu *sadhus;* white Jews and black Jews from their centuries-old settlements; beggars with the monstrous appendages of elephantiasis, so common in the area that it was known as "Cochin leg"; and occasionally the splendid spectacle of the Maharajah with his limousine and mounted guards and painted elephants, descended from his residence in the Hill Palace five miles away.

Mary had caught glimpses of it before, but now she was a part of it. Like third sister Thankamma, with whom she roomed in the

Y.W.C.A. the first year, she soon became as accustomed to the motley confusion as to the coconut groves and brimming rice fields of home. The Y.W.C.A. was virtually a hostel for non-Catholic Christian students from both Cochin and Travancore, most girls from the latter state attending other colleges than the Maharajah's. Hindu women students usually lived in the government hostel. There was a Christian hostel also for men students, where Babi resided.

The Maharajah's College, in 1940, was one of three institutions in the state of Cochin where women were permitted to enroll. A state institution, it was affiliated at this time with the University of Madras.

Knowing that it was her parents' plan to give both college and professional education to their three sons and to give all their daughters at least a college education, Mary was determined to prove herself worthy of the maximum.

"It is possible," Appan had promised vaguely, "that if you do well in college, you might go on for higher studies."

"Higher studies" might mean one of two things. After the first two years of college, she could go on for the further two years necessary to take her B.A. examinations, or she could transfer to another institution for professional training in some such field as medicine. She was not sure yet which she wanted. But of one thing she was sure. She had a God-given talent for study, and she must make full use of it. Her courses were English and Malayalam, mathematics, physics, and chemistry. As always, mathematics was her favorite, but chemistry was a close second. In her second year she followed nearly the same schedule.

Her roommates at the Y.W.C.A. became two of her best friends, C. T. Achamma and Elizabeth Mathai, whom they called "Ammini." The latter's short vivacious figure, quick clear voice, and flair for public speaking were fitting complements to Mary's tall and dignified person, her low voice, her retiring manner. It was because of Ammini —eloquent, energetic, and intensely patriotic—that Mary suddenly found herself deeply concerned with the nationalist independence movement.

It was August, 1942. Britain and her allies seemed to be losing the war. Penang and Singapore had fallen. Refugees were pouring into India from Burma by the hundreds of thousands. India was in imminent peril of invasion by the Japanese. Still there was no indication of a change in British policy. Sir Stafford Cripps had come to India making proposals which offered vague promises of self-determination in the future but for the present gave the country no voice or power even in conducting its own defense. The hopes that had been roused by the guarantees of self-government outlined in the Atlantic Charter of 1941 were shattered. Tensions were at a peak. Finally on the eighth of August the All-India Congress committee meeting in Bombay passed the "Quit India Resolution," demanding immediate freedom for the country and sanctioning a mass struggle on nonviolent lines under Gandhi's leadership. Before this plan could be put into operation, thousands of nationalist leaders, including Gandhi and Nehru, were arrested.

All of India was swept into turmoil. It was like Kala Varshan, the June monsoon, which flung the world into upheaval, turning the fields into backwaters and the backwaters into treacherous arms of the sea.

"It's come!" announced Babi with grim triumph, arriving at the Y.W.C.A. late in the day on one of his frequent visits. Never had Mary seen him look so darkly handsome or so reckless. "Now at last we can do something. Have you heard about the *hartal,* the strike, that's called for tomorrow?"

"Yes," replied Mary. How could a roommate of Ammini Mathai have helped hearing about the *hartal!*

"We'll show them!" exulted Babi. "The time is past when one nation can make slaves of another. Mahatma Gandhi *ki jai!*"

It was one of the slogans everyone was repeating: Victory to Mahatma Gandhi!

"You mean you're going to join the *hartal?*" Mary was as uneasy as she was excited.

"Of course. Do you think I'm a coward or a traitor?"

"But—what would Appan say?"

Her brother sobered momentarily. "We can't help what he might say. Can't you see, Mary? He doesn't understand. He belongs to another generation. This is a new world we're living in." His dark eyes caught fire. "Or it can be a new world if we make it so!"

"But do be careful," she pleaded. "Suppose you got arrested!"

He nodded. "I'll only do—what I have to do."

He left Mary confused and uncertain. She knew that Appan would not approve of their taking part in the *hartal,* yet her sympathies were all with the striking students. It was a hard decision to make—love of father or love of country!

That night a woman lawyer active in politics came to the hostel and made an eloquent appeal to the students. Her arguments were convincing. Surely staying away from classes was a small sacrifice to make for freedom when hundreds of their Indian sisters, like Nehru's wife Kamala and Gandhi's Kasturbai, had spent years in prison! Mary did not need to be convinced. No sacrifice was too great if you had only yourself to consider. She lay awake that night long after Ammini and Achamma were asleep.

"Well?" challenged Ammini the next morning, as she gathered up her load of placards and posters. "Are you going to stay away from classes or not?"

"Yes," replied Mary.

Though there was an active nationalist group in the area called the Kerala Congress Party (Kerala being an ancient name for Cochin, Travancore, and Malabar), it was not in control of the local government. Therefore the colleges and high schools in Ernakulam, being government institutions, did not observe the *hartal.*

"We shall go to the high school to picket," said Ammini. She challenged Mary. "Will you come with us?"

Mary went. For hours she and several other girls stood in front of the high school gate and when students appeared urged them to go back to their homes It was an orderly but noisy procedure. Mary's voice became hoarse with the shouting of slogans.

"*Swaraj!* Independence!"

"Let the foreigners quit India!"

"Mahatma Gandhi *ki jai!*"

The students were not hard to convince. The whole city had become aroused. Streets were filled with shouting demonstrators. So many students stayed away from classes that the colleges and high schools had to close.

After the *hartal* was officially over, Ammini and many others continued the strike. They would file through the college corridors during classes shouting, "Mahatma Gandhi *ki jai!*" "Quit India!" and other slogans. Many of the students would get up from their seats and leave their classes, marching after them. The Maharajah's College finally closed for an extended period.

The jails were filled to overflowing. So active and outspoken was Ammini that her roommates feared she would attract the attention of the police.

"Suppose you get arrested!" Mary worried, almost as concerned for her friend as for her brother Joseph. Many of the men students had gone to jail. Others had been dismissed from college.

"I hope I do," retorted Ammini recklessly.

The immediate crisis passed, and with it the danger of the Japanese invasion. As after the monsoons, the floods ebbed. Though nationalist fervor continued to imbue the student body, classes returned to almost normal routine.

Only once again during her college course did Mary make an issue of her patriotism. A big pro-British War Day Exhibition was being held in the park at Ernakulam. The senior students living at the Y.W.C.A. were told that they would be given tickets for a party if they would sell Union Jacks at the exhibition.

"No," said Mary firmly. "I will not sell them."

By the end of her second year, Mary had come to a decision. She wanted a career, preferably in a field related to science. She would become a doctor.

Perhaps she was influenced by her roommates also, because both Achamma and Ammini planned to leave college at the end of two years and study medicine Already they had made application at the Christian Medical College in Vellore, a town about eighty miles west of Madras.

"We may not be accepted," admitted Ammini. "They say it's very difficult to get in."

"But why not a government college?" objected Mary. "You'll probably want to go into government service when you get through."

The girls explained. Vellore, which had been founded by a remarkable American woman, Dr. Ida Scudder, had an excellent reputation. The many Syrian Christians who had gone there all said it had something special you didn't find in government colleges. It was *Christian.*

Mary was convinced. She decided she wanted to apply for admission to Vellore.

Appan was not happy to hear of this. "Wait," he counseled. "Perhaps you want to be a doctor, perhaps not. Keep on in college and study for your B.A."

Nor did her brothers encourage her. Second brother George, who was studying medicine himself, was the most emphatic.

"It's no job for a woman. You might even have to make night calls."

When at the end of two years Mary took her intermediate examinations and ranked first among all women students from the state's colleges, her father and her brothers were even more averse to her making the change. For in addition to the honor, she had won a scholarship of fifteen rupees a month for her next two years of college study. Appan celebrated the importance of this achievement by giving her a wrist watch.

And after all, Mary was well satisfied to wait. It was study in general that she wanted, not medicine in particular. Her chief regret was that she must now give up mathematics as her main subject and replace it with chemistry, which was more pertinent to the study of medicine.

Sister Martha, Mary's beloved Kunjamma, came now to be her roommate. Other friends took the place of Achamma and Ammini, both of whom had gained admission to Vellore. And with the passing months changes came also to the family.

One day in August Mary and Kunjamma went home for John's marriage to Annie, a Cherai girl whom he had known vaguely and for whom he had expressed a preference. The wedding took place on a Sunday at Mary's home. She had a new green sari with a red border for the occasion. And the very next day the whole family, including many relatives, journeyed by steamboat along the backwaters to Pazaanji, another village, to see third sister Thankamma married to a prosperous young businessman, also named Verghese.

"The house seems empty," said Appan when they returned home, then added quickly at sight of Mary's crestfallen look, "*Nallathu,* it is good, my child. It is as it should be."

Now that she had decided to be a doctor, Mary became acutely conscious of physical conditions so common as to have earlier gone almost unnoticed: the scrawny bodies of children playing in the dusty lanes, the ravages of malaria, the high percentage of faces scarred by smallpox, the fevered emaciation of tuberculosis. As she passed the victims of filaria in the streets of Cochin Town and Ernakulam, their deformities became suddenly objects of curious interest rather than of repugnance. Only once during those years of studying for her B.A. was Mary dismayed by the thought of becoming a doctor.

One of India's foremost philanthropists, having donated a large sum to the Maharajah's College for a course in pharmaceutical chemistry, came to the college to inaugurate the course. As he stood on the platform with Dr. K. N. Menon, the chemistry professor, the girl sitting beside Mary leaned over and whispered: "Did you know that that man is a leper?"

Mary looked at her in shocked amazement. "No!" she breathed. And poor Dr. Menon had to shake hands with him!

6

The long anticipated, long dreaded examinations were over. Hard to believe that triumph and defeat could be two sides of the same coin! For she had almost won a medal. She had come out first in the whole university in all her science subjects, but she had failed in English!

The reason was simple. Though she had studied the language from her first year of school, the English standards had not been high in the schools she had attended. She felt her failure keenly. It was necessary to wait another five months before trying again. Then she stood once more in English, passed, and received the coveted B.A. degree. But a whole year had been lost. Now she must wait another six months before finding out whether she could be admitted to Vellore.

Her time was filled. After Thankamma's little daughter Omana was born in December, 1945, her sister fell ill with rheumatic arthritis, and Mary assumed much of the baby's care. Thankamma, back home with her parents, was moody and bitter, a difficult patient.

For Mary, it was a period of troubling uncertainty. Medical training would take another five and a half years. On the other hand, Mary had made a brilliant record in chemistry. With two years of graduate work she could qualify for a lecturer's position in college. But she did not want to teach.

Her brothers were of little help as she tried to make up her mind. John, now in America doing post-graduate study in engineering in the Polytechnic Institute in Brooklyn, New York, was noncommittal. George, the medical student, was still firmly opposed to her becoming a doctor. Babi, who had graduated with top honors in mathematics, only half-heartedly favored a medical career. Said Appan, "Your decision it is."

Mary made application to Vellore and found herself one of seventy-five candidates invited to the college to take pre-selection tests. Only twenty-five students, she understood, would be eventually accepted.

The photograph Mary sent with her application showed a tall poised girl in neat, narrow-bordered sari, slightly heavy of feature, with thick dark brows, full lips, a rather determined chin, a square forehead, and a wealth of black hair which in spite of careful oiling was escaping into short untidy tendrils. "Not pretty," she appraised it with dispassionate candor. But she probably did not even notice the eyes, set deep like Appan's and wide apart, shining black and steady as a king crow's in flight.

Mary left home outwardly calm. Amma cried a little, for to her the places beyond the mountains seemed almost as distant as those to which John had gone, beyond the seas. Even Appan's eyes looked suspiciously moist.

Her journey began across the backwaters by *vallam* to Parur, where she joined Cousin Kunjannam, who had also been called for the examination; then the rest of the ten miles by bus to Alwaye, with Kunjannam's brother Matthew going along to help with the baggage. Since each girl had been asked to bring everything necessary for permanent residence in case she was selected, it took more than two coolies' heads to balance their steel trunks, boxes, baskets, and handbags. Though they had bedding rolls and the Cochin Express was an overnight train, the third-class compartment, crammed with students for Madras, barely furnished space for sitting upright, much less lying down!

The train crossed the Ponnani River, leaving behind Cochin State's palms and lagoons and rice fields. As they swept through the Palghat Gap, the only real break in India's six hundred miles of Western Ghats, Mary gazed wonderingly at dense forests and bare towering peaks. Then suddenly the mountains were behind. The world flattened into a huge brown earthen saucer burnished with the red glow of sunset. She stared through the open windows in dismay. Where were the lush greens of grass, the jades of palms and plantains, the emeralds of rice fields? This land east of the mountains looked like a desert.

"Here they do not have so much Kala Varshan, June monsoon," explained an older student. "They have more Thula Varshan, monsoon in October."

"In few places but Cochin," volunteered another, eager to display knowledge, "do they have each year as much as one hundred twenty inches of rain."

Even if she had not been wedged so sharply upright, Mary could not have slept. As the train rocked and rattled through the darkness, her senses were alerted to new sounds and smells and shapes . . . air dust-dry instead of tangy with salt, bullock carts creeping in lantern-lit caverns, vague shapes and shadowy mounds, the blaring confusion of station platforms. Erode, Salem, Jalarpet. . . .

Even the whines of beggars and the shrill cries of vendors, heads laden high, outside the windows sounded only half familiar, for they were out of Malayalam and into Tamil country.

"*Vazaipazam,* plantains!"

"*Ammal, ammal, pasi,* hungry!"

"*Chai,* tea! *Cha-ai!*"

"*Thanni,* water! *Thanni!*"

"*Pan, bidi,* cig-rette!"

Dust, preferable to the suffocating heat of closed windows, drifted through the openings, settled in thick films over the mountains of baggage, over saris, arms, hands, even seeped through the meshes of tightly wound scarves into face and hair. Mary's eyes smarted. The acrid dryness burned her throat.

Dawn came. The vague shapes turned into villages, the shadowy mounds into huge rock heaps rearing out of a dead flat plain. The dry earth stirred into life. Cooking fires blossomed among squatting figures on the roadsides, scenting the air with cow-dung smoke. Crows started their raucous squawking. Water carriers trotted and sloshed. Farmers prodded and clucked at their bullocks and water buffaloes. Carts lumbered. Irrigation devices of a dozen kinds creaked and groaned, twisted or rose and fell.

"Katpadi! Katpadi Junction!"

It was still not long past sunrise when Mary and Kunjannam assembled their baggage, procured coolies, made their way through the crowded compartment, and plunged into the confusion of the station platform.

"Mary! Mary Verghese!"

To Mary's surprise and delight Achamma and Ammini, her college roommates, were among the upperclass students who had come to meet the train. Several candidates beside Mary and Kunjannam were bound for the Medical College, among them Thankamma, one of her college classmates, and Mariamma, who had lived at the Y.W.C.A. in Ernakulam.

A row of strange-looking conveyances called *jutkas* was waiting to take them to the college. Mary looked askance at the little horse-drawn wagon with its high platform and rounded canopy of reeds. It tipped alarmingly on its two wheels when she climbed the rear steps, then leveled off when she and the other girls settled themselves crosslegged on the thin matting. It looked a little like a *vallam* but was not nearly so comfortable. A *vallam* was cool and smooth-flowing like the water beneath it. This cage was stiflingly hot and so low it was impossible to sit upright, and it ground and jolted with the pounding hoofs of the jerky little horse.

"See, we're in Vellore now. And there's the hospital where we all go for our training." Achamma pointed eagerly.

Mary tried to peer around the reed canopy, but she could see nothing except a confusion of streets, traffic, bazaars, buildings, pedestrians. Relief that she was nearing the end of her journey was mingled with dismay at thought of living in this clatter, heat, and noisome dust. Visions of the Maharajah's College with its broad green lawns and sea-moist breezes blurred her aching eyes.

"Now," said Achamma cheerfully, "it is only four miles further to the college."

Four miles! Mary closed her eyes. The clattering wheels seemed to be turning in her own head. Every clop-clop of the little horse jarred through her body.

Achamma and Ammini chattered as they rode along, trying to condense into a half hour not only their own two years of experience in the Christian Medical College but all of its preceding quarter century of history. As they talked, Mary became conscious of two words recurring almost as incessantly as the clop-clop of hoofs, and as rhythmically. DR. IDA . . . DR. IDA.

Dr. Ida had started the Medical School back in 1918, long before Indian women in any numbers had left their seclusion to seek careers, and when medicine especially had been considered for women a degrading profession. She had had almost no money, no buildings except a rented house, no staff except herself. But did that discourage Dr. Ida? Not one bit. "If you can get six applications," the Surgeon-

General in Madras had told her, "go ahead, but I'm sure you can't get more than three." She had gotten sixty-nine, and her first class of fourteen girls in their first-year examinations had led all the medical schools in the Madras Presidency!

Mary listened with incredulity as the story unfolded. It sounded almost too fabulous to be true, like the exploits of Saint Thomas. How could one woman possibly embody all the energy and achievement that they claimed for this amazing Dr. Ida? Studying medicine because a half century ago she had been shocked by the needs of Indian women . . . creating a women's hospital almost entirely by her own efforts . . . starting a school of nursing . . . enlisting the help of women in her own country and others until the little hospital had grown to a huge medical center with nearly 400 beds . . . playing championship tennis at the age of seventy . . . becoming so well known in her adopted country that years ago a letter addressed simply to "Dr. Ida, India" had come straight to its destination!

"But that's not all," continued Ammini with as much enthusiasm as she had exhibited in the cause of independence. "Wait until you hear this!"

In 1938, when the Congress Party had come into power in the Madras Presidency, all medical schools in the state had been required to affiliate with the university and give a college degree. This meant that almost certainly Vellore, giving only a diploma, would have to close. To upgrade sufficiently it would have to add over 200 more teaching beds, at least twelve new professors with higher degrees than any members of the staff, and new laboratories and departments. To do all this would take at least fifty lakhs of rupees, in American money more than a million dollars. But did Dr. Ida give up? No. Over seventy years old, she trekked for three years up and down the United States of America, speaking sometimes two or three times a day, trying to save her college.

"And she did it?" breathed Mary, enthralled in spite of herself. Stupid question, she thought. If she had not done it, she herself would not be here listening to the story!

"Yes," replied Ammini. That is, it was almost accomplished. A year from now, in 1947, a university commission was coming to make a final inspection, although provisional recognition had already been given. It was Dr. Ida who had made it possible. Everybody said she had performed a miracle.

Due perhaps to her own weariness, Mary found herself beginning to resent this energetic foreigner who had taken it upon herself to solve the problems of India. What a domineering, insufferable creature she must be! And how could the ardently patriotic Ammini, dedicated to ridding her country of Western domination, have fallen so abjectly under her spell? Mary began to wish fervently that she had not come.

"We're almost there!" announced Achamma eagerly. "We call that round rocky mound there on your left College Hill."

Mary opened her eyes. She was suddenly conscious of a change in the atmosphere. The town with its clamor and confusion and dirt had been left behind. Even the clop-clop of hoofs was now less jarring. The air was so clear that on the rounded hillock to the left every stone was limned clearly, every patch of grass, each separate frond on the three tufted palm trees at the top. They had moved into a broad valley stretching away on all sides to join purple mountains and sky as clear bright blue as the Arabian Sea. Mary breathed deeply.

The *jutka* deposited them in front of a long stone building, its entrance surmounted by a white dome. A tall spare foreign woman came out to greet them, the restraint of her thin, slightly austere features belied by the lively twinkle in her eyes. Dr. Ida? wondered Mary, and was almost relieved to discover that she was Dr. D. L. Graham, an Englishwoman, the acting dean of the women's hostel. For she had resolved not to yield to the spell of the brashly energetic American, as had Ammini and Achamma. This Dr. Graham Mary liked immediately. She was kind but wasted no words.

"Welcome to Vellore, girls. You must be tired. Take them to their rooms, seniors, and see that they have *chota*."

Chota? Mary recognized the Hindi word, but its meaning puzzled her. How could one have a "little"?

Passing through the Administration Building's arched entrance, they came to a sunken garden, with a large round lily pool in the center. Mary caught her breath. Everywhere she looked there were green vines and shrubs, the yellows and oranges of lantana, pink and white antigonon, every shade of bougainvillea from pale pink to bright crimson. And especially were there blues. Blues in profusion.

"Dr. Ida planned it this way," said Achamma, sensitive to Mary's delight. "She made sure there would be flowers blooming here all the year round. And blue and white are our school colors."

DR. IDA again! Spoken as if in capitals, in the same tone of voice Amma used when talking of Saint Thomas! The beauty of the flowers faded slightly. Achamma's devotion to this insufferably superior foreigner seemed almost a breach of patriotic loyalty, as well as a surrender of personal independence.

Chota, she discovered, was a "little" breakfast. They ate it in the hostel dining room. To her relief two of her fears were not realized. They did *not* have tea instead of coffee, and they did *not* have to eat Western style, with awkward tools. They ate in the manner most Indians preferred, with their fingers.

"One time only do we use knives and forks," explained Ammini slyly. "That is after anatomy class, when we have been handling cadavers."

Several of the newcomers turned pale. But if Ammini had hoped to dismay her former roommate by this preview of future ordeals, she was unsuccessful. Mary was too much the scientist to be daunted.

However, she had plenty of other misgivings. Did she really want to spend five and a half years training in medicine, when with only two years she could qualify as a lecturer in chemistry? And was she sure that she preferred this Vellore school to a government medical school? Suppose these foreigners tried to indoctrinate her with their own exotic brand of Christianity! Wasn't that one of the objectives of their "mission" institutions? Already she felt rebellion stirring. Her ancestors had been Christians when the European forebears of this American Dr. Ida had probably been practicing the magic rites of the Druids or sacrificing to pagan Thors or Odins.

Fortunately she need not decide just yet. With seventy-five girls competing in the tests, many of them from English-speaking schools, some from mission areas which would no doubt be given preference, she probably had little chance of being one of the chosen twenty-five. She almost hoped she wouldn't be.

The candidates were housed five to a room in the hostel. Each was given a dresser. Desks had to be shared. There was one big closet. All the girls slept in one large airy room on the second floor or on the surrounding verandahs. Mary was not sure she liked this arrangement. Some of the candidates were so sure of acceptance that they unpacked all their personal belongings. Not Mary. She had carefully put everything she would need for a week in the top of her neatly packed trunk.

That day, Monday, June 24, 1946, became a kaleidoscope of things half remembered: bewildering introductions, tours of classrooms and campus, and the exchange of her name for a number, 20, which she was to wear pinned to her sari for the rest of the week. But one hour of that day she would never forget.

"I've come to take you to chapel," said Achamma, appearing in her room late in the afternoon.

Mary stiffened. "Do I have to go?"

Achamma smiled. "No. But I want to go, and I'd like you to be with me."

Mary went. Instead of taking her through the sunken garden, Achamma led her around the big quadrangle of college buildings, so that they approached the chapel from the rear. It was an octagonal structure of gray stone rising with simple dignity from a terrace of green shrubs and flowering trees. Its white dome, a twin to the one crowning the Administration Building, caught the light of the setting sun and shone with a translucent glow, like alabaster.

"I wanted you to see it like this," said Achamma. "Some people say it's a little like the Taj Mahal. It's so beautifully simple."

"Yes," said Mary, gazing at it.

"And do you notice how even the two mahogany trees on each side grow with the same symmetry, rounded like the dome? Dr. Ida planned it that way."

Mary began walking fast, so that the shorter Achamma had hard work keeping up with her.

A few minutes later she was sitting on a mat in a place of cool spaciousness. All about her people were worshiping, but it was not worship as she knew it. There was no high carved altar, only a simple platform, over it one quietly glowing lamp of pierced brass. The only incense was the fragrance of alyssum and roses and jasmine stealing through the many openings. The music was like nothing she had ever heard before: no solemn chants or ancient psalms inherited from another century. These songs were of simple joyous things which pertained to everyday living. They spoke of day dying in the west, the beauty of the earth, the joy of human love and friends, a pilot guiding a small boat on a restless sea.

The prayers also were different. They did not sound as if taken from a book. Even Appan, praying spontaneously after he had read from the evening prayer book, never seemed on such intimate terms with God as this. Yet Mary did not feel out of place. She sat quietly, poised, a little withdrawn, eyes lifted to the narrow grilled openings high up toward the dome, watching the crimson sky change slowly to pink, then to a soft pale lavender

Then suddenly she was no longer looking at the sky. She was looking at the woman who had just risen to speak. Not a tall woman, though for some reason her presence seemed to fill the platform. Her hair was white, and her face lined, yet she seemed to glow with youth. Perhaps it was her eyes that made her look so young. They were a clear vivid blue, the color of the morning glories climbing the garden wall outside.

Blue and white, thought Mary. No wonder she chose those colors for her college. She herself is like a banner flaunting them.

No, not flaunting. To flaunt, one had to be self-conscious, and this woman was obviously concerned with just one thing: the group of girls seated on the mats beneath her. If she possessed an over-confidence, it was born not of conceit but of inner power and energy. She was richly, vibrantly *alive,* and she wanted to share her abundance of life with other people.

"So you girls want to be doctors," she said, smiling. "Or at least you think you do. Do you mind if I tell you what made me decide to become a doctor?"

The story Dr. Ida Scudder told was almost incredible. And yet somehow, hearing it from her lips, Mary immediately believed it.

"I was nineteen years old," she began, "just the age of many of you girls, when I returned to my native India after studying for some years in my own United States of America. I came back for just one reason. My mother was sick and needed me. I had no intention of staying. As soon as she was well again, I planned to go back to my own country and lead a free and happy life. But something happened to me one night as I sat alone at my desk in my father's little mission bungalow in Tindivanam."

The words she used were simple; her voice, though warm, was undramatic. Yet when she paused the silence in the chapel was so complete that the *chuk*ing of a nightjar outside sounded startling loud.

"Hearing steps on the verandah, I went to the door. There stood a tall, dignified Brahmin gentleman. I asked him what I could do for him.

" 'My wife,' he replied, 'a young girl, scarcely more than a child, is in difficult labor. The barbers' wives can do nothing for her. Will you come and help?'

"I told him that I knew nothing about midwifery. I could do even less than the untrained barber's wife, but my father was a doctor and he would gladly come and help. But he drew himself up proudly and said, 'You expect me to permit a man to come into my caste home and care for my wife? She had better die than have that happen!' "

Ida had returned to her desk, disturbed and unhappy. Again hearing steps, she had gone to the door, hoping the man had returned. But it was not the Brahmin. It was a Moslem. Horrified, she had heard him make the same plea. His young wife was dying, and would Ida come and help? She had taken the man to see her father, and together they had reasoned with him, Ida even promising to go with her father and do what she could to help. But he had refused. It was contrary to the custom of his religion that any man outside the family should look on the face of his wife.

"I went back to my room," continued Dr. Ida, "with a heart so burdened I could scarcely bear it. I tried to read, to write, but I could think of nothing but those two young girls. Again I heard footsteps. This time another man stood there, another high-caste Hindu, and with the same plea. He also refused my father's help, as the others had done."

Quietly the voice continued. "I could not sleep that night. I think that was the first time I ever met God face to face. I knew that he was speaking to me. And I did not want to answer. I did not want to spend my life in India. In the morning, early, I heard the tom-tom beating, as a funeral procession passed our house on its way to the river bank. I sent one of our servants to find out what had happened to the three young girls, and he came back saying that all were dead. They had died because there was no woman doctor to go to them. After much agony and prayer I made my decision. This is why I am here in India. That is why I am a doctor."

Around Mary there was a sound like that of a long-held breath slowly released. Lifting her eyes again to the chapel's stone-latticed openings, Mary was surprised to find that the sky outside had darkened to deep night-blue in which stars were shining. She had been quite unaware of the passage of time. But she realized suddenly that in the brief interval she had traveled much farther than from dusk into evening. She was no longer uncertain. She knew that she wanted more than anything else to stay here at Vellore.

7

That year of 1946 the college, in the hope that the expensively high percentage of subsequent failures might be reduced, was instituting a new series of admittance tests. Success in the medical profession, it was explained to the seventy-five candidates, depended on many factors. Besides scholastic ability, a sound basis in premedical studies, and an integrated personality with an active social sense, the Vellore examiners would consider other factors: general scientific aptitude, physical capacity, knowledge of English, and in the case of Christian candidates, Christian knowledge, understanding, and commitment.

Mary looked forward to the tests with trepidation. Now that she wanted so much to succeed, the outcome seemed even more uncertain.

"As if you had anything to worry about!" Achamma said, walking with her to the Assembly Room on the first morning. "You who led the whole university in chemistry!"

"But who failed in English," Mary countered silently.

As much as possible she kept her fears to herself. Perhaps it was this very restraint, she thought with brutal self-appraisal, which would be her undoing. That and English! So many of the girls, coming either from mission or other English-speaking schools, spoke the language as glibly as their own native dialects!

Dr. Ida, acting in the absence of the principal, Dr. Cochrane, who was on furlough in England, presided over the written tests in the Assembly Room. She set the candidates at ease by telling them of her own school days in America when women had been considered so out of place in a medical career that the men students had stamped their feet and ridiculed them when they entered a classroom.

"Fortunately those days are over," she ended gaily, "both in my country and in yours. Let us be thankful that today we no longer have to prove that we have brains, only that we know how to use them."

Then, suddenly serious, she offered a simple prayer that every girl might be given the wisdom and strength to do her best.

Mary searched the radiant face carefully, fearful that the image she had formed would not stand the test. But the blue eyes were as candidly clear by daylight as they had seemed in the glow of the pierced-brass lamp. They showed no condescension or arrogance, no pride of achievement. The gleam that sparked them was more than lively interest and humor. It was struck from some unquenchable inner flame which had lighted the way to deep and high adventure. Mary was surer than ever that it was a gleam worth following.

She was encouraged by the nature of the tests in physics and chemistry. There were fifty multiple-choice questions in each subject, and she felt that she answered them with reasonable credit. After refreshment other tests followed—tests of general intelligence, verbal aptitude.

Many of the activities of the next three days did not seem like tests at all. The candidates were divided into leaderless groups of eight or ten, and asked to perform in a series of specific situations. They produced plans for a doctor's house, criticizing each other's efforts. Provided with hospital furniture, they quickly converted a sitting room into a sick room. Presented with a boy pretending to have a fractured leg, they administered first-aid treatment.

Mary was not sure how well she acquitted herself. She had ideas in abundance, but her shyness and her ineptitude in English often kept her from expressing them. She felt much more at home in the tests for mechanical aptitudes. Here quickness of eye and manual dexterity made full compensation for slowness of speech. And her logical, scientific mind was equal to every challenge except one.

Taken into a chemistry laboratory and asked to assemble certain articles of equipment in as short a time as possible, she thought: As a B.A. graduate who majored in chemistry I should find this child's play. But to her dismay the apparatus here was different from that to which she had been accustomed. She wasted so much precious time trying to locate the various parts that there was no time left for assembling them.

The three days of tests were over at last. Wide awake, Mary lay on her bed that night and tried to tell herself that the outcome really did not matter. If she did not have the ability to become a doctor, better to know it now. She would be a teacher. The tests had been fair. She did not take part in the grumblings which issued from some of the neighboring beds:

"We don't stand a chance. It will be those who studied in mission colleges who will be chosen. You just wait and see!"

"Or those who have had more contacts with Europeans," interposed another voice in Malayalam.

The June heat was so oppressive that the girls had dragged their cots out of the big dormitory to the upper verandah. Mary knew that the monsoons had already come to Cochin. She missed the tang of the sea air, but here the stars were brighter. The air was so clear that the elephant-shaped mountain near the college was plainly outlined even in the dark.

The Selection Board of eighteen members met on the following morning. It included not only faculty members but special advisers, among them a psychologist and a psychiatrist, who had spent late hours analyzing the material received. The close correspondence of their reports was a striking comment on the value of the new procedure. For in all but three or four cases the reports given by five different members of the Board on as many as eight varying aspects of each candidate were in such agreement that the group had little difficulty in reaching its decisions.

Meanwhile the candidates had gone into the town for a tour of the hospital. Like the other girls, Mary found it hard to concentrate on the details of the trip. The hospital, in the center of the town's congested area, was a huge sprawling maze of rooms, stairs, corridors, and courtyards, leaving in retrospect only a few clear pictures: rows upon rows of white beds with folded red blankets, an altar silhouetted against a sunlit courtyard, anterooms as crowded as third-class railroad carriages, bullock carts dragging loads of brick and crushed rock, burdened workmen mounting ladders, a gateway of wrought iron painted silver, the opening choked with people. Everywhere *people.* Mary was so busy looking that she registered only snatches of the guide's glib comments in the English which still demanded her full concentration.

". . . just 371 beds now, but by July, 1948 we must have 600. . . ."

". . . new pathology and research block, new maternity and gynecology, all growing fast. . . ."

". . . Administration Bulding, children's ward, dispensary, surgical block, all rapidly expanding, with new stories added. . . ."

New . . . growing . . . expanding . . fast . . . strange words to hear in India! No wonder Mary felt confused.

The town itself was less bewildering. Crowded bazaars, little shops displaying hand-crafted silver, snake charmers, Hindu peddlers of charms, hucksters with huge trays of merchandise on their heads, narrow streets solidly lined with whitewashed, gaily decorated houses, sidewalks strewn with sleeping or squatting figures . . . these were commonplace. Even the immense old fort with its unmortared stone walls and green-scummed moat speckled with lotuses seemed to belong to the slow and ancient tempo of Cochin and its sleepy lagoons. The gray stones of its richly carved Hindu temple, seven hundred years old, were more akin to the hoary relics of Saint Thomas than the whitewashed walls of the bustling, teeming Christian hospital.

Back at the college the fateful hour came. The candidates were summoned to the outer verandah of the Administration Building and asked to form a queue in the order of their numbers. As each girl's turn came, she was admitted to one of the offices near the front entrance. There, Dr. Ida stood waiting. Beside her was her niece, Dr. Ida B. Scudder, who was also a member of the staff and presently acting as registrar. If the girl had been accepted, she was congratulated by the two doctors. If not, she was thanked for coming to Vellore and cooperating in the tests. Later, if she desired, she would be given a personal interview with her group observer, who would try to help her understand her special abilities and limitations.

Mary, as Number 20, watched the girls ahead of her disappear into the office, then emerge with face triumphant, tearful, mechanically smiling, tight lipped and resentful, nonchalant, or studiedly noncommittal. Some of the girls near her joked and tittered to hide their nervousness. Mary stood quietly, moving forward with mechanical precision each time the line advanced.

"How can you be so calm!" marveled one of the others. "Anybody would think you didn't care!"

"I care," replied Mary, wondering why people always thought activity and words were signs of deep emotion.

Her name called, she entered the office. Dr. Ida B. Scudder greeted her warmly. "We have been glad to have you here this week, Mary. We hope you have enjoyed Vellore."

So this was the end. She had not been chosen.

"Thank you," she replied steadily.

Dr. Ida took her hand. Seen close at hand, her eyes were even bluer than Mary had thought They were the color of the Arabian Sea in bright sunlight. And her white hair was like a mesh of silk. Mary had a sudden inexplicable desire to touch it, to find out if it would cling to her fingers like cobwebs.

"Yours is the first chance, my dear," said Dr. Ida graciously. "That means you are next in line after the first twenty-five. We want you to stay here another day or two and see what happens. You may be chosen yet."

Mary left the room feeling dazed and uncertain.

"What happened?" demanded Achamma, waiting for her outside.

"I came in twenty-sixth," replied Mary flatly. "They want me to wait another day. But—" She stopped. Who wants to be second choice? she finished silently.

"Of course you'll stay," insisted Achamma.

Mary stayed, not because she had any hope of being chosen, but because it meant that she could postpone for a little longer telling Appan that she had failed. One after the other the unsuccessful candidates departed. Mary went to the station with Achamma and some other seniors and saw Cousin Kunjannam and Thankamma and Mariamma off on the Cochin Express. None of them had been accepted.

Some of the rejected candidates grumbled bitterly. "What did we tell you! We didn't stand a chance. It's lucky the government colleges aren't so fussy. You're just wasting your time staying, Mary."

Mary made no reply. They were probably right. But when she followed them, she determined, she would blame nobody but herself for her failure. She noticed with a little glow of satisfaction that even the most disgruntled candidates had no word of criticism for Dr. Ida.

She was surprised to find that she actually enjoyed the long ride back to the college. Already the jammed streets, the blaring radios, the dimly lighted shops, the shadowy gray fort had begun to seem like home to her. She had become so used to the big upstairs dormitory that now, with most of the candidates gone, it seemed strangely empty. The muffled sobbing of a homesick girl kept her awake that night only a little while.

"I don't want to stay here," she heard the girl lamenting softly. "I want to go home. I don't want to stay."

She felt a healthy contempt for the successful candidate. She was probably the same girl Mary saw sniveling outside the hostel after *chota* the next morning. Absurd to be so dependent on places and people for your well being! Mary pitied rather than envied her.

Already her own resilience was reconciling her to the fact of failure. She was almost eager for the interval of waiting to be over, so she could make her next plans. After all, she had come to Vellore uncertain whether she really wanted to study medicine. Now, fortunately, the matter had been decided for her. Failure in the tests was no disgrace. It was merely proof that she would make a better college lecturer than a doctor. In two years, instead of five and a half, she would be ready to start her career. Relief began to outweigh disappointment.

It was Achamma who brought Mary the news when she had returned to her room after *chota.*

"That girl—the one who was crying—she's going home!"

"Oh, I'm sorry," said Mary. "She will probably be even more unhappy."

"Better not be sorry. You know what this means? If she goes, you're next in line."

Mary gasped. Strange, it had not occurred to her that the sounds of crying in the night might determine her own future! The knowledge was both exciting and disconcerting. Just when she had succeeded in reconciling herself, must the uncertainty begin all over again?

The morning passed, and she heard nothing more. Since it was Sunday, the students followed their usual custom of having dinner with the staff in the hostel dining room. At this meal the new students would be introduced. Half in anticipation, half to divert her mind from its turmoil, Mary dressed with more pains than usual, putting on a favorite sari, brushing her hair carefully in an attempt to restrain all the loose ends which persisted in escaping.

Dr. Graham, her group observer, was waiting for her at the door of the dining room, angular body erect as an exclamation point, spare face beaming.

"Good news, my dear! One of the girls has dropped out, and you have been chosen. Congratulations! We shall be introducing you with the others very soon."

Mary bowed and smiled when she was introduced, her dignity an effective shield for her shyness. She shook hands with all the staff, including Dr. Ida. Though the blue eyes and glowing personality still cast their spell, Mary noted also the slightly stooped shoulders, the lines etched deeply by a lifetime of concern and stress.

"I'm glad you got your chance," said Dr. Ida, holding her hand longer than was necessary. It was almost as if she had read the uncertainty in the girl's eyes. "I believe you have what it takes to make a good doctor."

Did she? Though in the next few days she went through all the routines of the new student, Mary was still uncertain. At last she wrote to her father: "What should I do? You decide for me."

His answer came back promptly, firmly, comfortingly decisive: "Stay and study medicine."

Would he have been so firm, so decisive, if he could have looked into the future and seen what the decision was going to cost?

8

Once the issue had been decided Mary plunged into the new life with all her abounding vigor. With the other new students she was initiated into the medical sisterhood by the upperclass women, sprinkled with water from a hose pipe, and given a new name, derived from imaginative delving into mythological or scientific jargon. It was her friend Elizabeth (Ammini) Mathai, president of the Students' Union, who performed the ceremony.

"I christen you," she pronounced solemnly, "Mighty Atom."

There was satire as well as humor in the designation. The suggestion that the self-effacing Mary might embody the explosive quality of the awesome symbol was as ironic as it was ridiculous. Only long afterward did it occur to someone that there was also aptness in the nickname—that an atom is broken before it reveals its power.

Mary adjusted to her new schedule with a minimum of difficulty. While her four roommates were diverse of temperament, and their small room on the ground floor near the entrance of the hostel was overcrowded, there was little tension Muriel was usually deep in a book, and sweet of disposition when she emerged. Leela was almost as quiet as Mary. Rose was pleasant and good-natured, a bit more interested in clothes than in studying. Mary John, the only one of the four in Mary's class, was a kindred soul, shy, studious, and of the same Syrian Christian background as Mary. Her pet name, Lily, suited her short slight figure and pretty face. Mary shared a desk with Lily. They became close friends.

Mary soon became intimate also with others of her class, especially those from the Cochin area. Among them were two younger girls without B.A. degrees, M. P. Aleyamma and Mary Chacko. M. P., as she was usually called, was bouncing, lively, full of mischief. Being older and a bit more sedate, Mary often assumed a proprietary, older-sister air toward the two, as if, coming from the same area, she must be responsible for upholding the honor and dignity of their common heritage.

"Silly!" she reprimanded M. P, discovering her in the juvenile diversion of climbing a tree.

It was a kindly tutelage, forced out of a constraining shyness, and they did not resent it. Stubborn they often found her, unwilling to yield once she had started an argument, but never arrogant, never bossy.

It was the little adjustments that Mary found hardest to make, like eating *chota* at 6:20 in the morning and dinner at 6:20 in the evening, instead of at 8 00 or 8:30. But in time she became so used to the early dinner hour that when she went home on vacations she became ravenous before the evening meal was served.

At least she did not have problems of adjustment to strange foods, such as did the few Hindu students and staff members.

"Vegetarian or nonvegetarian?" the servers would ask.

But even this apparent differentiation was sometimes misleading. The vegetarian meals, provided for those who did not eat meat, often included egg. Once during Mary's student days a chemistry demonstrator, an orthodox Brahmin, was eating in the hostel. "Vegetarian," he responded trustingly to the routine question, and when an omelet was set before him, assumed it was some unusual vegetable. When, some days later, he discovered that he had eaten eggs, his expression resembled that of a Westerner informed that he has just dined on some such Eastern delicacy as grasshoppers.

At seven each morning, after chapel, classes began. There was a break for refreshments at nine, then for lunch at noon. At three in the afternoon tea was served. Occasionally Dr. Ida joined the girls for tea in the hostel, and once the first-year students were invited for tea with her in the principal's "Big Bungalow."

To Mary's intense disappointment she learned that Dr. Ida was not to remain as principal. Already in her seventy-sixth year, ten years beyond the usual retirement age, Dr. Ida was merely acting until the return from England of Dr. Cochrane, the British physician and specialist in leprosy who had been principal and director of the college and hospital since 1944.

"Come with me to Dr. Ida's Bible class," urged Achamma one Sunday.

Mary went reluctantly, afraid of being conspicuous. The group met in a small prayer room near the chapel. Dr. Ida read from the Bible and talked informally, then several of the girls prayed. Mary wondered uncomfortably if she was expected to take part also. Appan always did the praying at home. It seemed the proper thing for the head of the family to approach such an important and powerful personage as the Deity. And, though he often used words of his own instead of reading from the book of ancient prayers, it was always with phrases of dignity and respect, as if he were addressing a court official or a maharajah. Dr. Ida talked to God as casually and intimately as Mary might have talked to Appan.

But apparently no one expected Mary to participate. After the class was over, Dr. Ida gave her a little book of devotions called *Daily Light.*

"I want all my girls to have this," she said simply.

In August Mary helped celebrate Dr. Ida's official retirement from the college. The students rose early and made a love chair, decorating it with blue and white flowers from the sunken garden. Seating her in it, they performed a dance of love about her, white jasmine flowers in their hair, lighted lamps in their hands, almost burying her beneath garlands of jasmine and roses. There followed a pageant in which the students portrayed some of the high points of the nearly fifty years which the indefatigable and dedicated American had given to her beloved India.

After Dr. Ida had left for Hill Top, her summer home in the Palani Hills, close to the borders of Mary's own state of Cochin, the life seemed to have gone out of Vellore. Even the pounding of hammers, the pulse beat of the expansion Dr. Ida had inaugurated in order to save her beloved college, seemed to have a hollow sound.

But she isn't really gone, thought Mary, becoming ever more conscious of the amazing energy and dedication which had created the Christian Medical College. There's a little of her in every stone of every building, every tree and flower. In fact, there's a little of her in all of us. The discovery came with a sense of awe and challenge. If we live the sort of life she did, Mary thought, *we are Dr. Ida!*

She became impatient to finish the first six months of premedical studies and get on with the real work of learning to be a doctor. Especially did the time seem to drag when, after about three months, Dr. Ida B. Scudder notified her that because of information received from the University of Madras relative to her college proficiency in chemistry and physics, she was exempt from further study in both subjects. This left only biology.

"I would recommend that you use the extra time to learn typewriting," added Dr. Scudder, whose own multiple activities as registrar, clinic leader, and head of the Radiology Department made her a model user of time.

Mary took the advice to heart. With another B.A. graduate who was also exempt, she immediately went to town and made arrangements for a course in typing.

Though written examinations were given at Vellore, all the students had to go to the University of Madras for their clinical and oral tests. Here in December Mary discovered the disadvantage of having a name beginning with "V", for it made her alphabetically the last of her class. Even for the glib students the orals were a torture. And Mary had to endure in addition waiting two or three hours before her name was called!

But the trip to Madras was not all torture, for Babi was there studying engineering and incidentally winning for himself the highest rank in mathematics in the whole university. Before Mary left for home to spend the Christmas holidays Babi took her on a tour of the city, showing her all the important landmarks save one.

"Did you visit Saint Thomas' Mount?" Amma would be sure to ask.

"No," Mary wanted to be able to reply. "I decided to wait until I could see it with you."

On that first train trip home, as on most others during her medical college years, M. P. and Ammini George, another Kerala girl, were Mary's companions. They traveled third class as a matter of course, and not until long afterward did the other girls realize that Mary could have afforded first-class accommodations had she wished.

It was a pleasant trip in spite of the noise and the crowding. The air was cool, the rice fields green after the fall monsoons.

M. P. and Ammini chattered about their college experiences, but Mary preferred to remain quiet. Nights, she believed, were for sleeping—even in a railroad compartment where they were packed as tightly as lentils in a pod. Since there was no room for Mary to curl up on one of the benches, she finally wrapped herself in a sheet, crawled under the seat, and, with the folds of the sheet pulled over her head to keep out both noise and dirt, went soundly to sleep.

The shocking news came while she was stopping in second brother George's rented house in Cochin, where he had recently established his medical practice: Appan had been stricken with a heart attack. Joining first sister Aleyamma and her doctor husband, George and Mary hurried home to Cherai to find Appan slightly improved but still very ill. After two days they were able to bring him and Amma back to George's house in Cochin.

Mary found it impossible to conceive of a world without Appan. She hovered helplessly about the room where he lay, wishing she were already a doctor like brother George and Aleyamma's Verghese. Surely if she had enough knowledge and skill, she could help protect the ones she loved! Vacation was a torment, Christmas a mockery.

But Appan, like his daughter Mary, was stubborn. The frail thread of life did not break. And though he thinned and aged distressingly in a few days, his eyes remained as piercing-bright as ever, and he subjected her to their full intensity. Stronger even than the possible imminence of death was his deep concern for his children.

How had Mary done in her exams? he wanted to know. Was she sure she had been well prepared? And how could she possibly study properly in that room with four female chatterboxes?

Amma also, while outwardly calm, managed somehow to combine motherly solicitude with the torturing worry of a wife. Had Mary been getting enough to eat, with those strange Tamil foods? And was she able to sleep properly with all those roommates? And Amma wanted to hear all about that wonderful Dr. Ida!

When Mary went to get the copy of *Daily Light,* to show it to her parents, and found it gone, she felt a sense of loss quite incommensurate with its value. She must have left it in Madras. She could buy another copy, of course. Later she did this, but it was not the same.

At the end of vacation Mary returned reluctantly to Vellore, leaving Appan. In the years that followed, Appan never regained his health but by observing caution was again able in time to supervise his coconut groves. For Mary, as for all her brothers and sisters, FAMILY became a unity more precious because of its uncertainty, a blessing no longer to be taken for granted.

Back at Vellore in January, she was now a fully registered student, beginning two years of pre-clinical study, a course which included anatomy and physiology. organic chemistry in the first year, biochemistry in the second.

"I hope you like anatomy better than I did," Achamma told her with a shudder. "You may not believe it, but I almost fainted the first time I went to the dissection room."

Mary did like it, for she had the curiosity of the born scientist. She found it interesting, a little awesome, but not disturbing. A mechanic would expect to take his machine apart to study its function. Why not a physician?

But there was one prospect of her clinical training which she found intensely disturbing. Ever since her arrival in the Vellore area she had been shocked by the amount of leprosy in evidence. Riding into town, she saw the victims along the roads. They thrust their hands toward the windows of cars and buses, and she noted with horror that the fingers were often mere stumps or curled into a claw. They appeared at railroad stations, lifting sightless eyes and distorted features and whining their beggars' jargon.

"*Ammal, ammal, pasi, pasi! Kan theriadhu! Ammal ni yen tai tahapan!* Lady, I'm hungry, I'm blind! You are my father and mother!"

In answer to her questions Mary was told that the area around Vellore had perhaps the highest incidence of leprosy of any place in the world. But it was not until she paid a visit to the hospital one day during that first year that she realized the full implications of the fact. Achamma, now in her third year, was in clinical training and going to the hospital every morning. One day she invited Mary to meet her there after classes.

Turning south near M Ward on their circuit of the grounds, they passed a group of low buildings somewhat apart from the others. On the verandah of one of them stood a queue of ill-clad, dejected-looking patients waiting their turns for treatment by a doctor who sat at a small table. Other figures, seeking shelter from the heat, were squatting or lying in the meager shade of a nearby tree.

"Our new leprosy clinic," explained Achamma casually.

In spite of the heat Mary felt suddenly cold.

"Do the students have to do clinical work here?" she inquired faintly. Strange, in all her calculations about becoming a doctor, it had never once occurred to her that she might have to work with leprosy victims.

"Yes," replied Achamma without apparent emotion. "At some time we all work in the clinic. And also we get some training in the treatment of leprosy on Roadside—you know, the mobile dispensaries which go out each week into the villages."

"You mean we—we actually have to *touch* them? The way that doctor is doing over there?"

Achamma looked surprised. "Of course. Why not?"

Mary was dumbfounded. A girl who almost fainted at the prospect of dissection but was unruffled by the idea of treating leprosy! Memories of Joseph, of the empty path, of a rough hand pulling her arm, of the glint of fear in Amma's eyes, sent an old chill through her veins.

"But—how can you?"

"Wait till you've heard Dr. Cochrane on the subject," Achamma reassured her.

Soon after this discussion Mary did hear Dr. Robert Cochrane, now back from England, give a lecture on leprosy at a public meeting. Former Medical Secretary of the British Mission to Lepers, he was one of the foremost authorities on the disease. In 1944 he had left his work as medical officer in charge at Lady Willingdon Leprosy Sanatorium in Chingleput to perform the gigantic task of upgrading Vellore to university status and changing it from a women's to a coeducational college. Mary regarded the dynamic, intensely serious, and forceful speaker with morbid fascination. She felt the same pitying emotion as when she had watched her college chemistry professor shake hands with the philanthropist who was a leprosy patient.

"Leprosy is one of the oldest diseases known to mankind," Dr. Cochrane began. "Wherever it has appeared, it has been surrounded by myth, superstition, dread, and fear. It has been described as the most loathsome of diseases, and the idea of guilt and sin has been perpetuated in the words 'moral leper.' Here in India it has from earliest history been known as *majarog,* curse from the gods."

Mary shivered. *"Adukkallai,* don't go near!"—Theresia's cry was as chilling as if she had heard it only yesterday.

"But leprosy is not a curse," Dr. Cochrane declared with almost harsh impatience. "It is not a mark of sin. It is not a moral or a social stigma. That is why we leprologists object so strongly to the word 'leper,' as tuberculosis workers resent the word 'consumptive.' 'Leper' and 'tainted' and all such words represent a medieval outlook that is erroneous and unscientific. For leprosy, like tuberculosis, is a disease caused by a bacillus. 'Hansen's Disease' we call it, after the Norwegian physician who in 1875 made observations of the organism which causes it It is an intensely interesting disease demanding the attention of the best minds, and offering a rich and as yet unexplored field for research."

And, contrary to popular belief, continued Dr. Cochrane, it was only mildly infectious, much less so than tuberculosis. Adults were relatively unsusceptible. It was usually acquired in childhood, through close and prolonged contact with an infective case. The beggar with leprosy ran little risk of infecting those from whom he begged. Those in real danger were the children who lived with him year after year in his crowded and unsanitary hovel.

Mary was impressed by what she heard. Her reasoning mind accepted Cochrane's professional opinion, even while her physical senses, conditioned by childhood fears, remained only partially convinced.

After the lecture the appreciative audience crowded around the speaker, questioning, commending, shaking his hand.

"Shall we go down?" asked Achamma.

"No!" blurted Mary. Then, at Achamma's look of surprise, she added hastily, "It's late, and I have studying to do."

Even to herself she would not have admitted her reluctance to clasp a hand that made a business of such contacts.

9

1947 was a year of change for India, change more momentous than had shaken the land for centuries. Colonialism was ending. A new nation was being born. For the first time in over twenty-two hundred years, since the reign of the peaceful Asoka, the country was to be united and free. United, that is, if a dismembered body can be called united; free, if a people with colossal problems of illiteracy, hunger, and disease can be called free.

Vellore was in step with this spirit of change. The college's new principal, Dr. Hilda Lazarus, was an Indian, the quintessence of that high quality which was to mark the top brackets of Indian national leadership. Formerly chief medical officer of the women's branch of the Indian Medical Service with rank of lieutenant-colonel, holding seven medical degrees earned in India, Ireland, Canada, and the United States, decorated four times by the British Crown, she brought to her new office not only a remarkable training and experience in both medicine and education, but the selfless dedication of a Christian devoted to the service of her people. It was fitting that in this new country committed to democratic principles based on equality of race, religion, and sex, an Indian woman of this caliber should preside over this Christian institution in the first year that men were admitted.

So far had the building program progressed that in 1947 Vellore was granted permission by the university to admit ten men students. Four hundred applied for the ten openings! Eleven were finally admitted, including the grantee of an annual scholarship furnished by an American woman in memory of her war pilot son who, while training in India, had become concerned over the poverty and sickness he saw.

If there was sex discrimination, it was the men who suffered. The girls of Mary's class, their immediate seniors, planned as grueling an initiation as their imaginations could devise. The men were required to wear saris. A senior, dressed like a king, was waiting for them in the sunken garden. Conducted to "his" throne, each new student was given a name—Cleopatra, Baby Hercules, Knight of the Operating Table, or some such ridiculous title—which was pinned to his shoulder. The ensuing ceremonies were a cross between a quiz program and the stunts of a Western Halloween party.

"What are the seven wonders of Vellore?" the men were asked.

To many the "three wonders" were well known: a river without water, a temple without a god, a fort without a garrison. To these stock answers the examiners had added several others more pertinent to the occasion, including "girls without beauty" and "boys without brains."

Another ordeal for the men was a chamber of horrors, designed to exorcize any lurking spirits of timidity. This was Mary's province. Blindfolded, the victim was exposed to gelatinous substances and fed delicacies suggestive of the more unpalatable portions of animal flesh. Blindfold removed, he was given helpful previews of the pleasures awaiting him in anatomy and physiology: a dissected frog, jars of pickled embryos from the museum, an illuminated skeleton.

In spite of the unaccustomed satisfactions of female superiority, both in numbers and in experience, the girls did not find the advent of males an unmixed blessing. Temporarily, the men were obliged to eat their meals in the women's hostel. This ended abruptly the girls' comfortable habit of eating breakfast in their housecoats.

But as August 15, Independence Day, approached, new students and old, men and women, staff and student body, foreigners as well as Indians, were joined in a unanimity of emotion that recognized no barriers. There was sadness in the emotion as well as triumph. For the sweetness of freedom was mingled with the bitterness of a country divided, of bloody rioting instigated by the jealous leaders of religious factions, of tragic massacres and migrations.

But there was no conflict in Vellore. Hindus, Moslems, Christians, all rejoiced in a unity which in a truly free land could be achieved only through diversity. Dr. Lazarus determined that for her students August 15 should be a never-forgotten day. An organizing committee was appointed. Imaginations worked overtime. On the evening of the fourteenth the sunken garden was a blaze of color, oranges and reds, purples and greens. Hundreds of little golden lamps were glowing.

Dinner also did justice to the coming holiday, with a rich and spicy *pilau* and plenty of ice cream and fruit.

On the gray stone walls of the Assembly Room hung a large plaque, reading "Magnificent India," made by a group of students. Against this backdrop student presentations drew on the wealth of their national heritage, in colorful drama, in tableaux depicting India's fight for freedom, in Tagore's great dramatic poem "Sacrifice."

But Dr. Lazarus had seen to it that the display of patriotism was not all words and symbol. The big event of the evening was the opening of a night school for the campus servants, an attempt to bring to actual fulfillment their dream of a better life for all of India's people.

During much of that evening Mary was riding seven miles in a bus to and from the Katpadi railroad station, all for the joy of seeing brother John, home from America, for the few brief moments that his train was in the station.

The train compartments were even more crowded than usual on this evening before Independence Day, and Mary inched her way, becoming more and more frantic. The train stopped such a short time! Suppose they spent all the precious minutes trying to find each other! Then she saw him.

"Valiangala, Big Brother!"

He had changed during his two years in America. He looked older, stouter. His voice, too, was different. He talked more like the American doctors at Vellore than like the English ones. But he was as mischievous and laughing as ever.

"Oho! So the little sister has become a doctor! Well, I must say it agrees with you. With that husky body you ought to be a coolie, carrying trunks on your head."

They talked of Appan's sickness, of Thankamma and her little Omana, of Amma, and especially of Gita, his own little daughter whom he had not yet seen. Then as suddenly as he had come, he was gone, and Mary was rattling back to the campus in the town bus. She was with the other students at midnight when there came over the radio the voices of Gandhi and Nehru, emotionally torn as the country was being torn, but bidding all Indians to go forward with courage and love in their hearts.

Mary awoke the morning of August 15 sure that she was hearing drums beating, bells ringing. Strange what a difference it made knowing that you belonged to a free country! Perhaps it was her own fierce need of independence that made her so exultant in the new nation's achievement. Never had the sky seemed so blue, the sunlight so golden. As she walked through the sunken garden to the early chapel service of thanksgiving, she felt taller, stronger. She held her head with a new dignity.

After the service the whole student body marched to the pole in front of the college buildings for the raising of India's flag. It was fitting that the procession should be led by Dr. Lazarus, herself a symbol of the remarkable emergence of Indian womanhood from its age-long seclusion, and that the rapt faces lifted to the rising tricolor flag, emblem of the new democracy, should include dark and white, men's and women's, Hindus', Moslems', Christians'.

If only I could sing! thought Mary, as the words of the "Jana Gana Mana," Tagore's stirring national anthem, soared with the saffron and green and white banner into the sunlit air of the new free India.

"Thou art the Ruler of the minds of all people,
Thou Dispenser of India's destiny . . .
Victory, victory, victory to thee!"

If only I could speak! she thought a few moments later as Dr. Lazarus and her own friend Elizabeth Mathai made moving speeches.

"India," declared Ammini, her voice ringing, "has only one doctor for every seven thousand people. One of her greatest needs is for strong, healthy bodies. What an opportunity for you and me!"

A strong, healthy body, thought Mary with a surge of triumph. Yes, I have that. And sometime I shall have the skill and knowledge to bring health to others. I'll be glad to give them to my country.

It was hard to believe in the months following independence that in the north the new nation was suffering birth pangs of riots, flights, and massacres. Among the first institutions in South India to offer its services to the suffering, the college sent a doctor and two nurses to help combat the appalling disease in the refugee camps. Still the ravaged north seemed incredibly far away. Only with the assassination of Gandhi on January 30, 1948, were the students stunned into awareness of the nation's tragedy. Shocked and silent, they huddled about the radios, in the shadows of the garden, on dormitory cots.

"The light has gone out," announced the Prime Minister brokenly to a country fused by grief into a far stronger unity than could possibly be accomplished by the joy of freedom. "The darkness surrounds us. Yet this light will still shine a thousand years from now."

Mary wished she could begin serving her country at once. Five years seemed like such a long apprenticeship!

It was a relief to her when she finally began her clinical studies. Now she spent each morning at the hospital, attending classes or working in some department, returning sometimes again in the afternoon. Every morning there was the rush to finish breakfast in time to make the seven o'clock bus, but the four-mile trip to the hospital in town afforded leisure for confidential exchanges which the rigid classroom and study schedule had not always permitted.

This figurative "letting the hair down" was some compensation for its literal prohibition, for Dr. Lazarus did not permit braids at the hospital. Up went the long glossy ropes of each new clinical student into a *kondai,* the thick coil which anchored all loose ends at the nape of the neck . . . all but Mary's. The stubborn tendrils of childhood remained stubborn, as difficult to subdue to meekness as her own strong will.

"*Kashtam,* a pity Mary always looks so untidy!" she overheard one friend lament to another.

Suddenly appearance-conscious, she tried to compensate for the deficiency. Though she had always worn chains and bangles and earrings, she wanted something specially her own. She designed a chain of gold beads, graduated in size, with a pair of matching earrings, and had it made by one of the goldsmiths in Cherai. When it was finished, she wore it with great satisfaction. For it was an expression of herself, simple, dignified, elegant. And nobody else in the world had one like it.

Of all her clinical subjects Mary liked surgery the best. Perhaps part of its appeal lay in the personality of one of its lecturers, Dr. Paul Brand, a young orthopedic surgeon. Totally dedicated to his profession and to India, where his family had been missionaries for five generations, Dr. Brand made of surgery more than an art and a skill. Watching him perform an operation on the limbs of a child crippled by polio, Mary was suddenly reminded of Joseph Achan bending to administer the Holy Qurbana.

But, much as she liked surgery, Mary felt strongly that it was no career for her. It would mean the necessity of working in a large hospital where there was ample provision for laboratory work. She might very well prefer to locate in a small hospital. Next to surgery, her favorite clinical subjects were gynecology and obstetrics, and she soon felt she might wish to specialize in these areas. With her first experience in the delivery room, she was sure of it. The excitement of preparation, the suspense of waiting, the struggle of new creation to achieve being, finally the exultation of holding in one's hands the warm wriggling bit of human flesh and imparting to it the breath of life . . . what could be more fulfilling, except possibly the triumph of having given birth oneself?

Compassion was tinged with deep respect as she regarded the poor, ignorant village woman who had just become a mother. This was the destiny accepted by her Indian sisters from time immemorial: early marriage and motherhood. Amma had married at the age of twelve. She had found fulfillment in the life of her children. In postponing marriage for a career, were Mary and others of her generation exchanging greater for lesser values? But it was only briefly that she wondered.

Had she not been so certain of the wisdom of her own choice, she might have asked the question again when she went home in the summer of 1949 to attend the wedding of her youngest sister, Kunjamma. The groom was a young doctor, N. M. Mathai, a cousin of second sister Annamma's husband George. Having studied medicine at a mission school in Miraj, he was now working for a diploma in children's health in Bombay. The wedding was held in his home in the hilly country of Travancore, east of Alwaye.

After the ceremony in the Jacobite church the party filled the compound of the groom's house, where a big canopy of palm leaves had been erected. Mary sat with her family at a table laden with curries and other delicacies, and stared at the couple seated side by side on the flower-decked platform. Impossible that the gaily smiling figure, half buried beneath silver-threaded garlands of roses and jasmines, was her baby sister Kunjamma, the Small One!

She looked around the family circle. John had his Annie, George his Kunjani. There were Aleyamma and Verghese, Annamma and George, Thankamma and her Verghese, and now Kunjamma and Mathai. Apart from Babi, who himself was soon to be married, only she, Mary, seemed alone. And she was twenty-four years old. A generation ago a normal Indian woman her age would not only have acquired a mate and borne a half dozen children, but would already, like as not, have lived four-fifths of her life span. Even now many of the women in this group were undoubtedly pitying her because she chose to postpone marriage. For a moment her fingers fumbled with a mound of rice and curry.

She looked again around the family circle: Aleyamma, immersed in children, husband, embroidery; Annamma, enclosed in the walls of her neat, efficient household; Thankamma, a little worried and discontented because of her frequent bouts with sickness; Kunjamma, looking smaller and more delicate than ever under her garlands. Envy them? No, she felt gratitude, instead, for her own independence and abounding strength. Making a neat ball of the rice and curry, she popped it deftly into her mouth. Never, she thought, had anything tasted so good.

In spite of her superior physical strength during her Medical College years, Mary was never a champion in any of the sports—badminton, net ball, throw ball, tennis—in which she participated. In one of the annual field day contests she came very near it. One of the events was a sack fight. Feet securely bound inside big jute bags, the contestants formed a circle and attempted, without using their arms, to upset the balance of the others. The last one to fall would be the winner.

For once, Mary's sheer physical strength was at a premium. One after the other her opponents went down There was a large audience, including Dr. Ida, always on the sidelines of any sports event whenever she was in Vellore. Mary set herself to win. She had recently seen Dr. Ida, now nearly eighty, trounce an opponent less than half her age in tennis, sending serves across the net with the speed and accuracy of Mary's own champion brother John. Mary felt a fierce compulsion to prove her own supremacy. Her desire to emulate Dr. Ida extended even to this comparatively unimportant area of athletic prowess. It was as if by making herself as much like her ideal as possible, she might discover the source of the older woman's inexplicable energy. Besides, Mary coveted the spark of approval in the lively blue eyes, the "Bravo, bravo!" which was the highest accolade any Vellore contestant could hope to receive.

Finally there were only two girls left beside Mary. One of them, Mary Ali, would offer small competition. The other, Susan, was a more formidable opponent. Hastily Mary determined her strategy—to oust Mary Ali before tackling the more difficult Susan—and moved in for the assault. Her legs were long and her balance excellent. She was sturdy of shoulder, strong of hip. Advancing in a series of short leaps, being careful not to come too close to her opponent, she moved into attacking position.

All three of the girls had their fans on the sidelines, and the cheering was almost as competitive as the battle.

"Come on, Mary, you can do it!" Mary recognized Lily's voice.

Mary bounced in, swung her shoulders, and the battle was on. Once she almost lost her balance, but John's gymnastic training saved her. She had not stood on her head all those mornings for nothing. Her opponent, Mary Ali, became unsteady. Just as Mary became confident of winning, she was thrown off balance by an upsetting jolt in the rear. Susan had joined forces with Mary Ali to eliminate her from the contest. She felt a blind anger. Surely that wasn't fair. Susan could have chosen to help *her* against Mary Ali just as well. She fought doggedly, but toppled. After that Susan made short work of eliminating Mary Ali, who came in second.

"Brave, bravo!" congratulated Dr. Ida, smiling with equal warmth at all three girls. "You all fought nobly."

Lily laughed at Mary's moodiness over the episode.

"It wasn't fair," insisted Mary. "I'm stronger than Mary Ali. At least I should have come in second."

"Oh, what difference does it make?" Lily's tone was more teasing than comforting. "It was only a game. What do you care whether you got a prize or not?"

Mary made no reply.

IO

Early one Friday morning Mary climbed into a big ambulance backed up to a side entrance of the hospital. She explained to the nurse in charge that she was taking the place of a student associate who was unable to fill her weekly assignment with the mobile clinic.

"Good!" replied the nurse, smiling. "Is this your first time on Roadside?"

"Yes," replied Mary. "I expect I have much to learn."

"Indeed you have," was the cheerful response. "But have no fear. You will find out what to do by doing it."

Mary watched curiously while the cupboard backing the driver's seat was stocked with medicines, another big wooden chest equipped with dressings and other surgical supplies was put aboard, and the lab box was stowed under a seat.

"That red box on the floor," explained the nurse, "is for ears, the blue one for eyes." Her own dark eyes twinkled. "Eyes shouldn't be red, that's how we tell them apart."

Soon, the rest of the team had arrived; two young women doctors, another medical student, two seniors in the School of Nursing, two pharmacists, a religious worker, the driver, and Dr. Ida B. Scudder, who was in charge. They almost filled the narrow seats running lengthwise along the sides of the bus.

Swinging out of the hospital gate, the bus moved through the Vellore streets, already congested with bicycles, lorries, bullock carts, and ambling cows, and turned off at the edge of the city on the road to Odugathur, some twenty miles distant. It was a narrow, bumpy road, full of ruts and potholes, yet in spite of scanty rains there were gems of beauty along its sides—fields of waving sugar cane just springing into silvery tufts, an occasional rice field reflecting the blue sky, carefully irrigated little plots of land embroidered with every shade of green from pale lime to deep emerald. Sometimes they had to turn out at a narrow place to let a caravan of bullock *bandies* pass, their small reed frames topped by incredibly lofty piles of grain bags or green manure or bamboo poles from the distant forest.

The hospital team was jolly and good-natured, and, though too shy to take part in the gay banter, Mary enjoyed it in her quiet way. Roadside, started by Dr. Ida herself nearly fifty years before, was one of Vellore's unique institutions. Mary had been hearing a great deal about it. "You think Out-patient Dispensary is a madhouse? Wait till you see Roadside!" "You'll never guess how many treatments were given on Roadside last year. Over forty-three thousand!" "Now I've seen everything. I've been out on Roadside!"

Always challenged by the new and the difficult, Mary approached the day with a sense of high adventure. Yet she feared it also, for it meant venturing into a strange new world which she had seen only from a distance, the world of huddled mud huts and half starved children and smoking cow-dung fires and women with sun-bleached hair and saris the color of earth. It was one thing having them come into her world of the hospital or of the safe comfortable compound among the coconut trees. It was quite another to enter theirs.

Suddenly a huge crowd appeared ahead, gathered in the shade of an arch of banyans. The ambulance pulled up under a tree at the side of the road. The team poured out and were immediately surrounded. Bewildered, Mary found herself the center of a clamoring group, all talking excitedly in Tamil. Soiled hands clutched her white sari. An arm with a fearful ulcer was thrust close to her face. To avoid its stench, she turned quickly, only to come face to face with a naked baby, hair matted, eyes gummed and running, small body riddled with sores.

"Dr. Ammah, please! Help my baby!"

Managing to escape, Mary fought her way toward Dr. Ida B. Scudder, who, surrounded by a similar group, seemed quite unperturbed. Mary watched while the older woman called the different patients by name, patted a skinny leg, pressed down a small eyelid and clucked sympahetically when it revealed the dead white conjunctiva of anemia, prodded a tiny bulging stomach. Mary's head whirled. Hundreds of them, there must be! Chaos! Surely they would be here all day, a week, before all of them were treated!

But suddenly, order emerged. Tables were unfolded and set up under trees. Another, with dressing tray, was placed by the rear steps of the car and stocked with medical supplies. The roadside had become a fairly efficient dispensary. However, they were not yet ready to start. The crowd tightened into a circle. Heads were bowed. The religious worker—Bible Ammah, they called her—began to pray. Mary listened in wonder. The woman sounded as if she thought there was a holy Presence standing beside her in the dust.

"Here we are, Father," she said simply in Tamil. "You see us. You see our weak bodies. You see the tired men and women, the sick children. You know our troubles. O Lord, our Brother, you lived with us once as a man. You were hungry and thirsty and knew pain and sorrow. Father, help us."

The team swung into action. Everybody except Mary seemed to know just what to do, even the crowd, which was rapidly increasing. Many gathered about the front seat of the bus, where dried milk from UNICEF and CARE, vitamins from Church World Service, and rations of grain and rice would be distributed. Around a table set some distance from the bus were ranged all the patients requiring dressings or surgical care. Farther away under a tree stood another table where injections of chaulmoogra oil would be given to leprosy patients. Under another tree the Bible Ammah was telling a story to a group of children, a story about another dry stony country called Palestine and a man who healed lepers.

Mary was relieved when Dr. Ida B., as she was usually called to distinguish her from her famous aunt, beckoned her to a place beside her table. At least she would not be expected to work with the leprosy patients! In spite of Dr. Cochrane's assurance she still turned cold at the thought of actually touching the stumps of hands, the distorted features, the festering feet. Helplessly lost at first, she was soon following Dr. Ida B.'s matter-of-fact directions, taking down names, writing "chits" or prescriptions, repeating instructions over and over in the best Tamil she could muster:

"*Illai,* no, *ammah!* Take the medicine out of the paper before you swallow it."

"You understand? Put the ointment on for three nights—*mundru,* three. Then give the child a bath. On the fourth morning wash him all over. Wash even his clothes."

"Each day give the baby one of these pills that is bright red. Crush it and put it in his *conjee,* his porridge. Each day. Understand?"

As the day wore on and the Roadside procedure was repeated at a half dozen other stops Mary found herself engaged in many other activities—dressing ulcers, bathing sore eyes, cutting hair so that ointment could be better applied to festered scalps, holding a wailing girl while the American doctor opened a painful abscess under the hard horny flesh of her heel, helping to examine a pregnant woman as she lay on the ground, a group of obliging females securing a bit of privacy for her by making a curtain with their saris.

"I call this the Gynecology Department," commented Dr. Ida B. cheerfully.

Mary watched her wonderingly. There was no need for Dr. Ida B. to do this. Surely it would be easier to stay back in Vellore in her own well-run Radiology Department. Why had she come to this country at all? What did she see in these wretched, ignorant riffraff of another race that she could remember and call them by name, as if she cared personally about them?

"Look, Mary, this is Panchala. And here is her baby Pushpam, such a lovely clean baby. Doesn't she look like a flower? Panchala had so many miscarriages before finally she was able to have this baby! Her husband is crippled from leprosy and can't work. No wonder he is bitter and unhappy. See that Panchala, who is still nursing, has powdered milk from the CARE parcel and shark liver oil. She has had it for a year now. That is why Pushpam is so fat and healthy."

"What is it, *Pattiammal,* Grandmother? You cannot see? Ah, yes, you have cataract. Come to the Eye Hospital. They can make you see again. . . . No one to go with you? Then here is this 'chit.' Wait here until we return tonight. We will take you."

"Your son, *ammah?* Chills and a bad headache every morning for ten days? . . . Yes, his spleen is definitely enlarged. Write him a chit, Mary, for antimalarial medicine. And be sure to come next week, *ammah.* Bring his medicine chit and another bottle."

"Oh, no!" Mary saw the older woman take a thin little face between her hands. "You have coughed blood, you say? Please, please don't have tuberculosis!" She turned to the young student in distress. "She's one of my own little girls. I've followed her family through so many years. I'd be just sick if I found she had T.B.!"

Mary did what she was told, capably, with ever increasing efficiency. At Dr. Ida B.'s request she treated a case of fluid in the abdomen by tapping it with a needle. She went with the American doctor to examine a Moslem woman, hidden inside a bullock cart behind a curtain which protected her from prying male eyes. She helped treat ulcers varying in size from one as large as a small saucer to one which extended from the toes to the knees. Carefully she wound the slender filament of a guinea worm from a woman's hip on a little roll of plaster, knowing that if she broke it off it would cause painful infection, and tried to explain to the woman that the water from her infected village well must be boiled. She treated a severe burn, removed a peanut from a little boy's nose, put drops in hundreds of infected eyes. There were no sore eyes like this in Kerala. She hadn't supposed there could be so many dust-reddened lids and white-filmed eyeballs in the world!

Long before the day was over the patients had ceased to be people, with names, families, individual ailments, and had become endless queues of bodies, blurs of squatting figures, upturned faces, red-rimmed eyes.

It was late when they reached Odugathur, the last stop, where another crowd was waiting for them. Must we treat them all? wondered Mary in dismay. It was so late! Why could not the ambulance have turned back sooner?

"Once," said Dr. Ida B., as if in answer to her unspoken question, "we almost decided to turn back before we got to Odugathur. It was so late, and we were all so tired. But we came on, and here was a boy lying on the ground with his head in another boy's lap. He had been gored by a bull. His intestines were exposed, but his friend had had the good sense to cover them with clean plantain leaves. They had been waiting for hours, knowing we would come. Fortunately we were able to save him. I've never had the temptation to turn back again."

It was over at last, the last patient treated by the light of a flaring lantern, boxes repacked, many of them empty now, the tables slid into their apertures, hands scrubbed. It had been an average day: 575 patients treated and 106 children given milk and vitamins.

In spite of the team's weariness they had a gay ride home through the dark. The two young nurses sang love songs in Malayalam, making Mary homesick. She wished she dared join in. It might make her forget the arduous, discouraging day. But she contented herself with a rhythmic clapping of hands. One of the pharmacists improvised a drum from an empty milk powder can. A container of puffed rice kernels was passed around. Then the mood changed. Somebody started to sing "We are climbing Jacob's ladder," and the team all joined in . . . all but Mary. She was suddenly glad she could not sing, for she had no heart for it.

So this was the new India she had been so proud of, the brave free country that she had talked so glibly about serving! She knew that she had never really seen it before, smelled it, felt it. Though she had scrubbed her hands until they felt raw, the dirt of it still clung to her stained and dust-stiffened sari, was crusted on her arms, ground into the pores of her face. She wondered if she could ever wash herself clean.

"Every round goes higher, higher," sang the team with soft sweet optimism.

Every round! Once each week, fifty-two weeks a year, and for how many years had buses like this been going out on Roadside? Almost half a century! And suppose they kept going for another fifty years, how much farther would they have climbed up the ladder? She had never known such misery existed.

A lantern flickered in the dark beside the road. The bus stopped. The back doors were opened, and a small shrinking figure was hoisted up the steps. The old woman blind with cataracts. Someone helped her to a seat beside Mary, where she crouched, pulling her bare feet under her gray-white sari and burying her head as deeply as possible in its folds. The dirty clawlike hand clutching the two edges trembled with fright.

Here were the dirt and stench and misery of the day all over again. Instinctively Mary moved away, recoiling from them.

Dr. Ida B., who was sitting opposite, leaned across the bus and patted the blind woman's trembling hand. "It's all right, *ammah*. Don't be afraid. I'm right here and I'll stay with you as long as you need me."

Mary looked at her again in wonder.

II

It was during the early part of Mary's clinical years that Dr. Paul Brand began making his surgical experiments that were to revolutionize the treatment of leprosy. Born in India, educated in England, he had just finished his medical training preparatory to returning to India as a missionary doctor when in 1940 bombs had begun to fall on London. Assigned to casualty clearing stations, he had acquired such interest and experience in repairing shattered arms and legs that in 1943, qualifying as a Fellow of the Royal College of Surgeons, he had sought and obtained an appointment to the Children's Hospital in London. Here, he had specialized in the treatment of polio cases. Reluctantly, for he enjoyed this work, he had yielded finally to the insistence of Dr. Robert Cochrane, then Director of the Medical College, that he come to Vellore. He had joined the staff in 1946, a few months after Mary entered the college.

Paul Brand's interest in leprosy was at first ordinary though he knew that Vellore, under Dr. Cochrane's direction, was successfully experimenting with the new drug D.D.S. (diamino-diphenyl-sulfone) which was soon to outmode the clumsy, painful, and much less effective chaulmoogra oil injection, for generations the standard treatment. Then one day Dr. Brand visited the leprosy sanatorium at Chingleput, near Madras, with which his friend Dr. Cochrane had long been associated. There for the first time he became suddenly, acutely conscious of hands.

Everywhere he saw them outstretched, as the patients lined up to greet him, some with the fingers reduced to stumps, others with fingers clenched stiffly toward the palm.

It was on these latter that the young doctor's sensitive eyes became riveted. He had always loved well-formed and skillful hands, and the mute appeal of the useless claws stirred him.

"Yes," agreed the specialist who was his guide, "it's a pity, isn't it? Almost half of all leprosy cases suffer crippling paralysis, usually in the hands or feet. And there's no real treatment possible. All we can do is try to prevent them from getting worse."

Fascinated, Dr. Brand approached one of the patients, lifted his hands, and examined them closely. Then on a sudden impulse he placed his own right hand in the right hand of the patient.

"Squeeze my hand, please," he said, "as hard as you can."

The man squeezed. Since leprosy produces hands without feeling and therefore without reaction pressures—he had no idea of the strength of his grip. To the doctor's amazement it was like iron. The clawed fingers crushed his palm; the long nails bit into his flesh; he felt as if the bones of his hand were being broken. It took all his self control to keep from crying out.

But his excitement was greater than his pain. There was still plenty of muscle power in that hand! In that revealing moment he began the activity that was to change not only his own life but that of thousands of others. He had planned to remain in Vellore only long enough for the hospital to secure another surgeon, then return to his primary concern of reconstructing crippled arms and legs. Now he envisioned possibilities even more challenging. There were many orthopedic surgeons ministering to victims of polio, but for the twelve million leprosy victims of the world there was not a single one.

Dr. Cochrane was equally excited. He had always believed, contrary to prevailing opinion, that surgery might be useful in treating leprosy. Urging his colleague to go ahead and try, he put a small research team at his disposal.

So Paul Brand began his months of research. He and his team studied the entire literature on hand surgery, and they tested thousands of leprosy-paralyzed hands. Triumphantly he came to two conclusions: First, the leprosy-induced paralysis was not indefinitely progressive, and since certain muscles affecting the hand and arm were rarely paralyzed, it was a mistake to assume that healthy muscle used for transplantation might later paralyze. Second, the bone absorption was not caused, as popularly believed, by the disease bacillus itself, but by the frequent injuries, such as cuts and burns, that were the natural result of the lack of feeling. His problem now was to transfer good muscles and tendons to do the work of the paralyzed ones. He was ready to begin his experiments in surgery.

"Send me a patient," he requested the sanatorium at Chingleput, "with hands so bad they could not possibly be made worse."

He came to Vellore, a young Hindu. "I'm no surgeon," said Dr. Cochrane, who brought him, "but I can tell you that the tissues of leprosy patients heal well after minor operations, and if you think you can transplant tendons and reshape bones to turn these miserable beggars into useful citizens, it's just what I've been wanting to do for years. There are a million suitable cases waiting for you."

Dr. Brand looked at the young man. There were ulcers on the soles of his feet that exposed the bones. His hands, fingers curled into the clawed position, were unable to grasp any object except by a pathetic attempt to pinch between the thumb and the side of the index knuckle. The doctor's heart sank, but not because of the apparent hopelessness of his patient's physical condition. It was because, looking beyond the deformities, he saw the young man's cringing, broken spirit.

The patient had been well brought up and had a good education. There had once been humor, alertness, ambition in those dead eyes, liveliness in the voice tuned now to a begging whine for the next meal. Was this what leprosy did to a man's mind and spirit? No, not leprosy. Men. For it was the thoughtless multitude, acting with herd instinct of self-preservation, that had robbed a good intellect of its will to think. Ironic that during much of his exile, like most of the worst-deformed cases, this sufferer had most certainly been noninfectious! Dr. Brand took the boy's hands. "Will you permit me to operate on these?" he asked gently.

The young Hindu regarded his claws without visible emotion. "Do what you wish with them," he said. "They are no good to me."

Mary and her fellow-students knew about this leprosy patient. They stole glances at him when they passed his bed in the surgery ward. Even though Mary knew now that fear of contagion was in large measure a myth, the habit of childhood was still strong. She kept as far away as her duties allowed. But with many other students in the popular young surgeon's classes, she followed his experiment with enthralled interest.

The operations were not basically new. The same technique of replacing an injured muscle tendon with a sound one had been used for war injuries and polio; it had simply not been used for leprosy.

Dr. Brand and his assistants operated on two fingers at a time, opened them out, fixed the transplanted tendons in their new positions, tested the tension, and then closed the wounds and prayed. After weeks of waiting and cautious testing, the excitement of success began to sweep through the hospital.

"Have you seen Dr. Brand's patient? He can bend his hand now at the knuckles!"

"Today he picked up a block of wood . . . a small bottle . . . a pencil. . . ."

"Today he lifted a glass of water!"

The young Hindu was a new person. His eyes brightened again into keenness. His laughter rang out. One day he looked down at his new hands, now strong and useful, and said to Dr. Brand, "These hands do not belong to me. They belong to your God, who made this miracle possible."

The patient remained in the hospital a year. During that time he became a Christian and was baptized. When he was finally dismissed, he went out with two good feet, two strong and able hands, and a hopeful face.

Two months later he was back again, dejected and half starved. "These are not good hands you have given me, Doctor Sahib," he told Brand mournfully. "They are bad hands."

The young doctor stared at him aghast.

"Bad *begging* hands," explained the boy sadly. Nobody would employ him, because he still bore the marks of leprosy. Nobody would even give him a place to live. Before, he had sat under a banyan tree, and, taking pity on his useless hands, people had thrown him coins to keep him from starving. Now they had no pity. They saw that his hands were whole. Now he had nothing.

It was possible to save this patient. Taken into the hospital, he was nursed back to health. He had learned to type before contracting leprosy, and, encouraged to develop the skill again, he was soon earning money by doing odd jobs of typing for patients in the hospital. But what about the other patients who were now being given new hands? Dr. Brand realized to his consternation that his job was only half done. Minds must be healed as well as bodies. The men must be taught skills and trades so they could lead independent lives. *Rehabilitation*. But where? How?

It was "Mother" Eaton who helped find the answer.

An eighty-four-year-old former missionary severely afflicted with rheumatoid arthritis, Mother Eaton had come to the hospital as a patient. Little could be done for her except give her some relief from pain. But Mother Eaton displayed no sharpness, no bitterness. She was always sweet and smiling.

One day she said to Paul Brand, "I couldn't sleep last night, Doctor, because of the pain, and I got to thinking about this problem of yours. I have five hundred pounds in the bank. It shouldn't be lying idle. Please take it and use it for these patients of yours."

Mary watched the cluster of thatch-roofed huts being built in a far corner of the college campus, little knowing how profoundly their purpose was to invade her own life. *"Nava Jeeve Nilayam,"* "Place of New Life" they called it, this village of white huts surrounding a training shed, the first leprosy rehabilitation center in the world, where reconstructed hands could learn little by little to become useful. Carpentry, masonry, painting, and toy-making were skills especially suited to the limitations of hands without cutaneous sensation. Special tools were designed; pliers and scissors were fitted with springs to insure easy opening and a firm grip, and all tools were stored in such a way that they could be grasped without friction.

Because of the important discovery that the loss of fingers in leprosy was due to persistent injury rather than to any disease-induced wasting of the flesh, the patients were trained to observe the utmost care in protecting their own fingers. Long handles for cooking utensils were designed, wooden rings to hold hot coffee tumblers, wicker baskets to hold metal plates.

Here also were taught skills of spiritual living. Caste barriers were set aside. Among the first twenty-four patients in Brand's initial New Life group were an engineer, a chartered accountant, a B.Sc. student, a former Brahmin, all living in harmony with uneducated villagers, sharing food at the same table, taking turns in doing the menial tasks of cleaning the compound, drawing water, performing sanitation duty, growing their own grain and vegetables. It was a Place of New Life for the reconstruction not only of bodies, but of minds and spirits.

The medical students helped by giving a chapel for the center. They spent a week building it, aided by students from other Christian colleges. It was a simple building, with low walls and thatched roof. The openings between its square stone posts looked out across the plain toward the distant mountains.

In Paul Brand, tireless, self-effacing, and utterly dedicated, Mary caught the flare of that same inner light which radiated from Dr. Ida. She saw it in many of the people here at Vellore. It mattered little what country they came from. Dr. Graham had it, an Englishwoman. So did Dr. Carol Jameson, an American, head of Mary's own chosen Department of Gynecology. But so also did Dr. Lazarus, an Indian. As she observed and reflected, Mary saw that it was more than just a sort of inner glow that lent sparkle and zest to the adventure of living. It was fire instead of light, a compulsive force that exploded into unusual, sometimes almost incredible action.

It was what sent Dr. Ida B. Scudder out on Roadside after a busy week in her understaffed and ill-equipped Radiology Department; what drove Dr. Victor Rambo, the American eye specialist, out into some squalid village outpost to spend his weekends removing cataracts. It got Treva Marshall, the cheerful, buxom, outspoken Dean of Women, up at midnight to see if a homesick first-year student was still crying into her pillow. Yes, and it was what made Ranjeetham, a Vellore graduate, go into a village to live and spend the money given her for a wedding present to build a small mud and thatch house which could be used for a hospital.

It fascinated Mary, whatever it was these people had, but it also frightened and repelled her. She wanted it, and she didn't want it. Always adventurous, she desired anything which would add excitement to living. But—suppose it made demands on her ambition, her career, above all, on her precious independence!

Religion, as she knew it, had made few demands on her, certainly no unpleasant ones. It had provided comfort, a rich and satisfying culture, security. It continued to occupy the same place of importance in her life at Vellore. Every few weeks Kuriakose Achan came from the Bethany Ashram in Travancore and conducted services for the Syrian Christian students and staff members. There were a score or more of them among the medical students, and many of the nurses came from the Syrian Christian group.

"Who else applies for nursing?" Florence Taylor, head of the School of Nursing, once demanded humorously. "There are Annammas and Aleyammas in almost every hospital in India!"

There were the Wednesday morning Bible classes, the morning prayers conducted each day by a staff member, the evening prayers led by students. When in Vellore Dr. Ida often conducted morning prayers, and Mary always attended when she was going to speak, determined to discover the secret of her vital faith. It was a search as much mental as spiritual, intriguing as a problem in chemistry. Dispassionately she analyzed her own motives and actions, as brutally honest as if they were elements in a test tube.

"Jesus, I my cross have taken,"

sang the students lustily in chapel,

"All to leave and follow thee.
Destitute, despised, forsaken,
Thou from hence my all shalt be.
Perish every fond ambition. . . ."

No, thought Mary, closing her lips tightly, I will not say those words. People should not repeat words they did not mean.

There was another hymn, Dr. Ida's favorite, in which she also refused to participate. It began, "Be thou my vision, O Lord of my heart," and went on to declare:

"Riches I heed not, nor man's empty praise. . . ."

It would be hypocrisy, Mary felt, to sing it. For she *did* want to make money. She *did* want men's praise. Why not? Was she not working hard to earn them?

And then in her fourth year of medical college, 1950, she discovered the secret.

Rev. Harrie Scott-Simmonds, at one time Precentor of Melbourne Cathedral in Australia, but now for three years connected with the Dohnavur Ashram in South India, came to Vellore to visit his friend Dr. John Moody, another Australian who was lecturer in dentistry. Simmonds was persuaded to give a series of sermons. An eloquent evangelist, he soon inspired in the whole student body a deepened sense of spiritual awareness.

Mary was ready for just such a stimulus. Long dissatisfied and questioning, she was fertile soil for the preacher's evangelical seed. One night Simmonds spoke simply but dramatically on the theme, "Behold, the Lamb of God." Mary went out of the chapel with every fiber of her sensitive spirit quivering.

Until this moment God had seemed an impersonal being, benevolent but vague, to be approached through a bearded *achan* or through sonorous prayers phrased by men of another century. The cross, symbol of his love, had been an elaborate stone carving, a wooden altar decoration, a figure stamped on a round piece of bread, to be eaten solemnly at communion. Now, suddenly, both seemed as close and as much a part of life as breathing. As she walked along the narrow white path through the sunken garden, Mary felt life surging about her, life in the act of creating, life in the act of dying that other life might live. She felt an agonizing desire to be a part of it.

Each day, going out on the terrace outside the sleeping room for her private devotions, she saw two of her classmates sitting together, enjoying what seemed to be fellowship in worship—Mariamma Thomas and a Ceylonese girl, Lily Lawrence. Mary wished she dared join them. Perhaps if she were not so terribly alone. . . .

"Won't you join us?" asked Mariamma one morning.

Mary was overcome. Suppose they expected her to take part, even to pray out loud! Her feet lagged. But desire for fellowship conquered. Timid at first, tongue-tied, she found to her surprise that prayer could be as natural as conversation. These girls believed God was actually a part of their little group. They were asking him to guide them in their daily living as simply and trustingly as they would have asked one of their teachers to help them solve a problem in chemistry.

Now that Mary understood Dr. Ida's secret, the knowledge brought only dismay. Submit one's will completely to another's, even to One who was all wise and loving—*especially* to One all wise and loving! Jesus had done just that, and look where it had taken him! Would this not mean, Mary wondered, not caring whether you ever made any money in your career or not? It might even mean—she shivered—going into a filthy village to work instead of into a government hospital, going out at night to make calls! Worst of all, it might mean, it *must* mean, giving up your independence!

For days she wrestled with the problem, her adversary as formidably tangible as Jacob's angel, for it was her own indomitable will. When finally the end of the conflict came, there was nothing dramatic about its conclusion. She simply awoke one morning knowing it had been decided.

"I am willing." She could not even speak the words aloud in the crowded dormitory. "From now on I will seek Your guidance. Help me to do what You want me to do."

It was strange what a difference the simple decision made. As on Independence Day, the colors in the sunken garden seemed sharper, brighter. Riding to the hospital in the bus, she was more aware of all the little details along the way, a bush of flaming bougainvillea, a mother nursing her baby, children's laughter, a ray of sunlight flashing on the ancient ruin on top of Fort Hill. It was as if everything in the world had been brought into sudden clearer perspective.

But even more profound was the change that came in her attitude toward people. It did not happen all at once. Perhaps she first became aware of it when a certain patient was admitted to B Ward.

The man was a poor villager, and he had broken his back falling from a tree. The students would have found the case of little interest had it not introduced them to a surgical problem not yet encountered. The villager appeared to be a victim of paraplegia.

"That means his spinal cord is damaged," explained a senior clinical student to a junior. "He has no movement at all in his legs, no feeling below the level of the injury. You could cut him with a knife below the waist, and he wouldn't know it. In over half his body he has no more feeling than does a leprosy patient in his hands and feet."

The case became the subject of avid discussion.

"You mean—he'll never be able to walk?"

"There's a chance he may. The doctors are talking about performing a laminectomy."

"A lam—What's that?"

The senior students were glibly superior. "It's the removal of the laminae from the spine to release pressure on the cord, which is probably caused by the displacement of the fractured vertebrae."

"But there's no assurance that it will do any good. Even with laminectomy he may or may not be able to walk."

A day or two later there was more news to share.

"That paraplegic. What do you think? He's gone home!"

"The laminectomy didn't do any good?"

"They never performed it. His family refused to let them."

"*Ayoh!* Why not?"

"Who knows? Can anybody ever tell why these ignorant villagers act as they do? Probably the doctors told them there was no certainty of his being able to walk even if he had the operation."

"What a pity! Now we'll never know how the operation would have succeeded."

Mary shared their clinical curiosity. Not long ago she would have expressed herself exactly as they did, her interest in the case bounded largely by its opportunities for further professional experience. Now she found herself thinking quite different, more disturbing thoughts.

How was the patient feeling now, at home in his thatched hut? What would it be like, never being able to work, having to be waited on—bathed and fed—while watching your family become poorer and poorer, hungrier and hungrier?

With comprehension came a sudden dismay. Already she was beginning to realize the implications of the choice she had made. It was not going to be easy, being a doctor *and* a Christian. It meant that patients were no longer just cases. They had become persons!

There was even more curiosity among the students when later another patient of Dr. Chandy, Vellore's head neurosurgeon, appeared in B Ward. His name was George Mathew, and he had been a student at Union Christian College in Alwaye, in Mary's own state of Kerala. As the result of an accident, he had become a quadriplegic.

"A quadriplegic!" Mary and her student associates discussed the case excitedly. "That's even worse than paraplegia. It means his arms are paralyzed too, as well as his legs."

One day Mary stopped beside George Mathew's bed. The boy was in cervical traction in an attempt to reduce the compression. His young face was hard and bitter.

"Ha! Come to sympathize, I suppose, in Malayalam. Don't. Pity is as bad in one language as another."

"I didn't come to pity you," said Mary.

"Maybe you brought me something, then. There's just one thing I would like: a good dose of arsenic. Or do you have some new drug that works more quickly?"

In spite of herself Mary's eyes twinkled. "I'm glad to see you still have a good sharp tongue."

He glared up at her. "*Seri,* yes. And since that is all I have, I may as well use it."

"It is not all," she told him boldly. "You have good eyes. You have a good brain."

"And what are they good for? Eyes to watch somebody hold a spoon in front of my face? A brain to tell me when I'm supposed to open my mouth?"

Mary drew a long breath. "You have God," she said softly.

His lips curled. "I should have known! You came to preach."

"But I didn't! It's just that I've found out lately how much it means, knowing God cares—"

"Cares! Did he care about me when he let this happen? *Mathi,* enough! Don't talk to me about God, you who have good strong arms and hands and legs!" His eyes grew bleak with desperation, and the sweat stood on his forehead. "Do you know what it is to be alive and dead at the same time, to have to be fed like a baby, to strain and struggle hard enough to climb a mountain, and yet not move an inch, to—"

"Hush!" pleaded Mary.

At sight of her stricken face he turned bitterly triumphant. "No, of course you don't. All right, then. Don't tell me how I ought to feel."

"I—I'm sorry," said Mary.

She turned away helplessly. There seemed to be nothing more she could say.

12

That year of 1950 was Dr. Ida's Jubilee, marking fifty years since she had come as a doctor to India. The year had seen many successive triumphs: a huge celebration in January, with His Excellency the Maharajah of Bhavnagar, Governor of Madras, and Her Highness the Maharani in attendance; the dedication of many new buildings; the admission of 20 men students out of the 581 applying; and, at long last, the full accreditation of the college by Madras University. Now, crowning it all, in December, came Dr. Ida's eightieth birthday.

The students were up at dawn creating a gorgeous birthday chair and making the chapel beautiful with the blue and white blossoms she so loved. There were lacy *appams,* served with coconut milk, for breakfast; then an impressive chapel service. In the evening a huge public meeting was held in the hospital compound.

Adding her white flower to the massed blossoms and garlands which half buried Dr. Ida and her birthday chair, Mary felt a deep sense of fulfillment. Once, walking with this woman through the hospital corridors, she had seen a poor villager, his face drawn by sickness but now suddenly illuminated, reach out timid fingers to touch the hem of her dress. India had a word for it, *darshan,* the blessing gained by the mere sight or touch of a *Mahatma,* a Great Soul. Mary felt it in this moment. She could never hope to emulate the achievements of this remarkable life, but at least she now knew the secret of its power.

She wished she could share the secret with everybody. Especially was her third sister Thankamma the object of her concern, for recently Thankamma's long struggle with bouts of rheumatic fever had culminated in a serious heart malady, which now confined her to her bed.

Mary prayed long and fervently that her sister might regain her health. But, the answer seemed to come, if she is closer to God because of her physical ailment, who are you to say she is unfortunate?

Thankamma closer to God because of suffering? Mary almost laughed at the idea. Always a difficult patient, her sister had become increasingly bitter and complaining. Mary both dreaded and longed for her next vacation, fearful of the new tensions which Thankamma might have developed in her absence, yet hoping she could share some of her own spiritual experience with her sister.

She did find Thankamma changed, amazingly so. Though still an invalid, her sister was no longer morose. She listened with interest to Mary's eager witness to her newly discovered faith. She also asked penetrating questions about her work in the hospital and the problems of her patients. Especially was Thankamma interested in those who came to Roadside. Day after day she inquired about their poverty, their hunger, their diseases, and the kind of treatments given.

Her eyes grew more and more thoughtful. One day they followed little Omana, running and jumping on the verandah outside the window, and sharpened with a bright intensity.

"Suppose my child were like those you see on Roadside," she reflected aloud. "Suppose all she wanted to do was to lie quietly in my arms because she had no energy to run and play. I—I've never really thought about such things before."

Another day she said, "I have been thinking, Mary. There must be children like that here, too, all around us, and sick people with no one to care for them. The villagers who need help are not all over there near Vellore. There may even be some here in our own village."

"Athay, yes," agreed Mary, quietly exultant because of the new interest and compassion in her sister s voice. "Oh, yes, there are!"

But it was not only Thankamma who awakened to a new awareness of people and their needs. It was Mary herself.

"Praise to the Lord! Praise to the Lord!"

When Mary heard the cry, the years fell away, and she was a child again, cold with fear.

"It's Joseph!" cried Amma. She dashed into the courtyard, seized

Omana by the hand. "Come into the house, baby. Come in here at once!"

The child began to cry, frightened by the unmistakable panic in her grandmother's voice. Mary followed them into the kitchen.

"I'll take the food to Joseph," she told her mother reassuringly.

Standing in the gate, waiting for him, she tried to remind herself of Dr. Cochrane's conclusive statements about leprosy, but for the moment the habits of childhood were stronger than all her years of medical training. She was actually trembling. It was all she could do to keep from setting the basket down on the ground and retreating in a panic. "*Adukkallai*—don't go near!" Theresia's remembered voice drowned out all the others.

Then she saw him. To her surprise he no longer looked revolting. He was no longer a fearsome stranger, but only a patient badly in need of medical attention. She set down the basket.

"Let's see those hands, Joseph," she said, reaching for the bandaged stumps.

He must go to the hospital, she told him earnestly, and ask the doctors there to dress his hands properly. And he must learn to take better care of his hands. He must examine his hands every day for cuts, bruises, and blisters. He must use special handles and holders for hot articles. And he must never, *never* touch a hot coal or a burning stick with his bare hands. Did he understand?

Joseph nodded. *Athay,* yes, he understood. Seeing the bewilderment in his face, Mary carefully repeated her instructions. More dazed than grateful, the beggar finally picked up the basket of food and went his way.

After that experience Mary no longer dreaded Roadside. During her fifth year in medical school she looked forward to going out with Dr. Ida B. Scudder on Fridays and with Dr. M. D. Graham on Wednesdays. The treatment of leprosy patients became as routine to her as vaccinating for smallpox or washing out sore eyes. She learned to give chaulmoogra oil injections, and was thankful for the superior strength that enabled her to administer the painful dosage with as neat and swift a thrust as possible. She massaged stiffened fingers and showed the patients how to stretch them. She bandaged dozens of infected hands and feet.

These clinical years were the most satisfying Mary had yet experienced. Always challenged by the new and the difficult, she delighted in the constant variety of problems which each new case presented.

The more acute the case and the more difficult its problems, the better she liked it. Only once did she complain of getting more than her just share. During her service in Obstetrics one of her assignments was to officiate at twenty normal deliveries. She seemed doomed to frustration. After waiting her turn for hours—days—she would find herself involved in a forceps case or a Caesarean.

"I'll never finish the assignment!" she despaired. "All this time, and I have only twelve!"

"Don't get discouraged," sympathized Dr. Loenen, one of the older Vellore graduates who was working with Mary. "Just think how much more you're learning."

Mary was not a brilliant medical student. Though intelligent and conscientious, she won few honors. And she did not believe in burning the midnight oil.

"How can you!" marveled Grace Koshi, a younger student who became her intimate friend and roommate during the last half of Mary's fifth year. "Here you are having an examination tomorrow, and yet you're going to bed early as usual, and you'll probably sleep like a log. And you're in your final year, too, when everything depends on your passing. I'm only in my second year, but I'm terrified."

"You should have no worries," Mary consoled her. "Better to work hard and steadily for a few hours and then sleep. You will waken ready to do your best. Remember what Dr. Brand said in chapel service—those words from Daniel? 'He is able to deliver us. But if not. . . .' "

"Yes. 'If not'?" prompted Grace. "That's what I'm worried about. Suppose we do our best and fail. What then?"

"If not," finished Mary thoughtfully, "I suppose He will help us find some way to use our failure."

Grace sighed. Could she become as calm and poised in three years' time? It was hard being a second-year student and rooming with three fifth-year girls. Yet somehow in her quiet way Mary managed to harmonize the disparate personalities around her. It was surprising, too, how many of her classmates found their way to her room seeking advice and understanding.

Grace and Mary were roommates by mutual choice. Both were Jacobites, Orthodox Syrian Christians. However, Grace was discovering through Mary a richness of spiritual experience which she had not found in the formalism of the Syrian Christian service. She affectionately condoned the older girl's stubbornness, admired her quiet poise, marveled at her scorn for conformity, even in matters of dress.

One Sunday morning Mary came down to their room on the first floor from the big upstairs dormitory where all the girls slept. Unlocking the door, she found dresser drawers gaping, her locker door wide open and its shelves ransacked. A thief had evidently entered the room in the night, climbing in through the transom. Though he had stolen a suitcase from another doctor's room, it was Mary who suffered the greatest losses. But, asked to make an inventory of her missing saris and blouses, Mary was vague.

"Oh, maybe three or four," she ventured.

Later the thief was apprehended, a driver who had moved to Bangalore but had returned to exploit his knowledge of the college area. When summoned to court to claim her property, Mary discovered that seven saris had been stolen instead of three or four.

"Just like you," scolded Grace affectionately. "Clothes are about as important to you as to a Hindu holy man!"

This new sense of spiritual values dominated Mary's last year in medical school. Having volunteered in her fourth year to act on the Chapel Committee, in her fifth year she was elected chairman and became secretary of the Student Council's Committee for Religious Affairs. She took an active part in the social service conducted by the students, supported by their chapel offerings and conducted by the student Social Work Committee. One evening each week she went with four or five other girls to Agraharam, a village on the Arni Road, or to Idyanchathur, another village closer to the campus, where the student committee rented rooms for social work. Here the girls held a medical clinic for villagers, taught the women hygiene, and in the "eye fly" season treated hundreds of eyes.

But it was at Christmas that Mary's work as religious secretary became really inspired. Meena, a Bengali girl, suggested that for the chapel sing every language group represented at Vellore be invited to present one or more of its own carols. So successful was the experiment that it was to set a pattern for subsequent years. Seated on mats in the dimly lighted chapel, open on all its eight sides to the stars, the different groups embodied that diversity in Christian unity which was the genius of Vellore. Carols were sung in Bengali, Hindi, and Urdu; in Tamil and Kanarese and Telugu; in Marathi and Malayalam; in English with all its many varieties, British, American, Australian, Indian.

Before dawn on the day celebrated as Christmas the upperclassmen followed their usual custom of rising quietly, walking through the hostel with lighted candles, and singing carols. Surprised, the new students rose, dressed quickly, and joined them. All together, they went to the men's hostel and serenaded them, whereupon the men also joined the procession, now bound for its last stops, the inner courtyard of the Principal's Bungalow and the sunken garden.

It was then that Mary had her inspiration. Eagerly she turned to a friend, Annamma Verghese, who had been one of the most frequent visitors to the patients in the Leprosy Rehabilitation Center.

"Let us go first to the Place of New Life," she suggested.

It was done. Annamma leading, the procession wound through the darkness, candles glowing in a long bright chain, to the far end of the campus and its lonely cluster of huts.

> "O little town of Bethlehem, How still we see thee lie! . . ."

It really could be Bethlehem, thought Mary, leaving the singing to the others. *Place of New Life*—a little village of square white houses with thatched roofs!

> "Yet in thy dark streets shineth the everlasting Light. . . ."

Figures emerged from the huts. Dark faces appeared in the circles of lamp flames, radiant with the joy of being included. Hands, newly re-created, were raised in the welcoming palm-to-palm gesture, itself triumphant and evidence of their re-creation. For Mary this, not the service in the sunken garden, was the climax of the Christian Festival of Lights.

So came to an end the five and a half years of preparation. Mary acquitted herself well but not brilliantly. Out of twenty-seven in her class she was one of four who did not fail any subject, one of seven who completed the course without losing a year. As for her greater achievements of growth in spirit, there was no formal record of these.

13

Amma lifted her eyes to the rocky eminence and breathed a deep sigh. She was silent so long that Mary became anxious.

"It doesn't look the way you expected? You're disappointed?"

"Disappointed! *Illa,* no! Just to be seeing it at last—Saint Thomas' Mount!"

Amma climbed the one hundred thirty-two steps, entered the ancient church, and stood awe-struck before the great stone which formed the central altar, held sacred by all Syrian Christians as the exact spot where the apostle had been slain; gazed up at the remarkable cross with its centuries-old Nestorian inscription in Pahlavi: "Ever pure . . . is in favor with Him who bore the cross"; marveled at the picture of the Virgin Mary supposed to have been painted by Saint Luke and brought to India by Saint Thomas. And when she had seen all, she sighed again.

"*Nallathu,* it is good. Now at last I have seen."

Dutifully Amma viewed other sites of interest in and around Madras, while staying with her cousins Mary and her husband Philip, whose house she had never before seen. But she exhibited only mild enthusiasm. Even the great University Convocation that was the real object of the trip, with Mary appearing among all the other graduates of Madras State in dignified cap and gown, did not seem to impress Amma so much as her visit to Saint Thomas' Mount. Obviously, her manner implied, having lived her supreme moment, all else in her life from now on must be anticlimax.

Returning to Vellore with her mother, the only member of her family able to attend her graduation, Mary helped the other members of her class prepare the long white jasmine chains that for years had been traditional.

"Childish!" pronounced some of her classmates. "We used to carry garlands in primary school. Let's not do it this year."

"But Dr. Ida likes it," one of the girls pointed out.

That settled it. They donned white saris, festooned the jasmine chains over their right shoulders, then wound in a long procession from the women's hostel into the sunken garden, around the lily pool, on into the cool Assembly Hall, where they wreathed their garlands into great white masses on the stage before taking their seats.

Graduation was in August, 1952, eight months after Mary had actually finished her work as an undergraduate, the date being adjusted to include students completing their final year in April as well as in December. Already Mary had completed nearly two-thirds of her first year of rotating internship.

As a junior house surgeon specializing in gynecology, her first half year had been spent in "Gyne" under Dr. Lazarus, substituting for Dr. Carol Jameson; her second half year would be spent in Obstetrics. She was now living at the hospital on the third floor of the Administration Building, in a room so small as to permit only one other occupant. Grace, still in her third year at the college, felt bereaved at losing her favorite roommate, but the friendship of the two girls continued, and Grace was a frequent visitor at the hospital.

Mary was too busy these days to pay proper attention to food or sleep. Her hours of duty were long. Always overcrowded with patients, the hospital was chronically understaffed. Only once during her residency did she experience a time of comparative leisure.

Mary and Serala Elisha, from the Telugu language area, were assigned for two weeks to the Gudiyattam branch hospital while its regular doctor was away. The two girls, good friends, were delighted. Here in the same compound was the little yellow church where, fifty years before, Dr. Ida had come for a weekly dispensary, traveling first by train and bullock cart, then in her one-cylinder Peugeot automobile—such an innovation to South India that villagers had fled from its path, howling, "The devil is coming!"

"Just think!" marveled Mary as they explored the place. "This was the beginning of Roadside—almost half a century ago!"

Work in the little hospital seemed like play after the teeming bustle of Vellore, but after two weeks of it Mary was glad to get back to the more demanding schedule.

Even better than ward duty she enjoyed her work in the operating room. During her four months in minor surgery and the necessary apprenticeship as assistant with major operations, she impatiently awaited the opportunity to operate completely on her own. The day came at last. Her first operation was the excision of a hydrocele. The senior doctor who assisted her was warm in approval of her technique. After her second operation, the repair of a hernia, she felt as if she had been presiding at an operating table all her life.

For three months during these two years of residency Mary was the only house surgeon in Gynecology. During this period Dr. Jameson was her superior, but she worked also with Dr. Lazarus, who, in addition to her work as director of the whole institution, assisted in the clinical work of the department. A prodigious worker, the Indian doctor was no easy taskmaster. The girls loved and respected but feared her.

Yet this remarkable woman demanded far less than she gave. Not the least of the skills which she imparted to her students was the personal concern which brought her to the hospital each morning with flowers from her garden, to be carefully arranged by her own hands and distributed among the patients.

Mary exulted in the strength which made it possible for her often to do the work of two or three doctors. On operating days she was always ready for work, scrubbed and masked, by seven-thirty. On other days she made her rounds of the wards before the arrival of the "boss," or department head. Once in Maternity she was kept up all night by the fitful restlessness of an eclampsia patient, but her following day's schedule remained inexorably the same. There were many out-patients to be treated, and frequently she was summoned on night calls, possibly to spend the rest of the night delivering a baby, or attempting to repair the damage caused by an ignorant midwife. Thanks to the fifty years of education since Dr. Ida began her crusade against barbers' wives' obstetrics, in Vellore itself these encounters with ignorance and superstition were becoming rarer. Not so, however, in hundreds of outlying villages. The victims of crude and unsanitary midwifery were frequent occupants of both hospital bed and operating table.

Seldom did the hospital day end before eleven at night. Then, often too exhausted to relax, the house surgeons would go out to a hotel for coffee or serve it to themselves on the third-floor verandah near the Pathology Department, a strip which they facetiously dubbed the

"Marina." Never shy with her immediate friends, Mary was always in the center of these midnight larks, joining heartily in the lively chatter ranging from serious philosophy through cases, patients, and complaints about the "boss," to the group's latest romances.

Prema, who had been one of the earlier graduates, was the frequent butt of their teasing. Her admiration for Dr. Bhat, assistant to Dr. Carman, head of Surgery, was common knowledge, denied least of all by Prema herself. The romance, however, had little opportunity to flourish until Mary, as ardent a matchmaker as an adventurer, planned a weekend outing to Kailas, highest of all the mountains overlooking the college campus. All the junior medical staff were invited.

"I organized this just for you," Mary teased Prema, who had become a willing ally. "Now see that you make the most of it."

They made the three-and-a-half-mile climb on a Friday evening in February, returning late on Sunday. Except for the fact that Mary had forgotten the coffee and a coolie had to trot seven miles down and back to get it, the holiday was a success. The party took long walks, played games, cooked and ate quantities of eggs, splashed in a swimming pool. But, except for the fact that Prema and her young doctor walked part of the way up the mountain together, the success of the trip in romantic terms was less tangible.

Disaster proved more effective a matchmaker than adventure. In May, Prema and a friend, Ammini George, together with another girl who had come from Trichur for a hernia operation, took a walk outside the hospital compound. Passing close to the walls of a ruined temple in a nearby field, they were the sudden victims of a wind storm as one of the ancient walls collapsed. The girl who had come for the operation was fatally injured. The other two escaped with fractures and bruises. Prema's physician after the accident was Dr. Bhat. In December of that same year they were married.

Though Mary was friendly with many of the other house surgeons—Prema, Leela, May, Sarama, M. P.—bonds were strengthened these days with her even closer friends. There was Elsie Alexander, who was a member of the intimate prayer fellowship which continued from college days, as was also Mary's special chum and confidante, Annamma Verghese. There was Cheruchi, who had specialized in biochemistry. But Grace Koshi remained one of her closest friends, visiting her often and sometimes accompanying her on her rounds of the hospital.

It was to Grace that Mary confided her hope that she might be chosen by Dr. Jameson to do post-graduate work in gynecology and obstetrics at the University of Madras after her two years of internship should be finished in January. It was paid post, awarded on the basis of scholarship and other personal qualifications, and there were numerous applicants. If working long hours without rest and applying oneself with fierce intensity to each duty every moment of the day were proof of the necessary qualities, Mary felt sure she could win the appointment.

Slowly she developed the skill, the confidence, even the callousness demanded of a good doctor. Grace, accompanying her on her rounds, marveled at the patience with which she listened to every patient's complaints, then set his fears at rest with simple explanations; marveled also at the sternness with which she persuaded the parents of a dead child to permit a post-mortem examination.

"Did you have to be so *heartless*?" she protested. "You almost forced them to consent."

"It was necessary," replied Mary calmly. "It may save the lives of ten other babies. Someday you will understand."

For three months in this second year of residency she went out on Wednesday Roadside to Chittoor for Dr. M. D. Graham, a specialist in children's diseases. It was a heartbreaking experience. Day after day she sat perched on a narrow plinth in the hilltop hut which was one of the Roadside stops, the only fixed landmark in a tide of mothers, infants, children. Wave upon wave they surged against her consciousness, challenging her new knowledge, her yet untried skills, receded, surged again. She begrudged the few moments it took to eat lunch in the dispensary's tiny adjoining room, giving the team a hard-earned bit of privacy.

After a week or two familiar faces began to emerge. Another week, and she was able to remember names belonging with the faces. Lakshmi, who had lost seven babies before this scrawny mite which she now held out so appealingly . . . Nagamma, whose husband had gone away in the famine and never returned, but who was trying to keep her two children alive by doing coolie work . . . Hamsa, a thin three-year-old with huge dark eyes and eleven "cutties"—abscesses—covering her scalp . . . Hussain, a little four-year-old Moslem boy wearing a mischievous smile, a diminutive string about his much too protruding stomach, and a shining blob of tinsel pasted to each ear . . . Panchalai, a clean pretty baby, but with eyes showing the scarred cornea of conjunctiva . . . Little Bala, twisted from polio, with whom Helen North, the physiotherapist, worked patiently week after week, coaxing him to move his limbs another inch. . . .

Through the barred window behind her Mary heard the strains of a violin coming from the leprosy shelter where, the treatments now over, a religious service was being held for the patients. Progress here at least! No more the painful oil injections that she had given as a student! The sulfone drug DDS, an efficient white pill, had taken its place.

As the weeks passed and Mary became more and more involved, an idea took shape, frightening, challenging. Suppose she was called to go into a village to work! There were plenty of Vellore graduates anxious to work in India's towns and cities, but few were willing to devote themselves to her 500,000 villages. Certainly, this was not what Mary wanted to do. Her whole being recoiled at the thought. But long ago she had relinquished her will to that of Another. She began to ask earnestly for guidance.

Then suddenly, in August, such problems became temporarily unimportant. The telegram telling of little sister Kunjamma's sudden illness and operation came one evening, too late for Mary to catch the Cochin Express. Kunjamma's husband, Dr. Mathai, still studying in Bombay, flew to Madras the next morning, then came on by train to Vellore. Mary took the express to Cochin with him that night. They arrived in Ernakulam the next morning, but it was too late. Kunjamma was already dead.

Mary was stunned. Gay, chattering, irrepressible little Kunjamma! Her youngest sister had been closer to her than any other person in the world. She felt as if a part of herself had died. Now the safe reality of FAMILY was shattered. Doubt, uncertainty, rebellion, were all a part of her grief. Of what use the knowledge and skill she was acquiring if they could not even protect those nearest and dearest to her? Kunjamma had had a brother, a sister, and a husband whose business was to save lives, yet they had been unable even to reach her side.

Back in Vellore, Mary pursued her duties for many weeks with meticulous detail but without zest or commitment. Then slowly she discovered that because of Kunjamma she was seeing people with a new sensitivity. A little child mother, torn and fevered by an ignorant midwife's obstetrics, pleaded for help with Kunjamma's big dark eyes. An old grandmother, squatting stoically at the bedside of her last living son, a hopeless tuberculosis victim, was Amma, dry-eyed, unable at first to weep.

"Yes, yes, I understand," she was able to say again and again. It was sobering, a little frightening, to discover that she had become a better doctor because of losing Kunjamma.

Her year as Senior House Surgeon was drawing near its close. One day Dr. Carol Jameson, head of the Gynecology Department, called her aside.

"I must ask you a question, Mary," she said with her usual brisk approach. "Perhaps you know that you are being considered for the graduate appointment in Gynecology and Obstetrics at the University of Madras."

Mary's heart began to pound. "I was hoping so." She tried not to sound too eager. "I would like very much to have it."

She wished she could appear at ease with the "boss," joke with her the way Prema and M. P. did. She never understood why she couldn't, because Dr. Jameson, though the senior member of the faculty and as efficient an administrator as she was a doctor, combined a contagious and lively concern for people with a rare sense of humor. Perhaps it was her own reserve which gave Mary the impression that she was not one of the doctor's favorite students.

"You understand, of course," continued Dr. Jameson with her generous smile, "that we have to consider many things in choosing. And that is why I must ask you this question. After you finished your graduate work in Madras, would you be willing to come back and work here in Vellore?"

Mary stiffened. "You mean, would I *promise* to?" she asked.

"Well, yes, I suppose you might put it that way, although of course there would be no written agreement. It would just be an understanding between us. Vellore needs workers in obstetrics, as you well know."

"Yes," said Mary. She certainly did know. "But—" She felt an obstinate little core hardening somewhere inside her.

"And to one who loves Vellore as we do, certainly service here should be no sacrifice." The woman who more than a quarter century before had abruptly changed all her own life plans to follow Dr. Ida halfway around the world smiled at Mary. "Should it?"

"No," said Mary. "But—" The hard little core was steeling into a rigid backbone of resistance. Suppose when she finished graduate work she did not feel called to return to Vellore. Suppose she decided she was needed more in some obscure village. Suppose—

"Then shall we consider it settled? It's agreed that if you are chosen you will be expected to return for an indefinite term of service in Vellore?"

"No," said Mary, surprised that so quiet a voice could emerge from such inner turmoil. "I'm sorry, Dr. Jameson. It's very likely that I might feel called to come back here, but I can make no such promise."

She was not chosen. The honor went to her friend M. P. Mary was more hurt and grieved than angry. Stubbornly she refused to admit that she might have been in the wrong, that it was less conscience than her own fierce desire for independence which had prompted her refusal; or that probably M. P. had superior qualifications. Ironically, the successful candidate was unable later to keep her promise because of family problems. It was to the credit of both girls that they remained friends.

There were weeks of disquiet, of uncertainty. Dr. Mathai, Mary's brother-in-law, suggested that she go for post-graduate work to Bombay, where there were many more openings than in Madras. But it would not be a paying post. Mary did not feel able to ask Appan for more money.

It was Appan himself who solved the problem. "The coconut groves have done well," he wrote with a still vigorous hand. "They have provided for all my daughters except one. Whatever she needs is still at her disposal."

So Mary made her plans. After two years in Bombay she would sit for her examinations in gynecology and obstetrics. But first she needed more practical experience. She would finish her two years as a house surgeon in January. She accepted a new temporary position at Vellore, that of registrar, a sort of senior interne, to begin the first of February.

At last the new Internes' Quarters, so long under construction, were sufficiently finished to permit occupancy. Mary had asked for a room on the ground floor of the new building. When the residents moved out of their crowded quarters on the third floor of the Administration Building, this room was not yet ready, so Mary moved temporarily into another room on the second floor. Partly because she expected to move again shortly, partly because her schedule left her scarcely a moment of leisure, she left all her possessions packed, just where the coolies had set them down.

The move was made on the twenty-seventh of January, 1954. Later she remembered only that she had been asked to move and that the arrangements had been made. It was the last thing she was to remember permanently for many days.

14

It was January 30, a day of mourning for India, the anniversary of the assassination of Mahatma Gandhi.

But youth cannot mourn for long. The station wagon full of young people, swinging out of the hospital compound, was soon in a holiday mood. When after a few minutes the car pulled up in front of a bakery and the driver, Thambu, collected a large order of fancy cakes, the pleasure of the group increased to festive gaiety.

"A picnic!" exclaimed more than one young voice exuberantly.

Dr. Carol Jameson, who had planned the outing, nodded. A trip to Gudiyattam had already been scheduled in order to take two medical students, Maisy Mathen and a young man named Thambidurai, for a period of service in the small branch hospital. It had occurred to Dr. Jameson to make the trip an outing for the house surgeons who had just finished their internship in the maternity department as well as for those who would begin their term the first of February. When the group was finally assembled, it included twelve besides herself: the seven house surgeons past and future, the two medical students, a nurse named Mariamma, the driver Thambu, and a final-year student in obstetrics, Chandrahasan Johnson, who, because of a recent family bereavement, seemed in need of relaxation.

It was a perfect day for an outing. The hot season had not yet begun. The dust of the spring drought was still only a golden haze, not yet a suffocating cloud. Frequent showers had kept the rice fields green, and the mangoes were in bloom. Flame-of-the-forest trees had buried their nakedness beneath a riot of orange and vermilion blossoms. And the tamarinds, long unkempt with their old leaves half gone, were springing into fresh cloaks of brilliant green.

Dr. Jameson, sitting with the girls in the rear of the station wagon, was in a reminiscent mood. Over a quarter century ago she had first traveled this road to Gudiyattam on a Roadside pilgrimage with Dr. Ida. She could still vividly remember the horror, the fascination of that day—the swarms of people, her wonder at the tireless vigor of the white-haired woman performing miracles of healing, her own inept struggles with diseases she had never encountered at Stanford or the Mayo Clinic, her aching weariness. In her mind past and present became curiously intermingled.

A question from the front seat of the station wagon jolted her back to awareness.

"What's that? I'm sorry, boys. I'm afraid I wasn't listening."

"Thambidurai wants to drive," explained young Johnson, looking over his shoulder. "He is asking you if he may have permission."

"Thambu seems to be doing well enough," replied Dr. Jameson. "Suppose we keep going just as we are."

The two young men were sitting in front with the driver. With Dr. Jameson on the left side of the station wagon were three young doctors, Sojibai, Satyabama, and Mary. The other house surgeons—Ramabai, Achamma Abraham, Nalini, and Annamma—with Maisy, the medical student assigned to the branch hospital, and nurse Mariamma, were packed into the right-hand seats and the rear space among the weekly medical supplies bound for the Gudiyattam hospital. The discomfort of the crowding merely enhanced their gaiety.

"She'll be comin' round the mountain when she comes," someone started to sing, and the rollicking tune was followed by others.

Johnson, sitting between Thambu and Thambidurai, was the natural leader with his splendid singing voice. Presently he discovered that the horn, fastened to the windshield within reach of his hand, made an excellent accompaniment to the music. After a little practice he found he could follow the rhythm of the songs with fair accuracy. While the squawking monotone added little to the musical cadence, it added considerably to the festivity, as well as opening a necessary path through the intermittent stream of carts, animals, and pedestrians.

Occasionally Johnson glanced behind to see if Satyabama—Bama, as she was usually called—was responding to the jollity. His half cousin by marriage and a friend since childhood, she had recently suffered a disappointment in love and his concern for her had brought them even closer together. Bama had made an excellent record in the college, and Johnson, though he had managed to fail in obstetrics, was by no means a poor student himself.

"You'd better marry her," one of his friends had advised jokingly, "just to give your progeny a chance of getting some brains."

Though neither Johnson nor Bama had any intentions of profiting by this advice, their mutual interest at the moment was a bit more than cousinly. He was glad to see that she was now chattering in lively fashion to Mary Verghese.

Thambidurai refused to be diverted from his purpose. A handsome, self-confident youth, obviously accustomed to having his own way, he had set his heart on driving the station wagon. At every lull in the singing, his voice could be heard urging Thambu to let him take the wheel.

"There's no reason why Dr. Jameson shouldn't let me," he complained to Johnson. "I'm perfectly capable."

Though Dr. Jameson took no active part in the gaiety, she encouraged it with smiles and nods, occasionally joining in the rhythmic clapping of hands. She welcomed the rare opportunity of observing her young residents in this carefree environment and sat observing, listening, shrewdly appraising.

"I like your sari," she heard Bama remark enthusiastically to Mary Verghese.

Mary smiled. "It's one of my favorites. I had it for my brother John's wedding."

Her attention drawn, Carol Jameson silently agreed with Bama. The green and red did something for Mary, kindled sparks in her dark eyes, muted the slight heaviness of her features. With her usual poise and serenity, plus this vivid radiance and animation, the girl was actually beautiful! The older doctor felt a sudden pang of regret and uncertainty. A pity she hadn't been able to recommend Mary for the Madras appointment—she had seemed to want it so much! But she was not the highest in scholarship, which should be the determining factor. Or—should it? Of course there were other qualities, perhaps of even greater importance. If you could only put people in a test tube and study their reactions, subjecting them, perhaps, to great stress or crisis!

"Yes? What's that?"

It was Johnson again, smiling apologetically, sensitive brows slightly frowning under the shock of waving black hair.

"Thambidurai is very anxious to drive, Dr. Jameson. He insists that he is well qualified and has a license."

After some thought Carol Jameson relented. After all, this was an outing, and all the guests should enjoy themselves as much as possible. Probably her older generation was inclined to be too cautious.

"Very well," she agreed, "but be sure and drive carefully, Thambidurai."

The exchange was made. The new driver seemed to display both skill and caution. The holiday tempo of the party continued unabated. Other songs were sung. Johnson, still within reach of the horn, endeavored to improve his rhythmic proficiency by tentative renditions of "God Save the Queen."

The new driver had been at the wheel for some time when a large public bus appeared in the road ahead. Perversely its driver refused to let the station wagon pass. Each time Thambidurai made the attempt he would either increase his speed just enough to keep ahead or manage to crowd the station wagon to the side of the road. Thambidurai became more and more exasperated.

"Chi!" he exclaimed. "Would I like to show that driver! He has no brains!"

Johnson agreed. No wonder the youth was irritated and uneasy! Driving an unfamiliar car on a strange road through the melee of Indian traffic was hard enough without this further aggravation. He began to wish Thambu were again at the wheel. The impasse continued for another two miles, during which Thambidurai became more and more uneasy and Johnson more and more proficient in his squawking rendition of "God Save the Queen." The blasts were now more than recreational diversion. They served insistent notice to the bus driver to keep on his own left-hand side of the road.

Suddenly Thambidurai lost patience. "Here goes," he muttered. "He had better make room for me—or else!"

He stepped on the accelerator, and the station wagon spurted ahead. Johnson honked madly his now nearly perfect version of "God Save the Queen," but the bus remained well to the right of center, on the wrong side of the road. Thambidurai drew out to pass it. This time apparently nothing would stop him.

But something did. As they drew level with the bus, Johnson gasped. The wall of a culvert loomed toward them on the right. Because of the position of the bus, they had not even seen the narrow bridge ahead He was sure for a moment they were going to hit the abutment head on.

Thambidurai cut the wheel sharply to the left. How he avoided hitting either the bus or the abutment, no one would ever know, but miraculously he escaped them both. Then suddenly he seemed to lose all control of himself and of the station wagon. Attempting to apply the brakes, he stepped instead on the accelerator. The car swung sharply to the left, then veered to the right, then left again, each swerve accompanied by a shrill crescendo of feminine screams. Back and forth it reeled in almost perfect rhythm, as if practicing its own macabre version of "God Save the Queen." On its third mad swerve to the left, it toppled over a bank.

Dr. Carol Jameson reached blindly for something to hold on to, found nothing, felt herself tossed and jolted and twisted as the van continued its fall, turning over three times before it came to rest.

This is the end, she thought. It doesn't matter about me. I have lived my life. But what a waste of all these precious, well-trained young doctors!

With a final jolt the station wagon landed on its side, far down the bank, its superstructure broken to fragments. The frantic screams died into an even more sickening silence.

Returning to consciousness, young Johnson found himself lying at the foot of the bank below the road. Though he knew vaguely what had happened, he saw and felt little at first. He lay looking up at the sky. His head seemed to be remarkably clear.

Life, he told himself, how short—and how uncertain! Strangely enough, he found himself thinking not in his mother tongue of Tamil, but in English.

As consciousness of his surroundings returned, his doctor's training asserted itself. He looked at his hands and feet, waggled fingers and toes tentatively, and muttered, "Good, no motor loss." Finding a stick within arm's length, he ran the end of it over his leg, and exclaimed aloud with satisfaction, "No sensory loss, either!" Then gingerly he tried moving his body. *"Ayoh!"* By the sharp, almost unbearable twinges of pain he suspected that his back must be broken.

After cautious tests to discover the extent of his injuries, he decided that the damage was not irreparable and that others might be hurt more than he was. Shaking himself like a bear, he crawled to his feet and looked dizzily about him. Through the first haze of pain and horror he saw nothing clearly. Then objects loomed into perspective . . . the scattered fragments of twisted metal . . . the horrified faces of the bus passengers peering down from the top of the bank . . . the strewn bodies . . . *ayoh!* There was no end to them! The ground was covered with them!

Some of the bodies began to move, crawled to their knees, stood partially erect. One of them came toward him. He recognized Dr. Achamma Abraham. She looked at him in dazed fashion, clutching at her neck.

"Have you seen my chain?"

Johnson laughed, a dry croak that did not leave his throat. He thought: How like a woman!

Soon most of the victims were moving, either sitting dazed or stumbling about on their feet. Two, he noticed—Dr. Sojibai Samson and Dr. Mary Verghese—were lying close together, not moving. Somebody bent over them, then announced with matter-of-fact finality, "They are gone." Johnson saw another figure lying motionless. Forgetting his racking pain, he ran and knelt beside it. *Bama!*

She had a big swelling covering her right eye and cheek. It looked as if the eye was gone. He felt her pulse. It was barely perceptible. He began giving her artificial respiration. Then suddenly he stopped, fearing that she might have fractured ribs. He began to pray:

"Oh, God help us! Let them live, let all of them live. And let them keep their senses. God, help our minds and souls as well as our bodies!"

He rose to his feet. No time to wander about helplessly, as everybody seemed to be doing. Time was racing, and people were probably dying. Somebody must do something. The pain still racking his back with every step, he made his way up the bank.

The bus was parked beside the road. The passengers, crowded on the edge of the bank, stared at him stupidly.

"The driver," he gasped. "Where—?"

The man appeared, frightened, defiant.

"We're from the hospital in Vellore," explained Johnson urgently. "You must take us all back there, at once."

The driver hedged. How could he? His rules would not permit him to leave his route.

"Rules!" Johnson exploded. "Don't you realized that people are hurt, maybe dead, and it's partly your fault?" Noting the surly stubborn features, he took a different approach. "We'll make it worth your while, see that you get good compensation." Still the man hesitated, his face a battleground of wariness, cupidity, and—strongest of all emotions—fear. Johnson played on the latter. "You'll be sorry if you don't," he threatened. "I'll report you to some of my friends among the high police officials. I'll have you arrested—" Again he exploded. "Can't you understand, man? These people are dying!"

Dr. Achamma appeared at his side, apparently resigned to the loss of her chain. "I'll give you these bangles," she coaxed, jangling her gold bracelets temptingly.

By now the passengers were also urging him, and finally the driver agreed. Johnson directed the procedure of getting the victims safely up the steep bank and into the bus. Several needed no assistance. Thambidurai, pale with shock, seemed to have escaped with only a few superficial bruises. Thambu, the original driver, was running around wringing his hands and weeping over a small cut in his scalp that might prevent him from acquiring an attractive wife with a decent dowry. Dr. Jameson, heedless of a scalp injury and a fractured arm, gave efficient assistance. Her first dazed helplessness, which had sent her wandering from one to the other frantically taking pulses and often finding none, had passed. Now she was clear headed, equal to the emergency. She was even tempted to smile ruefully when one of the young doctors seemed more distressed over the loss of the picnic lunch than over her own severely injured back.

"Oh, those lovely, lovely cakes," mourned the girl sadly. "Those beautiful cakes!"

But, looking at Sojibai and Mary, Dr. Jameson was far from smiling.

At last all were up the bank and in the bus except the two girls lying motionless on the ground. The driver pointed at them and shrugged his shoulders. "Not them. No use. They're dead."

"What if they are!" snapped Johnson. "They go too."

In spite of the intense pain in his back, Johnson helped carry the two inert bodies up the bank, careful to jar them as little as possible, and saw to it that they were deposited in the bus. Sickened, he kept his eyes averted. The faces of both girls were barely recognizable. Sojibai's looked as if every bone in it had been broken. Mary's was split open in a deep gash from cheekbone to chin. He had not the slightest doubt that she, at least, was dead.

Johnson was the last to enter the bus. Pulling himself up the steps, he lay down on the floor, face up. "Have to be in hyperextension—"

he muttered, choking as something filled his throat. Hemoptysis, he thought. Wiping his sleeve across his lips, he was not surprised to find it stained bright red.

He heard strangled sounds and was sure they came from Bama. Not really conscious, but at least alive, he thought. Try as he would, he could not move to go to her. Gratefully he saw that Dr. Jameson was trying to help her. *Nallathu,* good. He had done everything possible.

Though every jolt of the bus racked his body, he did not resist its motion. It was almost a relief to be able to yield himself to the pain. He knew that he would not now be able to move if his life depended on it.

15

The bus lumbered through the gate of the hospital compound and up to the entrance of the Out-patient Dispensary. Even before it could discharge its burden, the news was spreading through corridors and verandahs, into wards and offices:

"Terrible accident! Have you heard? Station wagon turned over—full of staff!"

Fortunately the holiday observed at the college had not extended to the hospital. Many of the senior surgeons were on duty, including Dr. Jacob Chandy, head of Neurosurgery. It was Dr. Chandy who took charge, and presently all the victims of the accident, even those apparently uninjured, were lying side by side on hastily improvised examining tables.

"You take this one." He issued crisp directions to his team of surgeons. "I'll take that one. You take this one. . . ."

Swiftly they traveled down the line, questioning, prodding, testing, diagnosing, issuing orders, sometimes wheeling one of the patients away to the operating room.

"What's the matter with you?" asked one of the younger doctors, looking down at Johnson.

"Fracture of spine," he replied calmly, "but no motor or sensory loss, and hemoptysis."

"Huh!" the young doctor had been a fellow student. "Look who's talking. Not even a full-fledged doctor yet, and making your own diagnoses!" He regarded his comrade quizzically. "Didn't I hear you were carrying people up the bank? You don't do things like that, brother, with a broken back!"

"No?" replied Johnson faintly.

"Just lie still. We'll look you over later. If you ask me, there are others who need attention first."

Johnson lay still. He could do nothing else. Later his diagnosis was proved correct. He had a compression fracture of the eleventh thoracic vertebra, with lesser fractures of three others, and a blast injury of a lung.

Grace Koshi was studying in the college library when she became aware of a commotion outside the building. Looking out from the balcony, she saw people running, heard them shouting. The campus driveways came alive with cars, all streaming toward the road leading to the hospital. Finally the excited cries, the relayed exclamations, became intelligible.

Mary! she thought with foreboding.

She caught the first bus, already crowded with students, that set off for the hospital. It seemed to crawl along the four miles of winding roads, of congested streets. Arrived at the hospital, Grace rushed to the open gate of the Out-patient Dispensary and forced her way through the crowd and into the building.

The old OPD was often a busy place, but never had she seen it like this, bustling with so many doctors. Even Dr. Ida was there, moving from patient to patient pressing their hands, murmuring words of encouragement, smoothing back tangled hair, wiping away caked blood, and all the time bewailing her inadequacy.

"Oh, if I could only do something to help!" she kept mourning, not realizing that the touch of her hand, the agonized concern scored in her face, were at that moment of as much therapeutic value as any antiseptics, drugs, or bandages.

When Grace finally found the patient she was looking for, she gasped. "Mary!" she whispered. But, though the girl's head was tossing restlessly from side to side, there was no sign of consciousness. Grace stared horrified at the gaping wound in the right cheek, the hair soaked with blood. "Is she—?" In panic she turned to the senior doctors who were working over her friend. One of them was Dr. Mathai, Mary's brother-in-law, who had only recently joined the Vellore staff. He was administering transfusions of blood and gelatine.

"We don't know yet," he replied. "I've already asked that word be sent to the family."

One after another, the patients were wheeled away. Johnson was at last accorded the attention he needed. Sojibai Samson was less critically injured than had been feared at first, though she had suffered fractures of all her facial bones. Barna, still unconscious, had a deep cut through her right cheek and maxillary sinus, a fractured clavicle, and concussion. She was to remain in a coma for two days and after that retain not the slightest memory of the accident. Mariamma, the nurse, had a badly sprained back. Most of the others had severe bruises. Maisy Mathen, the medical student who had been bound for the branch hospital, had come through the accident without a scratch.

It was Mary who had been most severely injured. Studying the results of her transfusions, the doctors were pessimistic.

"She's not responding properly," one of them commented. "Unless her blood pressure comes up, we cannot touch her face."

Eagerly Grace intervened, remembering that Mary's blood pressure was always inclined to be below the average. With this assurance the doctors finally decided to do primary suture on her face. They found the right maxillary antrum broken in pieces. But luckily the orbital plate was intact. It was hoped that her eye could be saved.

Grace was only one of Mary's many friends who rushed to the hospital on hearing the news, then hovered about during the anxious hours that followed. M. P. was late in arriving, having been confined to her bed all day with a high fever. Except for the fever, she would have been one of the picnic party. Disappointed, for she especially liked picnics, she had listened enviously to the other residents as they prepared for the outing. Now, far sicker with worry than with fever, M. P. sat outside the door of the operating room waiting for news of her friend. Finally, unable to stand the suspense longer, she donned gown and mask and went inside. But here her worries were only increased, not allayed.

It might have been I, thought M. P. numbly, staring at the still figure on the table.

It was 8:15 in the evening when Mary was brought from the operating room to the ward where Grace Koshi and others of her friends were waiting. A little later a nurse brought her clothes.

Until now Grace had not been able to weep. Her stunned grief had been like a dry hard core dulling her senses, choking her throat. Only when she saw the torn, stained bundle of rags that had once been the beloved green and red sari did her tears begin to flow.

There was no dearth of volunteers—nurses, medical students, doctors—to take their turns sitting with the twelve injured patients. Dr.

Mathai and Grace remained all night by Mary's bed. Though she kept tossing restlessly, she still showed no sign of consciousness.

"Leave me, leave me," she kept muttering.

It was after midnight that Grace, trying to adjust Mary's mussed gown, noticed a redness and swelling on her right shoulder and called Dr. Mathai's attention to it.

"Looks like a clavicular fracture," he said. "Let's hope she is improved enough tomorrow to have it attended to."

Meanwhile in Kerala, for the second time in six months, Mary's family was being shaken to its foundations. Appan and Amma were at Annamma's house in Ernakulam when the telegram arrived, long after the Madras Express had gone. Appan, ailing, could not possibly make the journey to Vellore. Amma was torn between loyalty to him and desire to go to Mary.

"Of course you must go," he told her gently. "Your child needs you."

They looked old, both of them. Kunjamma's death was still an unhealed wound.

"Not my other baby," whispered Amma. "I couldn't lose her too!"

"Stay as long as she needs you," encouraged Appan.

"Which won't be long," muttered George in an aside to Annamma. "Not if I understand that telegram."

Hiring a taxi, they drove all night—George, Annamma, Amma, and an uncle who was very fond of Mary. By a coincidence, that same night John, then an assistant engineer at Alwaye and living temporarily in his parents' home in Cherai, went to Ernakulam to visit his ailing father. Hearing about the accident, he telephoned his brother-in-law in Vellore, and after talking with Mathai started out himself in a taxi. On the way he met Aleyamma and her husband, who transferred to his taxi and went on with him to Vellore. Babi, working in Trivandrum, received a wire the next morning telling him to come to Ernakulum. Believing his father must be sick, he rushed to Ernakulam, then telephoned Dr. Mathai in Vellore. It was his brother John who answered. The end, John felt sure, was near.

Babi took Annamma's large car and drove it to Vellore, knowing that a Kerala taxi could not be used as a hearse. It was unthinkable that his little sister Mary should not be brought home. On the island with its blue seas and coconut groves she had been born, and there she belonged. It seemed to be the only thing left that he could do for her.

So they came, FAMILY, separate interests forgotten, fused again by fierce loyalty into a single body.

George and Annamma and Amma arrived early on the morning of the thirty-first, to find that Mary was still unconscious. There was little change in her condition that day. The doctors worked merely to keep her alive. The clavicular fracture received necessary attention, and about noon a tracheotomy was performed to facilitate her breathing.

Amma sat by the bed, refusing to leave, even though she had sat up through all of the previous night. Hour after hour she gently stroked the hot restless hands, her dry eyes fixed intently on the heavily bandaged face.

"Please come and rest," pleaded John and Annamma. "You can do her no good. She doesn't even know you are there."

"*Illa,* no?" replied Amma. "How do you know she does not? A child can feel love even when asleep. I ought to know. Have I not held you sick children all night many a time?"

It was that day also that a nurse reported anxiously to the doctors: "I've been watching her. She's very restless, moves her head and arms constantly. But in all the time I have watched, never once has she moved her limbs. You don't suppose—?"

"Yes," said Dr. Chandy. "Her spinal cord has been injured."

But it was not yet possible to determine the extent of the injury. At the moment the neurosurgeon was as helpless as Amma. All anyone could do was wait.

16

It must be the monsoon season, for only then did the water run deep in all the little inlets and overflow the fields, even on the edges of the compound, lapping against the trunks of the coconut palms. Always before she had looked down at the waving grasses, peering over the edge of the *vallam* which John and the other boys surreptitiously borrowed in spite of Amma's worried injunctions to "keep away fom the water." And occasionally, through threats or bribes, they could be persuaded to take the girls with them.

But the floods were never so deep as this. If the boat had sunk or upset, then why was she not scrambling with the others to reach dry ground, the grasses slapping and tickling her legs until she was weak with laughter, then running in the hot sun until her frock was dry, so Amma or second sister Annamma wouldn't notice? Why was she lying here with the dark waters swirling about her head and the grasses winding about her body? No . . . not grasses, tougher than grasses. Roots . . . clutching her limbs, binding them so that, no matter how hard she tossed and strained, she could not move them.

Or maybe not roots. Snakes. The long spotted kind she had seen snake charmers in Ernakulam twine around their necks. Muthi had once run into the house screaming that she had seen one in a big pile of coconut leaves drying for fuel in a corner of the compound, but, though Sreedharen had beaten the leaves with a stick while his father Ikkannan had waited with a club, nothing had ever come out. It must be snakes, for she could feel their fangs striking at her cheek, her shoulder, every thrust sending a sharp agony of pain through her body. She struggled with all her strength to free herself, but it was no use. The coils were as tightly intermeshed as the coconut leaves the women of Cherai laced into fencing or thatch for their houses.

"Leave me, leave me . . ." she tried to cry out, but the waters choked the words back into her throat.

Slowly the waves receded above her head, and wavering shapes began to appear, distorted as if reflected in a troubled pool. Once she thought she saw Amma's face, not angry or reproachful as it should be after her child had disobeyed, but all quivering and broken, as if she had been crying. Only once had she seen Amma look like that, when Kunjamma. . . . But, no, Kunjamma wasn't dead, she couldn't be. They were still children, riding the flooded inlets in a boat, only there wasn't any boat now, because something had happened. . . .

Making a desperate effort, she struggled up out of the dark waters. The roaring in her ears gave place to silence, broken presently by a succession of half strange, half familiar sounds. . . . a crow cawing, the rumble of a bullock cart, glasses clinking, water sloshing, the slap-slap of sandals on a hard smooth floor. Where was she? The flat whiteness overhead was not sky. There were walls all around, not coconut palms. And she could not be at home, because in Vypeen there were no bullock carts. Attempting to lift herself on one elbow, the better to see her surroundings, she sank again into a sea of pain.

"My back!" she moaned. "My neck! My head!"

She floated on the surface of consciousness, vaguely aware of faces, of hands, of voices, yet recognizing none of them distinctly. She knew that things were being done to ease her pain, was dimly conscious of the plaster shell which brought relief from the aching pressure, of the revolving bed which made it possible for her to be shifted into varying positions.

The floods had long since receded. In brief moments when the haze of pain dissolved she knew that she was in Vellore, that she was lying in a hospital bed, that there were nurses about her. She tried to remember what had happened, but her mind traveled in hopeless circles. She was moving into a new room in the internes' quarters. Her boxes were packed ready to go. She was terribly tired, but there was still work to do, patients to check on, calls to make. She was moving into a new room. . . . It was no use. She could not remember.

Then suddenly she looked up and saw a familiar face.

"Lily!" To her surprise the exclamation sounded no louder than a whisper.

Mary John's round pretty face was a queer mixture of astonishment, relief, and anxiety.

"Mary! My dear! You do know me, don't you?"

"Of course, know—" She put her left hand to her throat. "What? Can't talk—"

"It's the tube in your throat," said Lily. "You had trouble breathing. They did a tracheotomy."

Mary's hand kept on exploring, fingered the heavy bandages that covered her right eye and most of her face. "Why here? What happened?"

"You went on a picnic with the other residents to Gudiyattam. Remember?"

Mary shook her head. Even that little effort sent waves of pain through her face and neck.

"And there was an accident, a very bad accident. The station wagon turned over. You were badly hurt. It happened five days ago."

"The others?" inquired Mary faintly.

"You would think of them!" Lily scolded, her eyes brimming. "They're all doing well. You were hurt worst of all."

"How bad?" whispered Mary.

Lily gently touched the heavily bandaged head and shoulder. "Well," she said, her voice a little too bright, "I'm afraid you have a badly smashed jaw and a fractured clavicle. And—they think you have a rather bad infection in your face."

Mary tried to smile. The pain of the movement made her wince. Poor Lily, she had never been good at keeping secrets. What was she trying to hide now? That Mary had lost her good looks, that as long as she lived she would never be attractive again? As if she couldn't tell that already, with her face feeling as if it had been slashed from chin to—Suddenly a frightening suspicion turned her exploring fingers cold.

"My eye?" she croaked.

"They saved it," Lily hastened to reassure her. "At first they were afraid, but it's all right. They had to wire the orbital plate."

"Good," whispered Mary. "God—very good to me."

She wondered why Lily turned away weeping. Looks didn't matter very much, her friends should know that. She lifted her left hand and looked at it. It was still a surgeon's hand: strong, supple. Her right hand was bandaged and she could not see it, but she flexed its fingers, one after the other, and drew a sigh of relief. Eyes. Hands. A doctor's tools.

"Thank you, God," she whispered. Waves of fresh pain engulfed her. Afterward she did not even remember that she had talked with Lily.

The next few days could have been hours—or years. Under deep sedation she existed in a state of half-awareness, emerging only long enough to smile at a familiar face, respond vaguely to a doctor's or nurse's question, endure in wordless but not always tearless agony the painful dressing of her infected face. She was scarcely aware when Aley Kuruvilla, her first nurse, relinquished her post to another, Gnanamini. She felt her mother's presence, as constant a reality as the white walls enclosing her small world, and during the restlessness of the long nights she learned to tell by the sound of deep breathing or by the lack of it whether Amma, on her cot close by, was sleeping or lying tensely awake.

Though she was conscious of other familiar faces and figures appearing and disappearing—brother George, second sister Annamma, her friend Grace Koshi, Mathai, M. P., doctors and nurses, a blur of blue and white with a soft voice and fragrance of flowers which could be only Dr. Ida—it was Amma's face which she saw oftenest and in the clearest perspective. It was always there, it seemed, when she emerged, sweating and panting, from the periods of sharpest pain. Sometimes it seemed to merge into the outlines of another Face, scored even more deeply with suffering, its brow rimmed with thorns.

"*Dayavu chedu,*—please," she protested over and over. "Don't grieve—Amma. It's going to be all right."

But finally came the chilling consciousness that it was not going to be all right. Just when she made the discovery she could not have told. It did not come all at once, rather as a creeping awareness, like the inching of the tidewaters in monsoon. . . .

The relentless probe of questions: "Tell me, can you feel this, Doctor Mary? . . . Does the pain extend to this area?" . . .

Fragments of conversation overheard: ". . . completely anaesthetic . . . watched all night for some sign of movement. . . ."

Her own futile straining to find release in motion. *It was her shoulder that was hurt, her face. Why, then, must her whole body be bound so tightly?*

And then at last came a moment of complete clarity. "Tomorrow," she heard a voice say, "we shall do the laminectomy."

She opened her eyes. The room and everything in it came suddenly into perfect focus, frozen as motionless as her own inert lower body. She saw an empty wall, its blank whiteness broken only by a shaft of sunlight. She saw the slender metal uprights of a bed frame, like the bars of a cage. She saw Dr. Chandy, dark, grave, head bent over a chart, and Nurse Gnanamini, hand caught in the act of replacing a bottle on the moveable table of medical dressings. She saw her mother sitting in a chair by the window, the fan of her *dhoti* slightly askew, face lined and anxious, hands folded so tensely in her lap that the knuckles showed white. For an interval, objects, even the throbbing pain in her own face, stood still. Then abruptly motion resumed. Dr. Chandy laid down the chart and turned toward the door. Nurse Gnanamini replaced the bottle. Amma's hands began a slow kneading motion, strangely foreign to their usual competence and briskness. The cheek began throbbing again. Even the shaft of sunlight wavered as a gust of air lifted the window drapes.

Everything had resumed its normal motion . . . except for a pair of once swift and sturdy human limbs.

Mary did not sleep that night. For the first time in ten days she was starkly conscious. The usual sedation had no effect. The room was hot and airless. Perspiring profusely under the heavy bandages, she felt as if her shoulder and chest were bound with hot compresses. The throbbing in her face had become as steady as a pulse beat. Fearful that if she moved she might waken Amma, she resisted the almost uncontrollable impulse to beat, to strike out with her left hand, the only weapon of rebellion she seemed to have left.

No, not the only one. Mind and spirit were weapons, too, and she battled with them fiercely, soundlessly. Fate, Life, God—call it what you would. It was not being fair. She who had been willing to give everything, now had everything taken away! Far better to have died than to be less than half alive! Tears of pain, of anger, of frustration, mingled with the sweat that already soaked the heavy bandages. Her throat was wracked with soundless sobs.

Impossible to believe that by sheer will she could not still force her limbs to do her bidding! Feverishly she concentrated all her attention on them. She pictured them in motion, pumping vigorously along the paths between the coconut plots, shinnying up the scaly trunks of palms, leaping across a goal line, walking briskly along a hospital verandah. By what alchemy had this miracle of motion been achieved? Her legs were still here—her mind, her muscles. She exerted all her will power, strained and tensed every muscle, until the sheet was sodden beneath her head and shoulders. No use. Her limbs might have been two dead palm trunks.

Then slowly the helpless fury passed. Her reasoning mind began functioning. Laminectomy. The spinal cord was injured, yes, but perhaps not irreparably. The removal of the laminae would reduce the pressure. God was still good. She could trust him. He wanted only the best for his children. She would not, she must not give up hope.

In the morning she was able to bring a wan smile to Amma's face. Still too weak to talk herself, she got Gnanamini to explain the operation to her mother in detail.

"*Nallathu,* good," she assured Amma.

Dr. Gwenda Lewis, the young English anaesthetist, arrived with her lilting voice and springing step, filling the room with her usual abundance of radiating energy and optimism.

"I'll be right there beside you," she promised with one of her glowing smiles. "We'll all be fighting with you. And remember, Mary, dear, whatever happens, life is still good and worth living."

Mary managed to smile back, but she felt swift resentment. Don't talk to me, she wanted to retort. What do you know about it, you who have good strong legs?

Somehow the words, though unspoken, seemed familiar.

The laminectomy performed, the waiting began. With the removal of the laminae from the spine to release pressure on the cord, probably caused by displacement of fractured vertebrae, it was hoped that the function of the cord might be restored. Each day Dr. Chandy or one of his associates came to test the level of sensation. First they would use cotton for the "light touch."

"Close your eyes, please, Doctor. Now tell me—do you feel this?"

Mary would press her lids together until they hurt. "No."

"How about this?"

She would hold her breath, tense the muscles of her arms and shoulders, even strain her ears, as if in the hope that one sense might transfer its power to another. . . .

"No."

Then would come the "heavy touch," the pin prick.

"Very well. Relax now, please. Can you feel this?"

Another eternity of agony. Then, "No."

"This?"

Ah! Surely now there was a brief stab of something. . . .

"I—I'm not sure."

Her pulses pounded like hammers until with brutal honesty she localized the sensation in her throbbing cheek.

have the experience of living in this amazing place. For the first time since her accident she did not feel strange, alone. Nobody looked at her curiously when she propelled herself along the corridors and porches, across the wide expanse of green lawn, because almost everybody else was in a wheelchair too. It was a city on wheels. She hadn't supposed there could be so many paraplegics and quadriplegics in the world! The only difference between herself and some of the others was that they could do so many things she could not do—walk with braces, move in their chairs with amazing agility, perform the most astounding athletic feats.

But she would learn! The fellowship of others struggling with the same problems was both consolation and inspiration. She started her rigorous discipline of training almost immediately, concentrated on it with all her keenness of mind and persistence of will.

Dr. Bedbrook, a rehabilitation specialist who had trained in England's Stoke-Mandeville Hospital under the famous Dr. Gutmann, had developed highly successful techniques in the training of paraplegics. It was not long before Mary began to note marked improvement in her various ranges of activity. After some weeks of arm and balancing exercises and weight lifting she was able, to her great delight, to bend forward and backward by means of arm and shoulder motions, and to change position in her chair. Practising pull-ups with the aid of the bar fixed over her bed, she developed such additional strength in her arms that she could move herself about with considerable facility, and even dispense with the irksome aid of an attendant to turn her in her bed at night. This increased independence alone would have been full compensation for all the hours of intensive discipline.

But, as for every other paraplegic in the center, one of the major goals of her program was to learn again to walk. It was with excitement, trepidation, and much doubt as to its pertinence to her own special needs, that Mary embarked on this phase of her rehabilitation.

Even before she was fitted with leg braces, the training began. With stiff splints bound to her knees to keep them rigid, she was made to stand, supported by a therapist on either side. It was a strange feeling, standing for the first time after nearly four years!

Then she received her braces. With these in place, the regimen progressed. First she walked between parallel bars, a narrow prison as rigidly iron-bound as the braces, their dozen feet of length seemingly as impossible of attainment as if they were as many miles.

own medical practice in Cochin, but her second sister stayed on. Trust the efficient Annamma to have a household that could look after itself! George, her eye-specialist husband, and her two sons, Paul and Verghese, Annamma insisted brusquely, could spare her for two months as easily as two weeks. Grateful for her sister's calm presence, her long hours of patient reading aloud, Mary remembered with remorse her childhood resentment of Annamma's bossiness.

The face mended slowly. Though the outer scar soon healed, there was a sinus in her mouth along the cheek and lip. Each day Dr. Shanti Fen, Dr. Case's assistant, came to drain it. Mary dreaded his visits. It was a painful process.

She had so many doctors looking after her that she would sometimes joke about it. There were Dr. Case, the general surgeon; Dr. Moody, the orthodontist; Dr. Chandy, the neurosurgeon; and Dr. Brand, the orthopedic specialist.

"Who *is* my doctor?" she would demand in mock despair. "There are so many of you I don't know which one to complain to."

Each day the tests continued. The light touch, the heavy touch. "Do you feel this, Doctor Mary?" . . . "This?" . . . "How about this?"

Each day the pounding pulses, the dry throat, the agony of straining.

"No . . . no . . . no. . . ."

She could not keep track of the days of testing, but there came a time when they seemed to have gone on forever.

"How long has it been?" she asked one day. She found it easier to talk now, for after the eleventh day the tube had been removed from her throat. "How many days since the laminectomy?"

Miss Effie Wallace, the American nurse in charge of M Ward, smiled brightly. "Let's see." She tried to sound casual. "The laminectomy was performed on February ninth. This is—why, it must be the twenty-second! How time does fly!"

Two weeks. Mary was a doctor. She did not need to be told that if sensation did not return in two weeks after a laminectomy, it was not likely ever to do so. This, then, was *it*. She was doomed for the rest of her life to be a paraplegic, to be less than half alive.

That night, again, she did not sleep. *Why?* Her world rotated to the word's recurrent rhythm, the beat of her pulses, the throbbing of her face, her mother's little moans as she slept, the echo of steps along the corridor. Why? . . . *Why?* . . . WHY?

The question was not, *Why* did this have to happen to me? *Why* is God punishing me like this? *Why* must I be the one to suffer? Rather, it was, Why, when I came so near going, could I not have gone!

Had Mary been a different person, that night she might have been tempted to take her own life.

She could have found some way. She could even have used the empty glass standing on her bedside table, catching the flare of the night lamp and winking like a dozen wide-open eyes. It was thin glass, and her left hand was strong.

But not even then, in her deepest despair, was she tempted to destroy such a precious thing. She was a doctor, sworn to *save* life. Once there had been a woman in this very M Ward who had lain unconscious for months, with no hope of recovery. "Why?" Even Dr. Ida had asked the question. "Why do they want to prolong her life? If it were I, I'd so much rather they didn't!" But there had been no question about the right thing to do. Life was sacred. "Thou shalt not kill" was as central to the code of medicine as to that of Moses.

"Why?" Mary asked again. But the word had become prayer now, rather than bitter complaint. Why was this suffering required of her? Why had her life been spared? Job had learned what suffering was. He had learned to say, "Though He slay me, yet will I trust Him." That was not so hard. She could easily have faced being slain. Somehow she had to learn to say, "Though He does *not* slay me. . . ."

17

One day Helen North, the Australian physiotherapist with whom Mary had often worked on Roadside, appeared in her room.

"Dr. Brand sent me," she announced. "He thinks it's time to start your physiotherapy."

Mary's welcoming smile faded. "You have plenty to do working with people you can really help," she said soberly. "You'd better not waste time on me."

"And what makes you think I can't help you?" demanded Helen.

"I'm a doctor," replied Mary. "I know all too well what has happened inside me. It would take a miracle to make these legs move again."

"Who said anything about making your legs move?" retorted Helen cheerfully. "Though I've seen plenty of paraplegics who have learned to walk, with braces. But wouldn't you like to be able to do more things for yourself, so you wouldn't be so dependent on other people?"

Mary's eyes brimmed with longing. "Wouldn't I!" she whispered. "Oh, Helen! You mean I really could?"

"Of course. But it will mean long hard work."

"I'm not afraid of work," said Mary.

"Then let's get going. But before we start, let's pray about it, shall we?"

"Yes," replied Mary gratefully.

Helen North's religion was as refreshingly practical as the small pool where her polio patients received their therapy.

"Thank you, God," she said simply, "for giving back Mary's life."

Mary turned away her face. She could not voice this sentiment as yet.

"Help us to make Mary as strong and independent and useful as possible."

"Amen," echoed Mary fervently.

At first Helen North came to her room for a half hour each day, later, as Mary's endurance slowly increased, for longer periods. She moved each limb through its range of motion. Even paralyzed limbs, she explained, would become stiff if left in one position, and regular systematic motion was necessary to build up the healthy muscles as well as to prevent deformities and pressure sores. To compensate for the paralysis of limb and lower trunk muscles, those of arms and upper trunk must gain three times their normal strength, in order to balance and support her body.

As the full routine developed, it became, as Helen had promised, hard work. Still very weak, Mary became exhausted almost beyond endurance. With March the hot season was approaching, and she soon found that she was perspiring only above the level of her injury, which greatly intensified her discomfort. Face dripping, shoulders drenched and itching, she would submit patiently to the seemingly endless exercises she could not perform herself, then doggedly pursue the more and more strenuous regimen designed to strengthen arms and shoulders—stretching, bending elbows, holding in her hands heavier and heavier sandbags for longer and longer periods.

Mary worked under no illusions. Being a doctor, she knew all the limitations of paraplegia. Also, having never seen a rehabilitated paraplegic, she had little conception of the possibilities. Despair rather than hope was her motivating force. Her creed these days was simple. She *would not* yield to defeat. She *would not* inflict any more of her suffering than necessary on other people. And she *would* cling to her faith in the goodness of God even though for the present it meant a blind groping. So, though Helen North and others often saw traces of weeping in her face, they could not remember a time when she had uttered a word of complaint or had failed to welcome them with a smile.

And then one day, some weeks after the laminectomy, Dr. Paul Brand came to her room. He seated himself beside her bed.

"I think it's time, Mary, that you began thinking about your future."

She smiled wearily. "Do you suppose I ever think of anything else?"

"I mean your professional future Your future career as a doctor."

She stared at him. It was not like Dr. Brand to jest about serious matters. "My—Surely you must be joking."

"I am certainly not. You don't think your professional life has to be over, do you, just because you'll probably never be able to walk?"

Mary's heart was pounding. "But how—?" she whispered.

"In a few more weeks you'll be sitting in a wheel chair. You still have your arms, good strong ones, and your hands, extremely skillful ones. And your mind—" His eyes twinkled. "Such as it is.

Mary's palms were wet. Her fingers closed tensely about a damp fold of the sheet. "I still don't see how—"

Paul Brand's dark eyes glinted. "I wish I could take you to some other countries besides India. In many of them people in wheel chairs are doing not merely acceptable but exceptional jobs in different occupations and professions."

"But—" Mary's head whirled. "A doctor—a gynecologist?"

"I'll admit the gynecology is probably out," agreed Dr. Brand. "It would be hard, wouldn't it, delivering babies or performing hysterectomies from a wheel chair? But there are other areas."

Out of her first incredulity there sprang a wild hope. They discussed several possible areas of medical work—pathology, bacteriology. Mary's first elation turned to disappointment. Working the rest of her life with post-mortems, dead tissues, bacteria?

"Of course I can't do any clinical work," she said wistfully.

"Why not?" returned Dr. Brand promptly. "You might be able to." His eyes lighted with understanding. "I know how you feel. I'm glad you like to work with people."

The tears came to her eyes. Rising to leave, Paul Brand took her hand. "I believe you're closer to God than you have ever been," he said simply.

Mary shook her head. Why, she still wondered, *why* had her life been spared? Suppose they did find her some excuse for living? What use if, while you were serving one person, you yourself must be served by three or four? But the seed had been sown. Slowly, in the weeks and months that followed, it was to take root.

In April Annamma left for home, but Amma, though torn between the duty of wife and mother, stayed on. She and Mary moved to another room in M Ward, one with a kitchen, and with the arrival of Komachi, an older servant woman who had worked for the family in Cherai, their life settled into a steady routine. They tried to cook her favorite foods, especially fish curries made with coconut oil instead of the peanut oil usually used at Vellore. Amma was a favorite around the hospital and mothered everybody. She and Helen North became great friends, conversing together in signs and broken Tamil, of which they both knew little. Though her courage was magnificent, Helen often found her weeping outside the door of Mary's room.

"Won't she ever get well?" she would ask piteously.

Once Mary was able to eat, her brothers lavished on her packages of food from home—sweetmeats, fried fish, fried shrimp—and on their frequent visits insisted on bringing her such luxuries as apples. Though Mary was not fond of the latter fruit, it was the highest priced of any in the market, and they wanted her to have the best. John's wife, who was the best cook in the family, often sent delicious *halwa,* made with banana, melon, jackfruit, *ghi,* and flour.

Dr. Ida was a daily visitor, stopping every morning on her tour of the hospital with flowers from her garden. Mary looked forward to her coming. There was no restraint in her joyous approach—healthy sympathy but no muted pity.

"You're looking so nice today, Mary," she would say, her blue eyes beaming.

She and Amma were kindred spirits from the first. Dr. Ida would try to talk to Mary's mother in Tamil, but might as well have spoken in English, for Mary usually had to translate for her.

Dr. Ida was only one of her many visitors. Besides her intimate friends—Grace, Annamma Verghese, Lily, M. P., Cheruchi—many of the student doctors and nurses formed the habit of stopping in. As she grew stronger, Mary took a lively interest in everything which happened in the hospital or college.

"How is the new building coming along up on the campus?" she would inquire eagerly. Or—"How is the sunken garden now? What flowers are blooming?" And often the girls would have to confess shamefacedly that they had not noticed.

They found her an eager listener and wise adviser. She was always ready to help them solve their problems, big and little. And, unlike most of the young doctors after graduation, who regarded the activities of the junior medical students with amused condescension, she seemed to enjoy the recountings of their silly classroom pranks. Some of these new acquaintances became enduring friends. For instance, there was Ramani.

"Try and keep Mary company as often as you can," Grace Koshi urged the junior medical student. "She loves to have people around her."

Ramani, sensitive and concerned, was glad enough to oblige. Paying visits at first out of sympathy, she soon found that it was she herself, not Mary, who benefited most from their relationship. When Mary discovered, some two months after the accident, that the junior student's knowledge of spinal injuries was not keeping pace with her curiosity, she determined to remedy the deficiency. During Ramani's next visit she gave her a thorough briefing on the spine and its functional disorders, using herself as the guinea pig. With impersonal frankness she detailed the site of her injury, its causes and effects, and the extent of her paralysis.

Ramani was both touched and embarrassed. Feeling that some expression of sympathy was in order, she blurted out, "I—I'm sorry, Mary."

"Don't worry, Ramani." Mary smiled understandingly. "It's all right. I'm quite happy and have reconciled myself to the fact that I'll never be able to walk." Then she added with a twinkle, "If some chatterboxes like you come and keep me company every day, I don't even mind lying in this room for a few more months."

Another time she said, "Ramani, take a look at my legs."

The young student, accustomed now to the casual way Mary referred to her disabilities, obediently drew back the sheet. "But—they're terribly swollen!" she exclaimed in dismay.

"Yes," said Mary. "That's what I wanted to show you."

Whereupon there followed another medical discussion, this time on edema of the legs.

Mary made her demands, too, often difficult ones, as when she would ask Ramani to repeat the whole substance of the previous Sunday's sermon. And she kept the girls singing for hours in her room, though by no means against their will. Somehow such hymns as "O Master, Let Me Walk with Thee," and "The King of Love My Shepherd Is" gained a new meaning when they sang them for Mary.

But though Mary managed to present a serene face to the world, she often felt far from serene inside. The most galling consequence of her disability was her dependence upon others. To have total lack of control over the basis functions of her whole body, to be helpless as an infant, forced to depend on an *ayah* even to turn her in bed—bitter medicine indeed for one whose proudest assets had been physical strength and self-sufficiency!

But she would be independent again if it was humanly possible. With dogged determination she followed the exhausting schedule of Helen North's physiotherapy program. Toward the last of April she was fitted to a perspex jacket, a brace made from a solid piece of stiff plastic to give back support. With the temperature soaring often to 110 degrees in this hottest season of the year and accompanied by a high humidity, the discomfort of the jacket was great. Not only was it irritating to her skin, it caused painful pressure sores. The overhead fan seemed merely to circulate hot air, and the *cascas* curtains —reed draperies hung on the outer wall of the verandah and kept moist with water—failed to bring much relief, though Amma patiently kept spraying them with a hose.

Nevertheless, day after day, week after week, Mary persistently increased her skills. Finally came the day when she was transferred for the first time to a wheel chair. It was an event not only for Mary but for many of her friends. Unfortunately for the triumph of the moment, she fainted. The second attempt was successful, and gradually, as days passed, she was able to sit up for longer periods, both in the chair and in bed, against a back rest.

Now her world widened. Instead of four white walls and a door and window, she could see through the window into a garden with green lawns and flowers blooming. She could ride through the door and again become part of the turbulent human stream that flowed through verandahs and corridors.

Ramani, Grace, Annamma, and others vied with the nurses to take their turns pushing her about in the wheel chair, but at first she did not enjoy these trips. It was humiliating to have to be wheeled like a baby, and the sympathy in strangers' eyes was even harder to endure than their curiosity. She smarted increasingly under her helplessness. Unable even to dress oneself!

Lying in her bed, she spent hours trying to figure out how to put on a sari without passing it around her body. She could not bend. It was as intricate a problem as one in mathematics, but she finally solved it. One morning Helen North walked into the room to find her patient sitting in the wheel chair wearing a sari folded and draped with apparent perfection.

"How in the world!" she marveled.

News of the achievement spread. Nurses appeared, attendants, students from the nurses' hostel, doctors, medical students from the college, all demanding to see how it was done. Soon all the nurses in M Ward were giving demonstrations on how she had performed the feat, taking the end of a sari, folding it over to get the correct width, passing it under her limbs, pinning it to the petticoat over her knees.

One of Mary's visitors during those early months was Thambidurai, the medical student who had been responsible for the accident. He was subdued, a little frightened, remorseful. Mary tried to put him at his ease. Now that the damage was done, she felt, recriminations would be worse than useless.

Her brothers did not agree. They wanted her to bring legal action against Thambidurai. Being of a well-to-do family, the young student might be forced to pay handsomely.

"You're not being practical," accused George. "The fellow was definitely at fault. He should be made to assume responsibility."

"It was an accident," insisted Mary. "He did not intend to hurt any of us. And he was no more to blame, perhaps, than the driver or some of the others who urged that he be given permission to drive."

"But he *was* driving. And he *was* careless. And I say he should be made to pay. Yes, and John and Babi and Dr. Mathai all agree with me."

Mary shook her head. She believed in forgiveness, not retaliation. Punishing Thambidurai would not give her back her legs. It would not make her cheek whole again. And it might do irreparable damage to another person—and to her own spirit.

"So if a person strikes you on one cheek," retorted George, "you believe you should turn to him the other also."

The allusion was so ironically apt that they stared at each other in shocked comprehension. Then George smiled a little sheepishly.

"All right, Mary, have it your own way. After all, you're the one who has to"—he grinned wryly—"lose face. And—there does seem to be some Christian precedent for your position, even if it isn't practical."

Sometime later the police took action against Thambidurai for rash driving. The young student secured a lawyer who obtained a petition that the case be dismissed. Thambidurai circulated the petition among all who had been passengers in the station wagon, and asked them to sign it. By this time all except Mary were well on the way to complete recovery. None of them wished to press legal action, and he was able to secure their signatures. He came to Mary last of all.

Mary was alone in her room at the time. Her mother was outside on the verandah. She took the petition in her hands and looked at it. Thambidurai held out a pen. He was still humble, frightened.

"You—you don't have to sign it, you know, even though the others did. After all, you're the one who has the most reason for complaint. I wouldn't blame you at all if you refused."

Mary had to think quickly. Even though she had been considering the matter for a long time and thought she had made up her mind, she now weighed the problem again. If she signed the document, she would be relinquishing all right to compensation. She was the only one with permanent injuries. She knew she would be perfectly justified in the eyes of most people if she refused to sign. She could make this boy suffer for having caused her suffering. She could have him punished. But—would that be the Christian thing to do? The answer was quite simple. It had been given a long time ago by Another who had suffered because of people's intentional, not accidental wrongdoing. *Father, forgive them. . . .*

She prayed for a long moment silently. Then she reached for the pen.

"Are you sure you shouldn't talk with your mother or someone else before signing?" asked Thambidurai nervously.

"Quite sure," replied Mary.

Mary Verghese. She signed her name decisively at the bottom of the list.

The case was taken to court, and all the other victims of the accident appeared to give evidence and attest their signatures to the petition. The court came to Mary—the magistrate, the lawyer, and Thambidurai. It was on the day she moved into her third room, a little way down the corridor in M Ward.

The magistrate showed her the petition.

"Is this your signature?" he asked.

"Yes," said Mary.

He tried to question her about further details of the accident.

She shook her head. "I'm sorry," she said. "The injuries I incurred caused retrograde amnesia. I remember nothing back to three days before the accident."

The magistrate nodded understandingly. "Ah! I see. Of course. The brain was so damaged!"

Mary frowned. She was not at all pleased with that remark.

18

As if her troubles were not already sufficient, in June she suffered an attack of jaundice.

"At least I haven't caught up with Job," she consoled herself in the presence of an understanding nurse. "I haven't had boils yet."

"No?" retorted the nurse. "If you ask me, those pressure sores are worse than any boils."

But, like Job's, her problems were more mental and spiritual than physical. There were family worries. Her sister Annamma, returning to the hospital for a serious operation, was in a room nearby, yet Mary, again confined to her bed, could not go to her. It was Annamma, convalescing, who came to visit her instead. Amma, trotting faithfully back and forth between the two rooms, could not hide from Mary's keen discernment her increasing anxiety. She was worried about Appan and wanted to be with him, yet she would not leave as long as she felt Mary needed her. Somehow, Mary knew, she must make herself more self-sufficient. But how?

Still totally dependent on two *ayahs,* who had been hired at her expense through the hospital, Mary was finding even them a problem. In time Kochammu, her day attendant, had to leave on account of a family emergency, and was replaced by Victoria. Then Saraswati, the night *ayah,* stole an electric light bulb from another room, and the hospital manager insisted that she had to go. At Mary's urging she was kept on for another month while Jiwa, her replacement, was trained. These periods of adjustment always created fresh difficulties. Her whole being revolted against her utter helplessness. She would gladly have done a ward aid's duty herself, even a sweeper's, if she could only have been independent. Every door in her life seemed to have been slammed shut.

It's time you were thinking about your future medical career, Dr. Brand had told her months ago. The idea still seemed incredible. A healer of bodies whose own body was worse than useless? *Physican, heal thyself!* What possible use a doctor with only a brain and a pair of hands!

"But a trained brain," some inner voice kept insisting. "A strong pair of hands."

Behind the bright façade of smiling serenity she wept and agonized and prayed.

"Take my life. . . ." The words of an old hymn kept recurring. They were easy enough to repeat. If only her life *had* been taken! It was the following words which came hard.

> "Take my life and let it be
> Consecrated, Lord, to thee.
> Take my moments and my days,
> Let them flow in ceaseless praise . . .
> Take my hands and let them move
> At the impulse of thy love."

Take my hands!

Finally a first small ray of light shone through the crack of a door. Dr. Jameson asked her to go to the Gynecology Department to help some of the students with their cases. The work was entirely of an advisory nature. One of the students would present the history of the case, then the case would be discussed. Mary knew it was a task created more for her own therapy than for any great contribution she could make, but it was better than nothing. During those brief intervals she was not completely useless.

Then another door came ajar. Midsummer saw the death of "Mother" Eaton, the elderly rheumatic missionary, and her wheel chair, a lighter, more modern chair than the hospital's standard wooden models, was offered for sale. Dr. Brand suggested that Mary buy it. She made the purchase eagerly, and found that in the new chair she could wheel herself for short distances. And when a bar was installed over her bed, instead of having to be lifted bodily by one of the hospital attendants, Mary found that, with some help from her *ayah,* she could transfer herself from bed to wheel chair. She was as triumphant as a baby learning to take its first steps. In August, after six months of constant attendance. Amma returned home. Though Mary missed her mother's devoted presence, she felt a vast relief. She had taken her first unsteady steps toward independence.

About this time she received an invitation from Dr. Ruth Myers, head of Bacteriology, to come and work in that department. Mary considered the offer gratefully, but without enthusiasm. Dr. Edward Gault, head of Pathology, also urged her to come to his department. M. P., who was now specializing in pathology, did not encourage her.

"It would be hard to do autopsies," she observed bluntly, "sitting in a chair."

Regardless of her friend's comment, Mary was still lukewarm about pathology. She wanted to work with *people*. Hour after hour she mulled over the problem, lying in bed staring at the blank walls, sitting in her chair staring out the window.

Since her mother's departure she had moved to a new room facing the front of the hospital. Outside her window was a big tree, and beyond the tree a path and a set of low buildings—the leprosy clinic, which she had stared at so curiously long ago with Achamma. Here Dr. Gass and his assistants treated patients three days a week. Sitting in bed or in her wheel chair, Mary could watch the patients squatting in the shade of the tree. So close were they that she could occasionally see the white patches of skin, the stumps of fingers, the hairless brows. Though her first horror and revulsion had changed long since to pity, she still preferred not to look at them. Resolutely she turned her gaze upward to the green foliage, the interlacing branches, the blue of the sky.

Then slowly her aversion to watching them changed to fascination. As days passed, she came to recognize some of the patients, and was then either concerned or relieved when one of them failed to put in an appearance. *Nallathu,* good! The little boy who used to come with his grandmother must have been dismissed as an arrested case. For two weeks now the grandmother had come without him. But where was the old blind Moslem with the terrible ulcers on his feet? He should not be going so long without having them dressed. And the little girl who always wore so many marigolds plaited into her long braid? Mary was sure she had only just begun her treatments. It worried her also because the clinic always seemed so understaffed. Sometimes the queues of patients stretched the full length of the verandah, while others squatted for hours in the shade of the big tree, patiently waiting.

One day when Helen North arrived for the daily routine of physiotherapy, she found her patient in an unusually serious mood. Instead of smiling her usual greeting, Mary kept staring out of the window. They began the exercises in silence.

Then—"What do you think of leprosy?" asked Mary suddenly.

Helen paused in her patient manipulation of the useless limbs. Her face beamed.

"Mary, that's it!" she exclaimed excitedly.

Together they discussed the possibilities. A few days later Helen brought Ruth Thomas, a therapist in the employ of the British Mission to Lepers, to Mary's room.

"Helen tells me you're interested in working in the clinic," said Miss Thomas with enthusiasm. "That's wonderful."

"I'm not sure." Mary's guarded response revealed nothing of her painful excitement. Anxiously she probed the cheerful gaze for some evidence of pitying patronage, but found none. "There are many things to be considered," she continued cautiously. "I know my limitations. How much use is a doctor who can't walk, can't even lean forward in a chair?"

"That remains to be seen," replied Ruth Thomas. "She might be a lot of use."

"And I know almost nothing about leprosy."

"You can learn. Even the experts know little enough about it."

"Suppose"—Mary was merciless with herself—"the patients resent me. The sight of a cripple might remind them too much of their own disabilities."

Ruth Thomas did not argue. "Try it and see. Let me take you over to the clinic tomorrow. I'll call for you when I go in the morning."

Mary was exultant—and terrified. Her whole future, she felt, depended on the next few hours. She would not need others to tell her whether she was capable of a doctor's responsibilities. She would know herself. And most of the test would come before she set foot—how the old language persisted!—*rolled wheels* into the clinic. How could she possibly be through with all the routine care of bodily functions, washing, and dressing in time? That night before sleeping she thought through the whole procedure, estimating to a minute how long each complicated step would take. Rousing Jiwa before it was light, she issued explicit directions. When Ruth Thomas came, she was in her wheel chair dressed and ready. She had passed the first self-inflicted test.

"It seems natural to be piloting one of these," the therapist told Mary cheerfully as she pushed her across a porch. "I have a friend in England who lives in a wheel chair."

To Mary's relief the staff greeted her arrival at the clinic with neither effusion nor solicitude. She might have been any volunteer doctor who had offered to contribute her services to a busy department. Dr. Job, the senior resident, formerly a fellow student, greeted her cordially. Dr. Gass said matter-of-factly:

"Morning, Doctor Mary. It's good of you to come. Miss Thomas tells me you may be willing to help us awhile. That's good news indeed."

He issued a few simple directions, easy enough for any trained doctor to follow. Unobtrusively, certain adjustments were made in facilities and implements to fit her convenience. But they were surprisingly few. The doctors were usually seated when making their examinations, and the patients stood or sat beside them. Mary's arms were long, her hands as strong and skillful as ever. Her first awkwardness and fears were soon lost in the exhilaration of being actually at work again. Having examined and treated leprosy patients on Roadside, she already possessed some knowledge of the disease and its commonest forms of treatment. She helped the other doctors examine the patients. She wrote chits for medicine. She issued directions to the nurses for the treatment of simple ulcers.

If the staff carefully diverted their attention from her disability, not so the patients. She was painfully conscious of their stares, their pointing fingers, their whispers, even fragments of their comments.

"*Ayoh!* Look . . . doctor, *our* doctor? . . . What's the matter! . . . not walk . . . whole body like our hands and feet. . . . *Pavum,* what a pity!"

Looking anxiously into the faces raised to hers, Mary thankfully detected no resentment. On the other hand, she failed to notice the absence of other emotions commonly found in them: self-pity, hopelessness, sullenness, a sort of arrogant hostility. But her colleagues noticed and commented among themselves:

"Did you see how they looked at her? Almost humbly?"

"Yes. There she was, far more disabled than they, and yet not thinking of herself at all, only of them and their needs."

"She did more for them in an hour than we could in days!"

Mary insisted on remaining until the last of the long queue had been examined and treated, then returned to her room so weary that every muscle in her arms and shoulders ached. But she was at the clinic on the next day it was held, and the next. Her presence soon became routine.

On one of these days as she passed along the verandah skirting the leprosy clinic, she saw Dr. Brand sitting in his office at the end of the building reserved for his Department of Surgery and Rehabilitation. She wheeled herself into the room.

"I've been working," she told him triumphantly.

He nodded with satisfaction. "I know. How is it going?"

Her eyes held a confident gleam. "You'll have to ask Dr. Gass."

"I have," he replied. "And I don't mean, 'How is the work going?' I know that. It's going well. You're showing a remarkable aptitude and endurance. I mean, 'How is life going?' "

Mary considered. "I'm beginning to think," she said earnestly, "that it may have a pattern, after all. At first all the threads seemed so—so tangled and broken."

The young doctor's dark eyes shone. "And now you're finding that the great Designer may be able to use even broken threads?"

"Yes," said Mary gratefully. Somehow he always knew how to put things into the right words. "Dr. Gass thinks he may be able to use me permanently, though nothing is certain yet."

"Don't decide at once," advised Dr. Brand. "You might come sometime, Mary, and visit my department. I'd like to see what you could do here."

Mary looked eager but doubtful. Rehabilitation, perhaps. But surely surgery would be out of the question. She shook her head regretfully.

"Wait," urged Paul Brand again.

For some weeks she continued working in the clinic, returning exhausted after each session, often with an armful of books to study on leprosy.

She was surprised to discover from her research how little had been known about the disease until very recent years. She was impressed to discover that much of the literature was by Dr. Robert Cochrane, and that orthopedic surgery and rehabilitation had been almost unknown in the treatment until the experiments of Dr. Brand.

As she read, she become particularly interested in the problem of insensitivity, since the dangers and precautions involved in the proper care of anaesthetic hands and feet so closely paralleled those necessitated by her own paralyzed lower trunk and limbs. The commonest cause of the loss of fingers, toes, and feet, wrote Dr. Brand, was heat. If your insensitive hand held a metal tumbler filled with hot coffee until you lifted it to your lips and found that the coffee was too hot, by the time you put it down you would have burns on your finger tips. Building or stirring a fire, you might handle a burning stick or even a red-hot coal without being conscious of its heat. Then, since the burns would not hurt, they would be neglected and probably become infected, leading to the eventual loss of a finger.

Mary well understood the problem. Must not every bit of her own paralyzed body be examined each day for the slightest sign of redness or abrasion? For without pain, that blessed monitor, there was no protection from injury except eternal vigilance.

But the most important task in the rehabilitation of leprosy patients, Dr. Brand wrote, was the preservation of personality. For the treatment of leprosy was a long, long process. It might be two, three, or four years before the disease was arrested, perhaps much longer. It was very easy for the afflicted to become bitter and apathetic.

"I feel that the most precious possession any human being has is his spirit; his will to live, his sense of human dignity, his personality."

Mary read the words over and over. How well she understood this —better even than Paul Brand, with all his sensitivity, ever could! The pattern of her new life was indeed taking shape. She was beginning to see that there might be some rare designs in the plan of the great Designer which could be created *only* with broken threads.

19

Mary had been working in the leprosy clinic for perhaps a month when Dr. Brand made his astounding suggestion.

The young Englishman brought it up so calmly that he might have been suggesting she take a new kind of medicine. "You always liked surgery, didn't you? It was one of your favorite subjects?"

"Yes. *The* favorite. But—"

"And you showed unusual promise in it. I've been consulting your records."

"But—" Mary was still breathless. "Have you forgotten? I'm a *paraplegic!*"

"What of it? You don't operate with your feet. In fact, the hand operation I'm suggesting is one of the few that have to be performed with the surgeon seated."

"Yes," said Mary. "So it is." Her dark eyes had struck fire. Already her mind was at work, planning the details, analyzing the difficulties.

"I'm doing a tendon transplant tomorrow afternoon at one o'clock," said Dr. Brand. "Doctor Fritschi is assisting me. How would you like to help us?"

A pulse in Mary's injured cheek throbbed painfully, but her face remained studiedly calm. "I would like to very much," she replied.

Long before one o'clock the next afternoon she was in the operating room making her preparations. All her senses quickened at the familiar sights and sounds and smells. She was at home again.

But it was not a time for sentiment or even for thanksgiving. Too much was at stake. Wheeling her chair under the small table on which the patient's hand would rest, she carefully tested its height, then added cushions to her chair to bring herself to the proper level. Using a gown that could be put on from the front, she finished dressing. Then she scrubbed and put on gloves. When Dr. Brand and his assistant, the Swiss surgeon Dr. Ernest Fritschi, arrived, she was ready.

"Good," said Dr. Brand, checking each detail carefully.

Her work that day was comparatively minor: hooking the threads, cutting, hooking the skin, holding the tendons. It was her tension and uncertainty that made the elementary tasks difficult—her inability to lean forward and to move her body at will, the problem of maintaining balance while her hands were otherwise engaged, the discomfort of her profuse sweating under stress of excitement. There was no ceiling fan in the room, and even though it was September, the heat was still oppressive. The hour which the operation consumed lengthened into a seeming eternity.

"Tired?" asked Dr. Brand when, reaching for a clamp, her fingers fumbled. "One of the juniors can take over."

Mary gritted her teeth. "No. I'm fine."

Sweat trickled into her eyes. Pains darted through her shoulder blades. For an instant everything turned black. She clutched at the edge of the hand table to keep from toppling.

"Cut," came the terse order.

The room righted itself. The floor nurse swabbed at her forehead with a piece of gauze, and Mary's vision cleared. She reached with a steady hand toward the scissors, grasped them firmly, and cut the thread. She did not fumble again.

"You did a good job," Dr. Brand declared when they were back in the scrubbing room. "All you need is practice. The next time Ernest operates I'd like you to be his assistant. Think you could manage it?"

"Yes," agreed Mary.

In the following days she assisted Dr. Fritschi with several operations. Each time she became a little more proficient, felt a little less awkward. But though each new experience was in itself a minor conquest, she was by no means satisfied. A doctor would be of little use in surgery if he must remain always an assistant. The real test was yet to come. *Could she perform such an operation herself?*

Watching Ernest Fritschi's fingers, she mastered each detail of the intricate tendon operation. Lying in her bed, sitting in her wheel chair, she performed each step over and over in her mind, attempting to anticipate all the difficulties. It was enough of a challenge to perform a new operation with all one's bodily functions intact . . . was it not presumption to attempt it with less than half of them? Would her arms and shoulders stand the strain of both performing the operation and supporting her own body without yielding to intolerable fatigue?

When the day of the test came, she faced it calmly. The faith which had supported her through all the preceding days of testing was equal to this also. If God wanted her to be a surgeon, he would give her the strength and ability to perform the task. If not, then He would show her some other task which she could perform. It was as simple as that. Of one thing only she was certain. There would be no frustration of divine intent for lack of her own desire and determination.

Dr. Fritschi, who was going to assist her, greeted her with a slightly too obvious heartiness. She could see the anxiety in his eyes. And why not?

"You'll get along splendidly," he assured her. "But just in case anything should go wrong or get too difficult, remember I'm here to take over."

Propped on her cushions, head high, propelled carefully by an attendant, Mary entered the operating room. The patient was already in position, his hand resting on the small auxiliary table. Wheeled under it, she rested her elbows on it to make sure that she was seated at the proper height. Good so far.

To quiet the nervous tumult within her she sat still for a moment, looking at the hand, its fingers grotesquely curled, as insensitive as much of her own body and almost as useless. She felt a sudden kinship with the hand. Ironic that, powerless to create motion in her own dead limbs, she might make these taut knuckles bend, these curled fingers straighten! No, not ironic. Wonderful! She prayed silently.

"Take my hands and let them move
At the impulse of Thy love!"

With steady fingers she made her first incision.

The operation was a sublimis tendon transplantation, for the fourth and fifth fingers. It consisted of freeing this good, unparalyzed tendon from its insertion and retunneling it through the hand to the fingers, to substitute for the paralyzed intrinsic muscle. This would make it possible for the fingers not only to be bent at the knuckle but to remain straight at the other joints. After a similar operation on the other two fingers, and perhaps another to restore the opposition of the thumb, the hand would regain much of its lost function. Instead of a useless claw it would become once more an efficient tool, able to pinch, to grasp.

Mary knew that swiftness as well as skill was essential. The tourniquet creating the bloodless field would have to be released after an hour to prevent nerve damage in the hand. After the first few moments her sense of compulsive haste was replaced by one of confidence. The very strangeness of her task became its fascinating challenge.

"Good," commented her assistant as she continued the delicate process of diverting the sublimis tendon. "If I didn't know better, I'd think you had performed the operation a dozen times."

Mary made no reply. Words would be a waste of her precious energy. She spoke only when necessary to give directions and then only in monosyllables:

"Clamps . . . skin knife . . . sutures . . . cut. . . ."

Before the operation was half finished, her arms were throbbing from the strain. Her elbows, tensed for the double duty of maintaining body balance and stabilizing hand motion, felt as if they were being prodded by knives. Sweat gathered under her mask, seeped into her eyes, turned the upper part of her gown into a clinging compress. If only her hands remained steady, deft! With all her will she forced them to remain relaxed, deliberate.

A nurse, noticing, wiped the rivulets of sweat from her forehead.

"How about my taking over?" asked Dr. Fritschi. "It would still be your operation. Just the loose ends to tie up."

Mary smiled at the words' aptness. "No," she said.

She *had* to finish. Giving up now would be an acknowledgment of defeat. She would have proved nothing, either to herself or to others. No one else could open this door for her into the future, not even God. He could only give her the strength to open it for herself.

"Help me." She prayed not in words but in every breath, every heartbeat, every motion of her hands. "If this is what You want me to do, help me."

With painstaking care she finished suturing the tendon to its new position, using a needle and fine stainless steel wire. A gauze dressing was applied, then a light plaster splint, and the operation was finished. Only now did Mary dare look at her watch. The entire procedure had taken just under an hour.

"Well done," pronounced Dr. Fritschi. "I wouldn't have believed it possible."

The attendant wheeled her into the scrub room. Her hands, firm and deft to the fastening of the last suture, trembled now, and she had to clutch the arms of the chair tightly to maintain her balance. Her whole body felt almost as drained and lifeless as her limbs. Yet her spirit soared with triumph.

"Thank You." This time her lips formed the words, even though they uttered no sound. "Thank You for helping me open the door."

The next operation she performed cost her less in physical effort, and she was soon taking her turn with Paul Brand and Ernest Fritschi in the operating room, as well as paying visits to the clinic. Though she usually returned to her room weak from fatigue, and though she experienced moments of deep despondency when it seemed impossible to face a professional life with all its obstacles, the resilient powers of faith and determination were strong. Dawn found her struggling again with the routines of bodily functions, washing, dressing, in order to be ready for the early morning schedule. Her colleagues saw nothing of the inner turbulence, only the calm, smiling, uncomplaining exterior.

One day in October, soon after she began operating, Helen North brought Mary an exciting bit of news. Ernest Fritschi was leaving Vellore to assume a position at the new Leprosy Research Sanatorium in Karigiri. This left a vacancy in leprosy research for which applications were now being received. What an opportunity for Mary! She must hurry and fill out the forms at once, for the deadline date for applications was only two days away.

Mary's excitement was tinctured with uncertainty.

"If Doctor Brand thought I was qualified and wanted me to apply," she replied, "why didn't he tell me?"

Helen thought she knew the answer to that. Dr. Brand, being himself the honorary officer of the program sponsored by the Indian Council of Medical Research, was probably hesitant about initiating applications. That was doubtless why he had suggested that Helen give the information to Mary.

Mary was now genuinely excited. "Doctor Brand really sent you to tell me?"

"Yes," said Helen, producing an application blank. "Can't you see, Mary? This is *it,* what you've been waiting for. With your interest and experience, you're almost sure to be chosen."

Mary's enthusiasm dimmed. "That's what I'm afraid of," she said soberly. "They'll choose me out of—" She hated even to speak the word—"out of pity."

"Nonsense! You're well fitted for the job, better than anyone else, and you know it. If Doctor Brand hadn't thought so, he wouldn't have suggested that I tell you."

But Mary was not convinced. She brooded over the problem until it was almost too late to send in her application. Attractive though the position was to her, she felt she had to be chosen because of her qualifications and ability. . . . But how did she know she wouldn't be, reason argued. She *was* qualified. At least, she could make herself so. Perhaps it was selfish pride which made her so sensitive and suspicious. If a door was set ajar in front of her, should she refuse to enter it? And this time she did not need to push it open. She need only knock.

At the last minute she sent in the application.

Helen North brought Mary other news during her daily visits. Dr. Gwenda Lewis, the young English physician who had given Mary anaesthesia for her laminectomy, she of the lilting voice and springing step, had been stricken with polio in September and lay gravely ill in her room over in N Ward a few yards away. Mary followed her progress with intense concern. They had become explorers in the same shadowy world, she and Dr. Gwenda, with the same giants of crippling paralysis to conquer. She wondered at first if she should visit the room in N Ward. Would the sight of her dead limbs, her wheel chair, be too vivid reminders of what lay ahead?

"Nonsense!" Helen North assured her. "Gwenda is made of as strong stuff as you are. Try her and see."

Mary did. On her first of many visits Dr. Gwenda greeted her with a warm, if rueful smile.

"Welcome, comrade. They tell me I may be able to ride around like that sometime. There are so many things you'll have to teach me!"

Mary felt an even stronger kinship with the young Englishwoman when she read in the college newspaper, *The C.M.C. Pulse,* a letter of gratitude which Gwenda Lewis wrote to her friends.

> I want to share with you [one paragraph confided] my wonderful experience of constant awareness of the Presence of God. Many times in the past I have thought that I was depending entirely on Him, but I realize now that I had never really done so before. To be brought to the place where one cannot do anything and is compelled to leave everything to Him is an experience for which one can be only humbly grateful.

Gwenda's only audible complaint to Mary was that she had been unable to give the anaesthetic when Dr. Ida came to the hospital in October for the one operation ever performed on her, a hernia repair.

"Why couldn't she have had it a month earlier?" Gwenda lamented, begrudging the privilege enjoyed by the Hindu anaesthetist who had taken her place.

Dr. Ida's presence in the hospital brought gaiety. M Ward looked more like a *durbar* than a place for the sick. The corridors were filled with visiting dignitaries. Smells of garlands and bouquets overpowered those of ether and antiseptics. Almost every nurse and doctor in the seven-hundred-bed hospital made occasion to visit M-2 at least once and most of them many times. White hair waving about her face like a halo, lacy bedjacket matching her blue eyes, Dr. Ida held court like a reigning maharani. She who had spent most of her life in serving now reveled in the luxury of being served.

Mary was one of her frequent visitors. Almost every day since the accident, whenever she had been staying in Vellore, Dr. Ida had come to her room in M Ward, smiling, encouraging, bringing flowers. Mary found deep satisfaction in being for this little time on the giving rather than the receiving end. In these days she lost some of her shyness with Dr. Ida, even shared with her a little of her torture of waiting for the decision to be made on her application.

For October sped by and still she received no word. Dr. Brand left at the end of October for a trip through India, visiting various leprosaria and giving lectures and demonstrations in hand surgery. Uncertain about her future, Mary continued both her clinical and surgical work, becoming more and more adept in performing the operations that were beginning to make Paul Brand famous. Now that she had made the decision and applied for the research post, she wanted desperately to be chosen. She was more and more convinced that she could fulfill its duties competently. And it was imperative that she find some form of profitable employment. Her whole being rebelled at her continued enforced dependence on Appan and her brothers. This might well be her one opportunity to pursue the work in surgery which she so loved. It was difficult to control her impatience.

Then suddenly, in a roundabout way, she learned the answer.

The college choir came to sing for Dr. Ida and Gwenda Lewis. Mary happened to be in the corridor when they came marching through on their way to M-2. Mrs. Brand, also a doctor and a member of the choir, stopped to speak to her.

"Welcome, Mary, to my husband's department," she said cordially, grasping both her hands. "We are very happy to have you. I was so glad to hear that you received the appointment."

Mary's happiness was shortlived. Though the appointment took effect on November 1, she was unable to assume the duties of her new position for many days. Skin breakdown, resulting in abscess and fever, a constant hazard for the paraplegic, confined her again to her bed. The torture of those weeks of inactivity was more mental than physical. She had a job to do. She had been entrusted with a position of responsibility. Yet here she lay, utterly dependent, unable even to sit up in her wheelchair.

The life of the hospital flowed past, as about a stone in midstream. She tried to quell her torturing impatience with an interest in the events which moved on without her.

Dr. Ida was up from her bed in time to open the new rooms for the Physiotherapy Department, so eagerly awaited by Helen North and her associates.

"She didn't want to cut the ribbon," reported Helen on a flying visit, "so she asked that a bow be tied instead. Then she drew on one of the bow strings and declared the rooms open. Oh, Mary, you should see them! Limited though they are, they will help us accomplish so much more! You have no idea of the untreated cases of polio and spastic paralysis which come to us."

The new quarters consisted of one long room containing four cubicles, each with a short-wave diathermy machine, and of another room in which infrared, ultraviolet, venous constriction, and electrical treatments could be given. Further, there was a splint room, an enlarged swimming pool, and a gymnasium.

"We haven't a roof over the pool yet," Helen said, "and you should see how the patients respond to the combined sun and hydrotherapy treatments! When the hot season comes, of course we'll have to put a roof on."

Later, when Gwenda Lewis' sister arrived from England prepared to take Gwenda back with her, Helen brought even more exciting news.

"What do you think! Gwenda's sister is so impressed by the care we're giving her and by our new facilities for rehabilitation that she's going to leave her here for treatment! Isn't that a good recommendation for the kind of work we're doing? If we could just do more of it!"

Mary was sympathetic, but she could not share Helen's enthusiasm Of course India needed physiotherapy. She needed leprosy specialists also. It took all her faith and determination to present a smiling face and calm exterior these days.

The only action she saw during that long month of November was her own transfer to M-2, the room recently occupied by Dr. Ida. The essence of Dr. Ida's personality, the fragrance of her mountains of flowers, seemed still to cling to its four white walls. But it was a disturbing rather than a comforting essence. Four walls and a bed had never been able to confine that inimitable energy. One could learn many things from Dr. Ida, but not patience.

Mary was just beginning to sit up in her wheel chair again when Dr. Brand returned from his trip. He was immediately concerned by the news of her skin breakdown.

"That jacket," he said. "It's very uncomfortable, isn't it?"

"Yes," admitted Mary fearfully. Was he regretting already that he had recommended her for the research post? "But once I've recovered from this setback, I'm sure I'll be able to manage."

She did recover sufficiently to do some work in the clinic during December, but a week before Christmas she was back in bed again.

Christmas was delightful . . . and heart-rending. Her friends outdid themselves trying to make it pleasant for her. The room was beautifully decorated. There were chrysanthemums and poinsettias from the Nursing School. Her little nieces—Omana, Gita, and Shoba—sent her hand-painted Christmas cards. Dr. Brand brought his four children to sing Christmas carols in her room; later they went to sing them again to Gwenda Lewis, still confined to her bed in N Ward.

But perhaps the most significant of all her Christmas gifts was a little wooden plaque made in Dohnavur, South India, and given her by some of the hospital staff. It bore a motto of just four words:

"I KNOW . . . FEAR NOT"

Hanging on the white wall facing her bed, a tiny landmark in a void of utter blankness, its promise was to sustain her during the long, almost unbearable months that were to follow.

20

Mary was disheartened but not surprised when Dr. Brand recommended a fusion operation on her spine.

"You'll never be able to function properly as long as you have to wear that jacket." His tone was almost apologetic. "I'm sorry, Mary. You've already been through more than a human being should be expected to endure. And I don't need to tell you, this will not be easy."

"I know," said Mary.

She tried not to show her dismay. Another operation, followed by weeks of immobility! And the hot season, with its almost unendurable temperatures and humidity, not more than a month away! But it was another factor that worried her even more.

"You will have to find someone else to fill my position?" She faced the fear with her usual stubborn directness. "I realize, of course, that it wouldn't be fair to ask you to hold it for me. It's work you need, not promises."

Paul Brand hastened to reassure her. It was Mary they wanted, no one else, and they could manage very well until she was strong enough to work again. Dr. Fritschi could assume part of the operating load, commuting from the new Leprosy Research Sanatorium, which was only ten miles away. Furthermore, Dr. Lane, an English surgeon who had come to Vellore for training in hand surgery, would be available for some months.

Then Paul Brand went on to explain the advantages of the fusion operation. With her spine rendered completely rigid, Mary would be able to sit up without support. She might even learn to lean forward and backward. And of course without the jacket, pressure sores would be less likely to develop.

But Mary did not need to be persuaded. If the operation would make her more independent, more useful, of course she had to have it. And as soon as possible after she made a visit home. She was determined to go home before the operation. She had not seen her father since the accident. He probably did not have long to live. She bought her railroad tickets and made her preparations. It would be her first trip away from the hospital since the accident. It seemed as far as the ends of the earth.

But again Mary's family cooperated. George came, with her two oldest sisters, and George's oldest daughter, Leila. They all went back on the train together. The journey was less difficult than Mary had feared. Saraswati, her present *ayah,* was as efficient in a railroad compartment as in a hospital room. Except for the strain and embarrassment of having to be caried bodily from automobile to train compartment, from compartment to automobile again, it was no great ordeal.

They went to George's house in Cochin, and her parents came there to visit her. The meeting with Appan was tender but restrained, each trying to conceal the shock and distress at the change in the other. Appan had aged and failed visibly. The knowledge that concern over her own condition was partly responsible for his added to Mary's sorrow.

But neither was the sort to inflict personal distress on others. Though Mary could tell that Appan was worried about her specializing in leprosy and did not really approve, he made no spoken objection. The decision was hers to make, and he would respect it.

"Just remember, daughter," he urged her in confidence, "that anything I have is yours for the asking."

Long afterward Mary was to discover that he had kept a special secret account book to detail the amounts spent on her care and rehabilitation. Not that his other children would have begrudged the extra expenditures! But he had wanted to avoid even the possibility of constraint among his children.

Mary had two weeks with her family. She reveled in the company of her nieces and nephews, especially little Shiela, George's second daughter and her own godchild. She admired Babi's twins, Kochuman and Mol, now nearly a year old, when they came on a visit from Alleppey, where their father made his headquarters as a construction engineer.

To Mary's delight third sister Thankamma had become a thoroughly changed person. The moody and bitter preoccupation with her own ills had been replaced by a lively interest in her home community's social problems. With Amma, she had formed a committee to do social work in Kerala. Through the Y.W.C.A. in Ernakulam they had obtained dried milk and multipurpose food from Church World Service. Amma was president of the new organization. Thankamma organized the committee which administered the food rations from the family home in Cherai. To Mary all this seemed an answer to prayer. When she said as much to Amma, her mother shook her head sadly.

"*Ayoh!* A pity, then, such prayers are not answered more often! If they were, you would be walking on your own strong legs again."

Mary made no comment. Some of her friends were strong advocates of faith healing. They had held prayer services for her recovery in her room. Though she herself was a firm believer in the power of God and the efficacy of prayer, she was both a scientist and a doctor. God did perform miracles of healing, she knew from experience, in accordance with His utterly dependable laws and through the knowledge and skill of human beings, and she had no doubt that, as a result of prayer, healing had often been effected which had at least *seemed* to transcend all known laws and knowledge and skill. But she was far too humble to claim any such preferential favor for herself. Let her friends pray for a miracle of healing if they wished. She herself dared not pray for that. Suppose in some mysterious way it should turn out that she could serve God better the way she was! She preferred to pray rather for a deeper faith and for guidance in finding the way she could best be used in God's service.

Not that she had always felt such resignation! At first she had prayed with demanding, agonized insistence and implored others to do so. She had even written to an Anglican clergyman, Bishop Pakenham Walsh, for many years associated with a Jacobite *ashram* near Coimbatore, who was widely known for his firm belief in the power of prayer to effect healing.

"I am so worried," she had confided, "about being a burden to my family, physically and financially. It isn't that I mind so much for myself, though I had wanted so much to be of service. Please, please pray for me."

His reply had been solicitous, understanding—and disappointing. Of course he would pray for her. But only one thing could he promise. God would give her strength and courage, if not healing. And He could use her handicap as a great blessing.

Returning to Vellore in March, Mary found to her surprise that

Bishop Walsh had just come to the hospital as a patient. Soon after her arrival he came to her room to visit her. A man of nearly ninety, his very presence was a benediction.

"Would you like to be anointed?" he asked her earnestly.

Mary considered. Anointing the sick with oil according to early church tradition was in accordance with Jacobite custom, but this man was not a Jacobite. And the Jacobites were supposed to accept sacraments only from their own priests. However, this was unimportant. If God wanted to heal her, Mary reflected, he could do it as well through Bishop Walsh as through Joseph Achan. In fact, He could probably do it quite as well without benefit of oil or the laying on of hands. She looked up at the old bishop with his kind eyes and saintly smile.

"Yes," she replied.

A time was appointed, and he came to her room early one evening, just two days before the scheduled operation. Many of her friends came also. The bishop anointed her forehead with oil and prayed that she might be healed. Mary closed her eyes. As she prayed with the others, her body tensed and strained, as if it depended on her, through sheer will and energy, to bring the prayers to fulfillment. Then slowly she relaxed. A deep serenity possessed her. She knew suddenly that it did not really matter how the prayers were answered. It would be all right either way.

So she was neither surprised nor disappointed when no miracle of healing was accomplished. Secretly, perhaps, she was even a bit relieved to discover that God was not the sort of being who could be cajoled into changing his physical laws to suit individuals, that he acted as dependably in a human body as in a test tube. She was far sorrier for her hopeful friends than for herself.

And yet who was to say that there had been no miracle of healing? For had not the good bishop prayed not only for healing of body, but for that of mind and spirit?

The fusion operation was performed on March 14, 1955. Bone chips taken from her hip were inserted between five lumbar vertebrae, in order to effect rigidity. As usual, Mary's stubborn body refused to cooperate. Her blood pressure became so low that the procedure had to be suspended for an interval. At length the operation was completed.

Body encased in two slabs of plaster, either one removable, Mary was again placed on a revolving bed. Twice each day she was turned.

In the morning the nurses would remove the top slab and bathe her. Then, turning her over, they would remove the other slab and bathe her back. For two or three hours she was left lying face down. The back slab was then replaced and the bed turned to leave her again lying on her back. The procedure was repeated in the evening.

It was for the hours of greater freedom twice a day, lying on her face, that Mary lived. Head taped and pillowed, a book lying on a low table below the open bed frame, arms resting on the table, she could read or study. Avidly she read book after book—*A Man Called Peter*, the biography and writings of Amy Carmichael, volumes on the causes of nerve paralysis.

Not that the longer periods on her back were wholly wasted. She used them to pray for other people and to strengthen her own spiritual life. She enjoyed the visits of her many friends. She shared the problems of students and nurses, listened eagerly to news of all the latest romances and even tried to promote a few.

One day one of Mary's closest friends burst breathlessly into her room. "What do you think! *He* has *proposed* to me!"

The girl, three years behind Mary in medical school and now in the middle of her junior residency, had for some time been enjoying a casual friendship with a young post-graduate student in medicine, whom Mary knew well.

"Well, why not?" countered Mary calmly. "I understand such things are likely to happen. Didn't you expect he might?"

"I suppose so, but—Mary, what shall I *do!*"

"What do you want to do?" asked Mary reasonably. "Do you love him? Do you want to marry him?"

"I—I don't know." The girl's bright eyes and flushed cheeks belied her uncertain words.

"You *will* know," Mary assured her. "He is a fine young man and a good doctor. I like him. If you decide to accept his proposal, I shall give you my happiest blessing."

In good time her friend did so decide, and the triumphant suitor soon paid Mary a visit.

"I believe it's because of you that she said yes," he told her half jokingly but with genuine gratitude.

Many people helped to make the waiting period less intolerable. Annamma Verghese, Elsie, Grace, and other members of the little prayer fellowship were sources of constant strength and inspiration.

She could not have endured the long weeks without their visits. Friends brought flowers every day, and one doctor even fixed a pot of blossoms under her bed so she could see it when she was lying on her face. Dr. Rambo, the American eye specialist, brought a travel poster of the Jungfrau and fastened it to the wall.

"You need something to widen your horizons," he told her with a smile. "This will help."

It did How it did! It stretched the walls to include unbelievable vistas. The pinnacle of whiteness was like a glimpse of heaven.

Nurse Effie Wallace, as ingenious as she was practical, had attached a mirror to a bar over Mary's head, reflecting not only her face but the trays of food set on her chest, so she could feed herself normally, with her fingers. Even better, the mirror could reflect objects outside the window: the big tree, a bougainvillea bush, people passing along the path toward the leprosy clinic. Sometimes Mary caught sight of Dr. Brand striding along to his work, and it took all her will power to stifle her frustration.

She did not always stifle it. M. P., tiptoeing into the room one day when Mary was lying on her face, saw a telltale shaking of shoulders and withdrew to make a more boisterous entrance.

"That's you, M. P.," called Mary gaily. "I can tell your step, like a bull charging."

Darting an anxious glance at the floor under Mary's head, M. P. noted, as she had expected, the traces of tears. It was all she could do to maintain the mood of gaiety.

"My wedding," she blurted, feeling guilty to be flaunting her own happiness. "I—I thought you might like to hear about the plans."

"Seri, yes!" Mary's pleasure was so genuine that her friend's constraint instantly vanished. "Tell me about it. I can't wait to hear!"

M. P. sat cross-legged on the floor within range of the eyes that were now bright with excited curiosity instead of tears. The wedding was to be here in Vellore, in May. M. P.'s mother and sisters were coming from Kerala, and, even if Mary could not actually witness the ceremony, she could almost be a part of it, could she not? And her wedding dress was all white and gold. She couldn't wait to show it to Mary. And did Mary remember how worried she used to be, afraid that young Dr. Bhaktavizyam was just playing with her affections, and now here they were actually getting married!

Mary laughed happily, as excited over her friend's good fortune as if it were her own. She was glad that M. P., recipient of the coveted

Madras scholarship, had never discovered how much she, Mary, had wanted it or what a severe strain it had once placed on their friendship. Such a small, unimportant disappointment that had really been!

"Just be careful you don't charge down the church aisle the way you came into my room," she teased affectionately. "Your Doctor Bhaktavizyam might yet change his mind."

She learned to tell others than M. P. by their footsteps. Rhythm of gait, lightness or heaviness of step, slowness or swiftness of pace, were as variant as each personality. Grace Koshi moved quickly, lightly, Annamma Verghese with steps rhythmically smooth, Helen North with a deliberation as methodical as her patient manipulation of crippled arms and legs. Dr. Brand's steps were youthfully swift, decisive, as if he knew just where he was going and could hardly wait to get there.

To the rhythm of one set of footsteps Mary's pulses always quickened. A slow rhythm it was, but with a hint of impatience for its lost briskness. In spite of its earthbound reluctance, it managed somehow to impart the cadence of soaring wings. She kept listening for it long after Dr. Ida, now nearly eighty-five, had fled to her beloved Hill Top to find surcease from the intolerable heat.

For Mary there was no surcease. Its torment was as constant and inescapable as the hoarse scream of the brain-fever bird, its harbinger. *Popiya . . . po-pi-ya . . . PO—PI—YA* . . . louder and louder it shrilled, beating an endless tattoo against one's eardrums. Higher and higher rose the mercury . . . one hundred, one hundred five, one hundred ten. The small room became an inferno, the slab of plaster the floor of an oven with her body as the fuel. Bathing brought little relief, for the cool water became tepid even before it touched her flesh. Even though there was a ceiling fan above her bed, the air it set in motion felt like blasts from a furnace. The reed screens hung over the verandah steamed with each spraying of water, so that instead of cooling, they seemed only to make the atmosphere of the room more hotly humid.

Unable to move, her whole inert body generating heat but perspiring only above the level of its injury, Mary lay in agonizing discomfort, day after day, week after week. But the hot season brought its compensations. There was the delectable savor of mangoes, cool and succulent, sweeter than anything except possibly the soft meat of coconuts. There was the song of the magpie robin, who, after months of plaintive "swee-ee's" and harsh "chr-r-r's", suddenly recovered his voice with the hot weather and burst into a torrent of melody. It was almost worth the brazen swelter of a May morning just to hear him. There was a spray of *gul mohr* which a thoughtful nurse brought her in a tall vase, a wide-spread fan of pale green lace sewn with blossoms of orange and crimson and scarlet, gorgeous indeed as a *mohr's*—peacock's—tail. And there was hope. Cool showers and fresh breezes were on their way. Slowly her taut spine was welding into strength. A new wheel chair had been ordered—one that would be easier to operate and make her more independent. And, best of all, there would be work for her to do as soon as she felt ready.

May also was the month of weddings. True to her word, M. P. shared her hours of supreme happiness with Mary. The ceremony was performed in the church inside the moldering walls of the old Vellore Fort, once a communion of the Church of England, now a component of the new united Church of South India. Straight from the wedding at five o'clock came M. P. to Mary's room in the hospital, in her glistening sari of white and gold, her handsome new husband beside her.

Mary exulted in their happiness. But she had to keep the mood light. Otherwise she would have cried.

"Are you sure it was fever," she teased, "that kept you from going on the picnic that day? If you ask me, it was just lovesickness. You were pining away for a certain doctor in Madras."

Even in her happiness M. P.'s eyes brimmed. "I wish you had had the fever, Mary. I don't deserve all this when you—"

"Nonsense!" Though her lips scoffed, Mary's eyes glinted with affection. "Life's hot enough for me already. I don't want any temperature of a hundred four—not even if it could get me another Dr. Bhaktavizyam!"

21

May burst into its final days with a crescendo of heat. With the coming of June, the thermometer seldom moving above a hundred, hope flared again for Mary. Surely now the long immobility was nearly over. She looked forward to Dr. Brand's return from his vacation in the hills.

He came, smiling, buoyant, radiating health both of body and spirit, and her courage soared. She submitted eagerly to the examinations. It had been three months now since the operation, time for even stubborn bones to knit. After he had read the X rays, he came to her room. Expectantly she waited for him to impart the good news.

"Mary," he said gently, "God has been with you in these long weeks. You have been very brave."

Something in his manner roused a chill of apprehension. "Was the operation a—failure?"

"A complete success," he assured her, "as far as it went."

He told her that a second operation, fusing the rest of the vertebrae below the injury, would enable her to sit up better and live far more effectively than she could do even at present.

At his words, the numbness of her lower body seemed to spread upward into her shoulders, creep down her arms and into her fingertips.

"I'm sorry," Paul Brand spoke humbly, apologetically. "Any of your friends would pay almost any price to spare you this."

Mary closed her eyes tightly, so the tears—she hoped—could not escape. She pressed her lips together to keep them from trembling. This was her battle. She would fight it alone, behind the closed doors of her body. She would not, she simply *would not* inflict her torments on other people.

"I wonder if you know," continued Dr. Brand with apparent irrelevance, "how much your Christian witness means to others in this hospital—patients, nurses, doctors, all struggling with their human pains and problems. 'Think of Mary.' I hear the words over and over. 'We think we have troubles, what about her? Yet always trusting, always smiling, never a word of complaint. . . .' "

Mary made a strangled sound. When finally, able to retain the tears no longer, her eyelids quivered open, she was relieved to find herself alone. Always trusting, always smiling! No complaints! They should see her sometimes—*now!* In wild relief she unleashed the storm of pent rebellion, expressing it in every way possible. She wept. She clenched her fists. She beat her arms against the mattress. Mutely, but with as much play of muscles as if she had been screaming, she indulged in an orgy of self-pity. It was not fair. She could not bear it. God was cruel to ask it of her. . . .

Exhausted finally, she lay panting, emptied of emotion, arms and shoulders as impotent as the rest of her body. What use rebelling? She would have to go through with it, of course. As useless to struggle against her fate as for a bird caught in a steel trap.

The battle over, she opened her eyes on the calm cool majesty of the Jungfrau, sun-crowned, rising serene above a layer of petty clouds. Beside it the little wooden motto bore its mute witness:

I KNOW . . . FEAR NOT

Mary wept again, this time tears of relief and thankfulness.

The second operation, performed on June 15, was for fusion of her lower thoracic vertebrae, utilizing bone chips taken this time from her leg. Back in her room Mary began again the weeks of immobility and waiting: the imprisoning slabs of plaster; endless hours on her back; the two shorter periods of respite each day on her face, the open book on the low table beneath her, the pot of flowers a splash of brightness on the bare cement floor; the cheering visitors; the young nurses and student doctors dropping in for advice and gossip; the praying for the needs of others; the sounds of hurrying feet; the reflections of a tree, a garden, striding figures.

The worst of the hot season was past. July, *Addi Masam,* the windy month, brought relief along with its racing petals and whirling dust. Occasional rain freshened the air with blessed coolness and the fragrance of moist earth. In the flooded paddy fields up near the college the farmers would be wading in mud behind their wooden plows and lean black buffalo cows or white oxen, treading new stripped green leaves into the worn-out soil, making the fields ready for the seedling rice. Closing her eyes. she could almost see them. Motion . . . it was all about her, in racing wind, in clopping hoofs and rumbling wheels, in hurrying feet. Only she, of all God's creation, seemed to be motionless.

"They also serve," she reminded herself with stern insistence, "who only stand—who only *lie* and wait."

"Stone walls do not a prison make," she quoted just as resolutely.

The arrival of the new wheel chair spelled both triumph and frustration, triumph because the difficulties of obtaining an import permit had been almost insurmountable until Mr. Savarirayan, the hospital manager, had managed to obtain the chair for her free through Church World Service; frustration because she could not yet use it. There it sat, with its detachable arms, shining, tantalizing, empty.

When in late August Mary began to suffer pains at the level of the spinal injury, she was both stunned and incredulous. At first, startled by sensation where previously there had been none, she nourished a wild hope. But Dr. Chandy, the head neurosurgeon, shook his head.

"It looks like irritation of the injured cord," he told her with concern. "I was hoping this would not happen. It sometimes requires"—he hesitated—"persistent treatment."

The pain increased, became constant. Even the rubbing of her gown caused irritation. The mild sedation of non-habit-forming drugs, which were all the doctors dared administer and all she was willing to accept, proved of little benefit. At times the agony was almost unbearable.

Now, for the first time since her accident, Mary took little delight in visitors. Her smiles were forced. It was all she could do to hold back the tears of self-pity. Even while responding dutifully to their sympathetic chatter she longed for them to be gone, so she could give vent to tears, clench her hands and lips and teeth. She almost ceased to enjoy the little prayer meetings which her friends liked to hold in her room—Grace and Helen and Annamma Verghese and others. The prayers she uttered these days were ragged fragments.

"Lord, help me . . . You who knew pain and suffering . . . forgive me for complaining because—had no feeling . . . help me use it—somehow—to help others. . . ."

Pain! *Sister* Pain! Oh, to be another Saint Francis, who felt kin to all of God's creation, even the most ugly and despised!

It was during these weeks that she remembered the discussions held in her final year of medical school, when she had been a member of Dr. Ida B. Scudder's Bible class. They had probed into the problem of suffering and how it could possibly fit into God's love. Mary had been concerned at the time about the pain of her sister Thankamma and the agonies she herself was witnessing daily in the hospital. Now suddenly it was no mere subjective problem. It was a devil—or angel—to be wrestled with.

"Do you remember the poem you shared with us," Mary asked Dr. Ida B. on one of her visits, "during that last year in Bible class?"

Dr. Ida B. brought her a copy of it on her next visit. "It was given me by my father," she explained, "many years ago. Its author is unknown. It was found written on the walls of a Denver hospital."

The simple words sustained Mary in the days that followed.

The cry of man's anguish went up unto God,
  Lord, take away pain!
The shadow that darkens the world Thou hast made,
  The close-coiling chain
That strangles the heart, the burden that weighs
  On the wings that would soar.
Lord, take away pain from the world Thou hast made,
  That it love Thee more!

Then answered the Lord to the cry of His world:
  Shall I take away pain,
And with it the power of the soul to endure,
  Made strong by the strain?
Shall I take away pity, that knits heart to heart,
  And sacrifice high?
Will you lose all your heroes, that lift from the fire
  White brows to the sky?
Shall I take away love that redeems with a price,
  And smiles at the loss?
Can ye spare from your lives, that would climb into mine,
  The Christ on his cross?

It was with both relief and dismay that Mary received Dr. Chandy's reluctant suggestion that he perform a cordectomy, the removal of a small section of the spinal cord in the area of the pain level.

"Not another operation!" she cried out in consternation. Then, with a surge of hope, "You believe it would take away the pain?"

The doctor could make no promises, but he believed that a cordectomy should effect relief. It was the next step indicated. But it was a serious step.

How well Mary knew it was serious! A cordectomy meant not only the severing of the spinal cord. It meant the severing of all hope. Henceforth no miracle of healing, no unexpected medical discovery, could possibly reactivate her lower body. What would it be like to live without hope? No, rather ask what would it be like to go on living in this constant pain!

She wrote home about the problem, asking advice. They wrote back doubtfully. All were still hoping that there might be a recovery. They did not like to see hope removed. And they worried about her submitting to another operation with more possible complications. But she was a doctor and a grown woman. She was old enough and wise enough to decide for herself.

She decided. She would have the operation.

Amma, John, and Annamma came. They were there on the evening of October 2, when Dr. Chandy came to her room for a final reassuring visit.

"Mary," he said, taking her hand before leaving, "tomorrow God will be with us."

"Yes," she replied gratefully.

But Annamma shook her head. "He looks worried," she murmured after he had gone.

The next morning Dr. Ida came to the operating room to offer prayer. Mary was humbly appreciative of everybody's concern, though she wished they would make less of a fuss over her. After all, she was not the first person in the world to have an operation.

Although she had to have the usual blood transfusion, the cordectomy was accomplished with a minimum of complications. She emerged from the anaesthesia with mingled fear and hope. Now to discover whether it had accomplished its purpose!

Hours passed, and, except for the discomforts attendant on the operation itself, she knew blessed surcease from pain.

"It's gone!" she announced triumphantly to Dr. Chandy when a whole day and night had passed without the pains recurring.

"Good," he returned cautiously. "But the spinal cord is still under shock. We can't know for sure for some time yet."

A few hours later, when Mary felt the familiar knife-thrust of agony through her chest, she turned faint with despair. The pain was not gone. It probably never would be.

"Dear God!" she prayed silently. "*How* am I going to live with it?"

But God was good. Somehow He made it possible for her to conceal her distress from the anxious eyes of Amma and Annamma and from many of her most intimate friends. Mercifully the pain was not constant, as it had been before. It came suddenly, without warning, sometimes with excruciating sharpness, then in a moment or two went away. Since she knew it would pass, it was much easier to endure.

"When I get back to work," she told herself, gritting her teeth and twisting her lips into a smile to keep the agony from showing, "and my hands are busy, I won't notice it so much."

Amma and Annamma returned home, confident that the operation had been a success. As October passed, the tiny world reflected in Mary's mirror was often washed fresh by the swift downpours of the fall monsoons. In her mind's eye she could see the brimming squares of the rice fields all along the roads, the bright red saris of the toiling women, hands and feet plunged into muddy water, stooping hour after hour to transplant the little green rice seedlings. They too must have pains in their backs. Because of her own pain, she understood suddenly, she would always be able to comprehend better how other sufferers felt. She would be a better doctor. Slowly her prayers began to change. She no longer asked, "Help me to bear this pain." She begged rather, "Help me to *use* it."

In November, for the first time in eight months, she sat up in bed, braced with a back rest. One Sunday morning two weeks later Dr. Brand told her, "Well, Mary, here's the day you have been waiting for. Any time you feel like it you may try sitting in the wheel chair."

Her heart bounded. "How soon can I go to work?" she demanded.

There was a hint of relief in his answering smile. "I was hoping you would ask that. Soon, I hope. But, of course," he added hastily, "we don't want to hurry you."

In two weeks, he explained, Dr. Lane, the English physician who had been training in hand surgery, was leaving, and the department would be again understaffed. If Mary could take over a few duties as she continued to sit up and became stronger, possibly make rounds with one of the other doctors. . . .

"Yes," said Mary, determined that she would be carrying a full schedule long before the two weeks were up.

Later that day she was sitting in her wheel chair.

"I'm going to chapel service," she told her amazed attendants.

It was not far along the smooth corridors and verandahs to the chapel, but she made the trip slowly, stopping often to hold court for surprised and admiring nurses. When her *ayah* Victoria wheeled her finally into the chapel, Mary's cup of joy was brimming. It was a beautiful place of worship, white dome curving upward into purple shadows, arched chancel of cool gray stone opening wide on a courtyard garden, altar curtain embroidered with green palms and white antigonon and flaming bougainvillea. The mats on the polished marble floor were filled with rows of blue-and-white garbed students.

Mary sat quietly on the edge of the circle, like a vessel long empty, letting the beauty and holiness of the hour flood her being. Dr. Inbanathan, the college chaplain, seemed to speak only to her. She remained for the whole hour and felt strengthened rather than wearied.

The next day Dr. Brand was amazed when she wheeled into his office, looking thoroughly professional in her neatly draped white sari, black hair for once glistening-smooth, the long braids wound into a *kondai* at her neck.

"Dr. Verghese reporting," she announced.

"Mary, you're incredible!" Dr. Brand threw back his head and laughed. "Wait here. The boys must see this."

At his summons all the members of his department dropped their work and came running: Dr. Lane; Furness, the Anglo-Indian clerk and typist, himself a one-time leprosy patient; the two physiotherapists, Palani and Namosivayam. None of them could believe his eyes.

"But—only yesterday it was you got up from your bed!"

"We were not expecting you for at least another two weeks!"

"Don't tell us you plan to work already!"

"I certainly do," retorted Mary, "starting tomorrow."

After that day she began working again regularly, with limited duties at first but gradually increasing the demands on herself. She admitted patients, dictated notes, made rounds of the patients in the wards with the other two doctors. True to her determination she was carrying almost a full load, with the exception of performing operations, when Dr. Lane left Vellore.

So busy was her schedule that on December 9, Dr. Ida's eighty-fifth birthday, she was late in arriving at the party on the lawn in front of the Administration Building. When she finally wheeled herself into the area, rainbow-bright with its gay paper streamers, its visitors in holiday dress, its bowers of flowers festive as a wedding *pandal,* the party was well under way. Seated in her bedecked birthday chair, a garland of pink roses and silver mesh about her neck, mounds of blossoms all about her, the guest of honor had already received the homage of a long procession of nurses, students, and doctors. To offer her small contribution, Mary realized with consternation, she must run—*wheel* the gauntlet of all those curious eyes alone. She would rather spend another week flat on her back in bed!

Suffused with shyness, feeling hot and unkempt in her working uniform, conscious of untidy tendrils of hair about her face, Mary started up the path. The bouquet in her lap seemed pitifully small. Then suddenly she stopped, staring at the blue-clad figure hurrying toward her. She gasped, finding herself enveloped in color and fragrance, as the garland of silver and roses fell about her shoulders.

"My dear!" Dr. Ida greeted her. "I've been saving this for you."

22

Mary began operating again in January, 1956.

Previously she had been raised to the proper level in her wheel chair by extra cushions, an awkward arrangement. Now a small movable platform with ramp attached made it possible for her to be wheeled under the operating table and work at the correct height. Though she was still unable to bend backward or forward or to maintain balance without the steadying of hands or elbows, her efficiency in performing hand operations increased constantly.

Only once in the operating room did Mary's physical handicap become a dangerous liability.

Her first operation over, one morning, she prepared, as usual, to be wheeled by the attendant down the ramp of her platform and into the scrub room. Assuming that he was behind her, she released the brake on her chair. Before she knew what was happening, she was sliding back down the ramp; then head and shoulders jerked back painfully against the floor as the chair overturned. Since her legs were tied in place, she remained in the chair. Nurse Alice David screamed and rushed to her side.

"Oh, Doctor Mary! Are you hurt?"

The quiet denial was not completely reassuring, especially since Mary left almost immediately for her room. Scarcely had the nurse found opportunity to share her fears with Dr. Brand, however, when Mary was back again in the scrub room, preparing for her second operation.

During Mary's months of incapacity Paul Brand had been refining his procedure, and it was now being spoken of everywhere as the

"Brand Operation." The new technique was being used in more and more cases at Vellore.

Mary mastered the details of the operation, first watching performances by Dr. Brand, then assisting him, and finally, after a couple of months, attempting the new technique herself.

With her zest for new adventures she found this free tendon graft a fascinating procedure. Confidently she followed each delicate step: freeing a good muscle tendon from the patient's forearm, making a curved incision over the back of the hand above the thumb and extending up the forearm, laying back the skin flap, and detaching the tendon of one of the muscles used for upward motion of the wrist. Then, grafting to this the free tendon from the forearm and splitting the graft into four slips, she proceeded to pass the slips through the proper tunnels in the hand and to suture them to the tendons on the back of the fingers. It was an effective and simplified technique, a great improvement over the former method. Stitching the skin flap neatly back into place, Mary regarded her handiwork with approval. Then her brows knit.

What a pity, she thought, for the patient to be left with such a scar! The leprosy sufferer wanted so desperately to appear like other people once the disease was arrested!

With Dr. Brand's increasing responsibilities necessitating his frequent absence from Vellore, more and more of the operating load fell to Mary and to Ernest Fritschi, who commuted twice each week from the Leprosy Reseach Sanatorium in Karigiri. Then, in April, Fritschi was involved in a motorcycle accident while traveling to Vellore, and for some weeks he was unable to operate.

With Dr. Brand away, first in Madras as an examiner for the university, and then on vacation, Mary was forced to assume full responsibility for the hand research unit. She had only one house surgeon as her assistant. With Vellore already an oven and the hot season not yet approaching its blistering climax, it seemed an impossible assignment.

"Coward!" she berated herself. "Last year at this time you would have given all you possessed to have a job like this. Thank God and ask Him for the strength to do it."

Somehow she managed to keep up the pace. Two mornings a week she operated on hands, from 7:30 to 12:30. During each session, she found, she could do two complete hands, or more if only the fingers were involved. Some days when the work was most pressing she returned to the operating theater in the afternoon.

In addition to her surgery she held the usual clinics, dictated all the notes on patients, and made rounds of all the wards. It was often a temptation to cut short these daily rounds, to discourage the ceaseless questions and petty complaints with which the patients greeted her. But, seeing the tortured faces light at her coming, remembering her own pain and loneliness, she could never do so. Her friends scolded, pleaded, and secretly marveled because she seemed never too busy or wearied to stop and listen to her patients' troubles.

Mary's own troubles, it often seemed to them, received far less attention. With the additional work load, she had long felt the need of moving from the hospital to a room of her own. But the hospital authorities seemed slow in recognizing this need.

The change was made at last, and after Mary moved into a room of her own in the new Internes' Quarters, her daily life became much pleasanter. There were more contacts with girls of her own age, gay informal gatherings reminiscent of the old midnight coffee hours on the "Marina." Her friends were able to visit her more often. Frequently Grace, now in her own residency, brought her lunch to Mary's room or enjoyed her siesta on Mary's broad bed.

Mary still required two girls to give her constant attendance. She could not even turn in bed without help. Though she could turn her body to the side by manipulating arms and shoulders, she needed help in straightening her legs. She had learned to push herself up a little in her wheel chair but could not move forward or backward. It was impossible for her to assume a comfortable position without help. Nevertheless, even with these limitations, she was carrying a full working load.

During Dr. Fritschi's period of incapacity, no foot surgery was being performed in the leprosy unit, and Mary felt this lack keenly. Many of the patients were suffering from foot-drop deformity. In her hours of enforced daytime rest and when she woke at night, she thought about the problem. True, the foot operation was always performed with the surgeon standing, but—*must* it be? She weighed all the difficulties. Her wheel chair would not fit under the operating table, only under the small hand table. She had limited motion. But she knew every detail of the operation. She had assisted at it several times. And it needed to be done. "I'll do it," she decided resolutely.

For many days she thought about methods, devised plans. Finally she was ready. In the operating room she made her preparations. She folded the foot end of the operating table, then placed the hand table in position to hold the patient's leg. She rolled her chair, as usual, under the hand table. She put a small cushion behind her in order to bring her body closer. And when all was ready, herself gowned, masked, and scrubbed, the patient in place, she closed her eyes and prayed.

The foot stretched out in front of her was misshapen, unable to take a step without drooping. It showed the scars of plantar ulcers, caused by undue pressure on weight-bearing bones brought on by lack of proper balance and absence of sensation. The corrective surgery consisted of removing a tendon from the inside of the foot and transferring it to the front of the leg, where it was attached to a bone. Four incisions were necessary, and the whole procedure, especially this first attempt, required intense concentration. Unable to bend forward or backward, Mary could not relax. When she had finished, she was desperately tired. But she did finish, successfully, and became almost as adept at this operation as at the procedure on the hand.

Her next challenge during the working months of that year was eyebrows.

Like the claw hand, the depressed nose, and the wrinkled skin, the missing eyebrow was among the stigmata of leprosy. Even after the disease was arrested and there was not the slightest danger of contagion, these outward signs often meant ostracism for a former leprosy victim. A man's hands might be fully restored to usefulness, but a prospective employer, seeing the collapsed nose, the missing eyebrows, would very likely refuse to give him work. To restore the patient's dignity and self-confidence, Dr. Brand had performed not only extensive surgery designed to reshape the nose, but operations to restore lost brows. There were patients in Mary's wards with brows as bare as the sandy bed of the Palar River in May. She was determined they should not remain so.

Again she made her preparations with care. She had the patient placed on the table as for a foot operation, but with his head instead of his foot on the small hand table. When all was ready, she closed her eyes and prayed.

This "island artery flap" operation, as it was called, was delicate and time-consuming. It involved tracing a blood vessel from just in front of the ear up into the scalp; measuring the distance from the vessel to the end of the eyebrow, then the same distance along the artery. At this point in the scalp the new eyebrow was then marked and an equivalent piece of skin removed from the brow The island artery flap from the scalp was then tunneled under the skin until it came into the proper position for the eyebrow, where it was fastened into place. When Mary had finished her first such operation, she was exhausted but triumphant.

"You'll have only one difficulty," she told the patient. "You'll have to keep clipping your brows because they will grow so fast."

The patient grinned happily. If he were like some proud owners of new eyebrows, reflected Mary, he would let them grow so long he could hardly see through them. More than once she had seen a patient come into a room, shoulders back and head proudly lifted, eyebrows leading and he himself following at a distance. She knew well enough how they felt. Would she ever stop running if she had her legs again?

Mary enjoyed the brow operations. As she became more adept she took pride in shaping her handiwork to suit the patient's face, occasionally drawing out an "Ajanta" brow, a bit slanted like those of the ancient Buddhist masterpieces in the Ajanta Caves. Once she teased her friend Grace Koshi, whose eyebrows were unusually thin.

"Better let me give you a graft. You need it badly. How about it? Any style you say."

"Why don't you give me half of yours?" Grace would retort. "You could surely spare that much."

With Dr. Brand's return in June, Mary was able to leave her work for a while and go home for the first time since her fusion operations. Mingled with her exhilaration at being joined again with FAMILY was another as yet unassessed excitement. Dr. Gwenda Lewis had recently returned from Australia, where she had spent some months in a world-famous rehabilitation center for paraplegics. Though still severely handicapped by her polio, she had widened the scope of her activities to an astonishing degree. She was now even talking about driving a car.

"If you could only go there, Mary!" she kept saying. "You'd be amazed at the things I've seen paraplegics learn to do. Many of them are actually able to walk. With braces, of course. They reach a surprising degree of independence."

Independence! The hope throbbed with every turn of the wheels as the train caried her homeward. Should she tell FAMILY about this possibility? No, she decided. Her father and brothers had already done enough for her. She could not burden them with this. But they knew Dr. Gwenda, having met her on their trips to Vellore. She could not resist sharing with them the news of her friend's good fortune.

"You remember Doctor Lewis," she remarked casually one day when her parents and brothers were together. "The one who had such a severe case of polio. She's just back from a rehabilitation center in Australia, and you should see how she has improved."

Instantly John's interest kindled. "Why couldn't such a place help you, too?"

"It could," agreed George, the physician.

"Then let's send her. We three can easily manage the expense." Babi, the engineer, was already making the plans. "I guess our little sister is going to have just as much chance to be rehabilitated as any foreign doctor!"

Mary's heart pounded. She was so choked with gratitude she could hardly speak. Finally she produced a letter she had recently received. Gwenda Lewis had communicated with Dr. Bedbrook, the rehabilitation specialist in the Royal Perth Hospital, telling him about Mary, and he had written, urging her to come to Australia for treatment.

"Then it's settled," said John, as much the executive as his brother Joseph.

But for Mary nothing was settled. Would her spirit of independence let her accept this largesse from her brothers? Would she have to resign her job permanently if she went? Could she possibly arrange all the physical details of such a long and frightening trip? And—what did Appan think about it all?

He waited until they were alone before he told her. "If you go, it will be I, not your brothers, who will send you," he said firmly. "I do not wish you to be under obligation to anyone else, even other members of your family. Remember, anything I have is yours."

Speechless, Mary absorbed every familiar detail of the fragile, beloved features, the deep-set eyes, the high prominent bones shadowing the sunken cheeks, the mouth as stubborn as her own. Could she possibly bring herself to travel so long and so far, knowing that she might never see him again?

It was harder to leave FAMILY this time than ever before. Amma and a servant girl traveled with her on her return trip to Vellore. As usual since the accident, Mary occupied a first class compartment. This luxury always made her feel guilty, when she thought of the shabby third class cars, jammed with people.

They almost failed to reach their destination. Just outside of Gudiyattam there was a crashing sound, and their compartment began to lurch crazily. The humid smoky air was rent with screams. Looking out the open window, Mary saw that the train was swaying on the edge of a precipice. Gripping the iron bars of the window with both hands, she closed her eyes. The servant, squatted on the floor, screaming, clutching her bedroll, even Amma, cross-legged and dignified as a Buddha on the opposite seat, seemed suddenly far removed and unreal. She hung suspended on a bare knife-edge of eternity. Strange, that it should happen here again, on this road to Gudiyattam, as if some grim fate were bent on finishing a job it had once bungled!

Mary clung to the bars with all her strength and prayed. "Not yet, God, please! Surely You still have work for me to do!"

The train finally came to a shuddering stop, still on the edge of the precipice. Three of its cars were off the rails. But there were few injuries to the passengers and no deaths. It had been a narrow escape. Several Vellore nurses were on board, returning to work after their vacations in Kerala. An ambulance from the hospital had been scheduled to meet the train in Katpadi, but a phone call soon brought it to Gudiyattam. Mary spent most of the twenty-five-mile trip to the hospital trying to calm the young nurses' hysterical excitement.

At the first opportunity, she questioned Dr. Brand about the possibility of her going to Australia. He did not appear enthusiastic.

"You are needed very badly here," he reminded her.

"If I went," she inquired with her usual blunt directness, "would I lose my job?"

Regretfully he told her it would have to be so. Mary's heart sank. Keenly disappointed, she postponed for the present all thought of taking such a momentous step.

But as the summer passed changes took place in the Hand Research Department that made her future even there uncertain. Dr. Brand had been invited by the Nigerian government to come to Africa and demonstrate his new techniques. Before his departure in September it was decided to combine the two departments of Hand Surgery and Orthopedics, with Dr. Selvapandiam, a young surgeon, in charge under Dr. Brand. Regretfully Mary was told that she could not occupy her present position permanently without a post-graduate degree in surgery. She would be able to hold her post only as long as her present sponsoring agent, the Indian Council of Medical Research, was willing to pay her salary.

It was a stunning blow. Even Dr. Brand's concern and understanding could not mitigate it. There was an opening under the British Mission to Lepers, he suggested helpfully, in the sanatorium at Vadathorasallur, ninety miles from Vellore. He urged her to take the position.

Mary rebelled. She would be the only doctor there, which would mean the end of her career as a surgeon. Besides, a remote town without good roads was surely no fit place for a person in her condition! Yet if she remained in Vellore, she would have no sure means of self-support. After much soul-searching and many tears, she wrote to her father asking advice.

"Stay on at Vellore," he replied with comforting decisiveness. "If your present means of support should fail, we will give financial assistance."

The college authorities offered another solution. She would stay in Hand Research in her present capacity until Dr. Brand's return from Nigeria, then enter the Pathology Department, starting her work there the first of January. Though nothing was promised, Mary knew that this might open up future possibilities of doing graduate work.

She felt lost, confused, betrayed. Her faith was strained almost to the breaking point. Pathology held even less appeal now than in those first fumbling months after her accident. Retire into a laboratory to work with dead tissues when her mind and hands had known the divine joy of re-creating human beings? It would be like turning from savory curries and coconut dainties to a diet of unflavored rice. She had something special to give these leprosy sufferers, with their scarred cheeks, their useless, insensitive feet so like her own. She had seen it in the sudden quickening of hope in their faces, the lighting of their eyes.

Especially had she seen it in the eyes of one young man, a former leprosy patient, now a physiotherapist working in the department. He had been in college when he had discovered that he had leprosy and was obliged to leave. He had come to the Place of New Life, and Dr. Brand had operated on both his hands. Keenly interested in the techniques of his own rehabilitation, he had taken a course in physiotherapy from Ruth Thomas, and was now an efficient and devoted member of the staff. While in Vellore he had become a Christian. Patiently now, he manipulated other hands as insensitive as his own, coaxed fingers into wider and wider ranges of activity, taught patients to substitute eye control for skin and joint sense, to prevent ulcers on their feet by the use of sponge rubber soles, to splint every wound in order to avoid the movement that pain would normally prevent, to routinely inspect hand and feet every night for thorns, blisters, and splinters.

Once, working in the clinic, Mary felt his eyes following her motions. Looking up, she saw their habitual somberness strangely softened.

"I used to pity myself for my hard luck," he said, smiling, "but not any more. Seeing you work from that wheel chair, how can I possibly complain?"

No, even in these days of uncertainty, life was not all confusion. During the hours in the operating room she forgot her worries. Once she rolled under the hand table, all sense of frustration vanished. Each new case, no matter how familiar the routine, was an all-absorbing challenge. Never was she too weary to feel the zest of excitement. The desires and demands of other human beings faded, all but the needs of the one patient waiting for the skillful ministration of her hands. There were only God and herself, His servant, working together, performing again the miracle of creation.

She had never been quite satisfied with the Brand Operation.

"It's good," she told herself over and over, "except for the scar."

People were so sensitive about scars, especially women! But men too were acutely conscious of the long red crescent left by the flap incision. How make the scar smaller, more nearly invisible? For months Mary pondered the problem. In a flash of intuition she conceived the idea of suturing the tendon graft outside the hand, then tunneling it underneath the skin.

She tried it, first on a hand with only two claw fingers, next on a full claw hand. The procedure, while exceedingly delicate, was as swift and simple as the old method, and to her delight it left only two very small scars. She could hardly wait to share her discovery with the other surgeons.

Once a week all the staff of the Hand Research Unit met for a clinic to discuss problems and patients. At these clinics the most interesting cases from both Vellore and Karigiri were often presented. Mary exhibited her patient. The staff crowded around, stared unbelievingly.

She explained the procedure, then later demonstrated it in the operating room. All were delighted, and the new method became the accepted routine. There was nothing unusual about the suggestion and adoption of improvements in the operations. All surgery for leprosy was still in the experimental stage, and seldom was an operation performed without some suggestion for improvement from an interested onlooker. However, Mary's refinement of the technique was a major contribution.

But her greatest satisfaction in the achievement did not come from the admiring approval of her colleagues, nor even from the warm commendation of Dr. Brand. It came from the kindling eyes and straightened shoulders of young patients who left the hospital not only with usable hands but self-confident in the knowledge that they again looked like other men and women.

23

Dr. Brand returned from his trip in December, 1956, after two and a half months of lecturing and demonstrating in Nigeria, the Congo, South and East Africa. Spending Christmas in his home, Mary listened with fascination to his reports of other new countries bravely making their way across the threshold of independence. She had thought India's problems of poverty and ignorance and disease so colossal as to be almost insurmountable. She learned now of countries where there were almost no doctors, and trained nurses were unavailable because few women were educated even to primary standard; where no form of the wheel had been heard of until the past few years and there was no counterpart of even the ancient bullock cart; where there was nothing to compare with India's heritage of learning and culture.

"We think we have problems here at Vellore, with lack of equipment and shortage of staff. We don't know how lucky we are," said Paul Brand.

Mary felt humbled, chastened. She had been worrying about her own petty problems! Suppose she did have to spend the rest of her professional career in pathology instead of surgery. She should be thankful she had been born in an enlightened country where careers for women were possible.

But January came, and she did not go into Pathology. Though she had submitted her resignation, no applicant had appeared to take her place in the Hand Research Unit, and she was asked to continue. In spite of the insecurity of her position, she decided to do so. For who could tell? Perhaps the very insecurity was evidence of the

Guidance in which she had such implicit faith. Sometimes all other doors had to slam in one's face before the realization came that another door was opening.

Australia! More and more legible became the word inscribed over the slowly opening door. In April, Helen North, who had been on furlough since October, wrote an enthusiastic letter urging her to come to Perth.

"Surely it's the best opportunity you could have anywhere in the world," she pleaded. "It will take courage to plan such a long trip, but you have never lacked courage. *Please* think about it."

Mary shared the letter with her family, and all urged her to pursue the matter further, assuring her of their support. Again she asked Paul Brand for his advice. Again he was not enthusiastic.

"There are two problems," he reminded her. "Finances, substitutes. But of course it is for you to decide."

She was not greatly concerned about a substitute, because Ernest Fritschi was still available for part-time service. Besides, her own job tenure was too uncertain to warrant a sacrifice of what might well mean a greater opportunity for future service. But finances were another matter. It required weeks of correspondence for Appan to convince her that he considered the expenditure a good investment. Even then the decision cost her hours of thought. Most of her friends encouraged her; a few were pessimistic. Did she know how far it was? How could she possibly travel that distance in a wheel chair? How get on and off an airplane?

One, Dr. Sakuntala, reminded her of Australia's reputation for race prejudice. "Don't you know they don't like dark skins there?"

Now that she had made up her mind, Mary refused to be dissuaded. She consulted Cook's in Madras and made arrangements for her trip by air from Madras to Calcutta to Perth. She asked Vellore to provide a trained nurse to accompany her at her expense. When the hospital was unable to grant this request, she managed with the help of Grace Koshi and other friends to find a young nurse willing to resign her job and go. A month before the date set for her departure she took her vacation and started a strenuous regimen of exercises designed for strengthening her arms. Helen North, now back from furlough and as excited as Mary over the coming adventure, came each day to help.

But a perverse fate seemed bent on preventing the trip. A week before her scheduled departure Mary developed an acute urinary inflammation, bane of the paraplegic. To add to the illness, there was delay in getting her passport. Swiftly both hope and courage ebbed. Not even in the days following her accident could she remember being so depressed.

"You can't possibly go!" insisted one after the other of doctors, nurses, concerned friends.

"Even if the fever subsides, you'll be too weak!"

"This is probably a blessing. You never should have planned the trip."

Driven by necessity, Mary called the travel bureau in Madras and explained the situation.

"Do you wish to cancel your reservation?" inquired the agent briskly.

Her brain whirled. Yes, yes, *yes!* Everything and everybody was putting the word in her mouth.

"No," she replied clearly. "I only wanted to inquire when I must let you know definitely."

"We can give you just one more day," she was told, "to cancel your trip with the price of your tickets refunded."

That night her fever went down. In spite of weakness and exhaustion she persisted in her plans, and on the scheduled day in November, 1957, she and her nurse flew from Madras to Calcutta, spent one night there with a cousin, and the next day boarded the plane for Perth, Australia.

For many a person with a normal body, such a long trip might have been trying; for Mary, with her constant worry over the artificially controlled functions of her paralyzed organism, and with her distaste of being dependent, it was a kind of torture. Yet seeing her sitting serene and smiling, hour after hour, no one would have guessed this.

Her pretty young nurse, Sushila Nambiar, was a treasure of dependable efficiency, plus abundant charm and friendliness. Though a Kanarese girl, she had an adopted father in Kerala, so she and Mary had much in common. Since she did not speak Malayalam and, of Indian languages, knew only Kanarese, they spoke together in English.

The plane descended into a strange world, but to Mary's unbounded relief it was not a world of strangers. Scarcely had the other passengers disembarked when four people climbed aboard, a short stocky man, a smiling, able-bodied woman who looked equal to any emergency, a nurse, and a middle-aged man who immediately assumed full charge of all details.

"I am Dr. Bedbrook," announced the latter. "Welcome, my dear doctor, to Australia! Meet your physiotherapists, Miss Sharp and Mr. Johnson."

Mary shrank back in dismay when the stocky little man, Johnson, prepared to lift her. "I'm pretty heavy—"

Miss Sharp laughed. "Heavy! You're nothing but a featherweight for that bundle of muscles!"

Mary felt herself lifted as gently and easily as if she had been a child. Amazed, she yielded herself to the unbelievable strength hidden away in Johnson's body. It had taken two strong-looking attendants to carry her onto the plane in Calcutta, and she had been sure they were going to drop her. This one pair of arms bore her down the steps with the greatest ease. Halfway down, she looked below to see a barrage of clicking cameras.

She shivered. Not from nervousness. The air was cooler than any she had ever encountered. She thought gratefully of the sweaters Grace and Cheruchi had insisted on knitting for her. It had been autumn when she left Vellore, where even the dead of winter meant only a slight relief from heat. Here it was spring. But what a spring! In India spring was the long drouth before the rains: brown fields, copper skies, trees and bushes springing into hot colors out of a parched earth. Here, everything seemed freshly washed and hung out to dry, and the colors, unlike India's, were muted, restrained.

Riding along the broad, amazingly clean streets, Mary gazed with wide-eyed intentness. How could there be so much *space*, so few *people?* Where were all the bullock carts, the rickshas, the burden-bearing coolies, the half-naked children, the ambling cows and scavenger dogs, the *beggars?* She marveled at the comparative silence. Even through the city traffic they moved swiftly and without confusion. No eternal and violent squawking of the horn!

Mary spent her first two days in the Royal Perth Hospital. Then she was taken to the hospital annex three miles out of the city, an area of spacious buildings and green lawns almost surrounded by bush. She found herself in a room with two beds, airy and comfortable, with a congenial roommate. Sushila was soon pressed into nursing service in the hospital and worked in Mary's ward all the time they were there.

It would have been worth the trip, Mary often thought, merely to have the experience of living in this amazing place. For the first time since her accident she did not feel strange, alone. Nobody looked at her curiously when she propelled herself along the corridors and porches, across the wide expanse of green lawn, because almost everybody else was in a wheelchair too. It was a city on wheels. She hadn't supposed there could be so many paraplegics and quadriplegics in the world! The only difference between herself and some of the others was that they could do so many things she could not do—walk with braces, move in their chairs with amazing agility, perform the most astounding athletic feats.

But she would learn! The fellowship of others struggling with the same problems was both consolation and inspiration. She started her rigorous discipline of training almost immediately, concentrated on it with all her keenness of mind and persistence of will.

Dr. Bedbrook, a rehabilitation specialist who had trained in England's Stoke-Mandeville Hospital under the famous Dr. Gutmann, had developed highly successful techniques in the training of paraplegics. It was not long before Mary began to note marked improvement in her various ranges of activity. After some weeks of arm and balancing exercises and weight lifting she was able, to her great delight, to bend forward and backward by means of arm and shoulder motions, and to change position in her chair. Practising pull-ups with the aid of the bar fixed over her bed, she developed such additional strength in her arms that she could move herself about with considerable facility, and even dispense with the irksome aid of an attendant to turn her in her bed at night. This increased independence alone would have been full compensation for all the hours of intensive discipline.

But, as for every other paraplegic in the center, one of the major goals of her program was to learn again to walk. It was with excitement, trepidation, and much doubt as to its pertinence to her own special needs, that Mary embarked on this phase of her rehabilitation.

Even before she was fitted with leg braces, the training began. With stiff splints bound to her knees to keep them rigid, she was made to stand, supported by a therapist on either side. It was a strange feeling, standing for the first time after nearly four years!

Then she received her braces. With these in place, the regimen progressed. First she walked between parallel bars, a narrow prison as rigidly iron-bound as the braces, their dozen feet of length seemingly as impossible of attainment as if they were as many miles.

Slowly she learned to make all the difficult motions with arms and shoulders which would shift the dead weight of her limbs forward by a few inches, both feet at the same time. Each motion required all her capacity, left her upper body drenched with sweat, her arms and shoulders trembling, her temples throbbing. After the bars came the crutches. . . .

"Come now, Doctor, a little more motion of the shoulder. . . . Fine, at least three inches that time! . . . Once more, please . . . remember, it all must be done with the shoulders and arms, and it requires a steady rhythm. . . . Good, much better than yesterday, wasn't it? You must have taken at least six steps today!"

Mary did not enjoy the disciplines of walking. Hour after hour, day after day, inch after frustrating inch . . . the bright encouraging voice, the grueling strain, the struggle to establish a rhythm . . . week after week, month after month . . . three inches, five inches, never quite reaching the impossible goal of six. And—*what real difference would it make if she did?* Would it make her any more independent in her daily living? Would she be more efficient as a doctor? Unconsciously, perhaps, she let this feeling of stubborn resistance temper her efforts. With a fierceness of energy that smacked of belligerence, she forced her half-body to full cooperation in the training, but her heart was not in it.

Then came a complication. She was given alcohol injections to improve functional bladder control, one of the major emphases in the rehabilitation program for paraplegics. As a result, spasms developed in one leg. In time this made the affected leg shorter than the other. Even though she was fitted to a shoe with a lift, the deformity and spasticity complicated the problem of walking, even of sitting, for the twitching foot persisted in slipping off its rest. A guard was attached to the back of the foot rest to obviate this difficulty, but the spastic limb was to remain a problem. No misfortune without some small blessing, however, for the authorities finally agreed that it was not practical for her to try to learn to walk! Mary felt greatly relieved.

The recreational program was a revelation. Mary had supposed that for paraplegics all active sports were out of the question. Here to her amazement she saw men and boys in wheel chairs playing vigorous games of table tennis and basketball. Rather than handicaps, it seemed that wheel chairs could sometimes be assets. Normal boys from town considered it great sport to come out to the center, seat themselves in wheel chairs, and compete with the paraplegics, more often than not finding themselves soundly beaten.

"This is nothing," said one of Mary's new friends, noting her surprise. "If you really want to see something, go to the Paralympics!" with eagerness and pride, he explained. "Like the Olympics International Only paraplegics can take part. They have all sorts of events, swimming, archery, basketball, snooker, field events like the javelin throw and shotput, table tennis, fencing—almost anything you can name. And every contestant competing from a wheel chair! It's something to see."

Mary saw a vast new world opening up before her. The Paralympics had been started, she learned, by Dr. Gutmann. Britain was the leader, with its annual International Stoke-Mandeville Games, but other countries had their teams, too: Germany, the United States, France, Greece, Italy, Switzerland, Norway, the Netherlands. . . .

"But not India," interposed Mary silently. No, of course not India. Sports for the disabled? Except in a very few places like Vellore, not even the most elementary forms of rehabilitation were available. She suddenly remembered the young quadriplegic in B Ward, his hopeless eyes and bitter, twisted lips. And India had thousands like him. If only they could come to a place like this!

Mary's chosen recreation was archery. In spite of long practice she did not become very good at it—never as good as Janet, another paraplegic who could sit in her wheel chair and hit a bull's eye at an incredible distance. Janet hoped to take part in the Paralympics if they were ever open to women and held in Australia.

"Janet puts me to shame," Mary remarked once, ruefully. "Miss Sharp is my only consolation." Miss Sharp, the director of recreation, a far better sport than she was archer, grinned back at her.

One day, however, Mary put a severe strain on the physiotherapist's good nature. She was wheeling herself down a walk toward the lawn where the archery session was to be conducted. Arriving at the one tiny step which separated the walk from the lawn, she paused as usual, waiting for one of the therapists to come and help her down. Her eyes measured the small step. A mere handbreadth! Foolish to wait. Turning her chair, she tried to ease herself backward down the slight incline. The chair tipped, and she found herself lying on her back, head smarting, helpless limbs thrust ignominiously into the air. Miss Sharp and Mr. Johnson, preparing the archery court, saw the mishap and rushed to her side.

"Silly child!" the woman scolded, badly frightened. "Impatient, stubborn! I could spank you for being so naughty."

Johnson said nothing, only picked Mary up, chair and all, and calmly set her back on proper keel. She was unhurt, merely deeply humiliated.

"I'm sorry. My mistake," she replied meekly. It was one of the few times in her life she had ever made such an admission.

Besides her own program of rehabilitation Mary was given excellent opportunities for increasing her knowledge and experience as a doctor. She went with Dr. Bedbrook and his team when they made their detailed rounds on Saturdays, and also attended their staff conferences. Her zest for learning was fired as much by professional interest as by personal concern.

Mary liked Australia. She relished its climate, deliciously cool after its hot summer. For the first time in her life she wore woolens and basked in the glowing warmth of a fireplace. She found the Australians friendly. Forewarned by the country's policy of granting only temporary visas to people of colored races, she had expected aloofness, if not discrimination, but encountered none.

Mary made many friends in Perth. One, a Mrs. Prosser, came with her car and took Mary, with others, to the Disciples of Christ Church each Sunday. Another, a wealthy gentleman named Mr. Finey, himself a paraplegic who had married his nurse, enjoyed coming to the center and taking other paraplegics for long rides in his car. From this luxurious vantage point Mary viewed the beautiful city of Perth, with its wide streets and comfortable homes, its spacious King's Park. In western Australia, she learned, there was only one person to every two square miles. In Kerala for each square mile there were a thousand! Mary marveled at the plenty she saw—the robust and well-clothed bodies, the lack of slums and want. It was India, not Australia, that she was seeing through new conscience-stricken eyes.

Though she had planned to stay only six months, the extent of her visa, so marked was her progress that she asked for a visa extension so that she could continue the treatment three months longer, until August.

It was in July that the brief cable came. Long though she had expected the moment, its stab was no less sharp. Appan was dead.

24

If only I had gone home when I planned! was her first stricken thought. But she knew Appan would not have wanted it. He had hated to be fussed over as much as she did. And he had gone suddenly, easily, exactly as he had hoped.

"Amma was by his side," John had added to the cable, knowing that the words would give her comfort. It was the one wish Appan had expressed the last time she had seen him, just a year ago—that he might go with Amma near him.

The zest had gone out of Mary's adventure. Even the sun-swept winter skies had lost their blueness. She was glad when the time came for sailing home.

Cousin Kunjannam, with her brother, met her at the dock in Bombay. *Dr.* Kunjannam now, for after failing to gain admission to Vellore in Mary's class, she had come to Bombay to study medicine. While stopping for three days in her cousin's home, Mary went to visit the All-India Institute of Physical Medicine and Rehabilitation. Sponsored by the World Health Organization, the Government of India, and the Bombay State Government, it was the only institution of its kind in the country. Mary met Dr. Sant, its head, and attended one of his clinics. To her disappointment she learned that he was trained only in orthopedic surgery, not in rehabilitation medicine, and that the institution offered merely out-patient care and training.

Oh, for a Dr. Gutmann or a Dr. Bedbrook, she wished fervently, to do for India what they are doing for their countries! Then, being Mary, she prayed earnestly that God would raise up some person for the task.

From Bombay she flew to Kerala for two weeks at home before returning to Vellore. The reunion was both heartbreaking and comforting. It was a relief to discover that, even with its chief cohesive agent gone, FAMILY was still a unit. It was like a living organism which, one of its cells removed, strengthens each member to fill the gap. Her brothers seemed to have absorbed Appan's tender understanding and concern. One by one, secretly, they assured her of their continued support. All that they had was hers. Amma, even in her grief, was strong and sturdy.

Strangely enough, it was Thankamma with whom Mary now felt the closest unity; Thankamma, who had needed neither the miseries of Vellore nor the clean abundance of Australia to open her eyes to the needs around her.

"Remember Joseph?" she asked one day. "He has been very ill. I got him into the hospital in Ayyampilly. At first the hospital refused to admit him. So outmoded in their ideas! But finally Dr. K. C. Paul convinced the authorities that leprosy was not as contagious as tuberculosis."

"Bravo!" murmured Mary. Was this third sister Thankamma speaking, the nervous girl who had hidden in the house, terrified, whenever Joseph's "Praise the Lord!" was heard at the gate?

When Mary reached Vellore, she found her old job waiting for her in the Hand Research Unit. Dr. Brand was on furlough in England, but Dr. Selvapandiam and his colleagues gave her an enthusiastic welcome. In the department she found the same overflowing wards and clinics, the same dearth of staff, and was soon plunged into the familiar routine of work. But these were among the few things which remained unchanged. In her absence the hospital had been putting down new roots and spreading like a banyan tree. There was a whole new floor in M Ward, a complete new ward called "L", new sections in "J", and part of the planned Neurological Extension had already been opened. New stories, new wings, new partitions or the tearing down of old ones to make more room, and the new Out-patient Dispensary, grown in her absence from a skeleton of bricks and bamboo staging into an impressive structure, long and white and gleaming, made the hospital compound barely recognizable.

Her friends were eager to report changes also, as well as to rejoice in the obvious improvement in her own condition. Dr. Gwenda Lewis, just back from England, was expecting a car fitted with hand controls, and she was going to teach Mary to drive it. Young Dr. Johnson and his wife Bama had a new son. A woman writer from America had been in Vellore and was planning to write a new biography of Dr. Ida. Ramani reported the arrival of a new doctor in the Neurology Department, a cousin of Elsie, Pulimood by name, who had become a most interested member of the Bible study and prayer group of which Mary used to be a part.

"Are you sure," teased Mary, noting the look in her friend's eyes, "it's merely this gentleman's religious zeal which makes him so attractive?"

"You and your matchmaking!" scoffed Ramani. But her high color and nervous laughter were sufficient answer.

Mary rejoiced once more in the fellowship of the little prayer group, and it was soon meeting in her room again. But she sorely missed the presence of her intimate friend Annamma Verghese. Annamma, now the wife of Dr. Mammen Cherian, who had been another devoted member of the fellowship. Annamma was now in Edinburgh, Scotland, doing graduate work in medicine with her husband.

In addition to her immediate friends and co-workers, others welcomed Mary's return to the hospital. One was Dr. Chandy, head of Neurosurgery.

For months Dr. Chandy had been working with a patient in N Ward, a man who had once earned a good income. Now, as a paraplegic, faced with his inability to support and educate his seven children, he had sunk into hopeless depression.

When Mary heard of how poorly the man was responding to therapy, she wondered if Dr. Chandy was right in wanting to introduce her to him.

"Are you sure the sight of me will not hinder you?" she asked.

Dr. Chandy did not understand. "How could it possibly hinder! You can show him what possibilities there are for a paraplegic—how it's possible to conquer such a disability, become self-supporting and independent."

Mary knew she could show the man the *results* of rehabilitation. What she could not do was offer him the means of getting them. For this was India, not Australia. What did she have to give this fellow paraplegic? Hope—or only worse frustration?

"I'll see him," she promised.

The results exceeded Dr. Chandy's expectations. Young Dr. Pulimood, Dr. Chandy's new house officer, reported enthusiastically:

"You wouldn't believe what a difference her coming has made! Our patient is a new person. Just the sight of Mary in her wheel chair, patient, courageous, *showing* not *telling* him that life needn't be ended for a handicapped person—why, one of her visits did more than all the lectures and arm-strengthening exercises!"

But, though somewhat reassured by her apparent success, Mary was far from satisfied. The patient still had no access to adequate means of rehabilitation, no possible source of employment even if he became rehabilitated. Furthermore, N Ward had other new cases of paraplegia. She tried to find time to visit them in her few hours off duty, but with each visit she found the problem more and more frustrating. There was so little she could do for them.

"If only we had one good department of rehabilitation here in India!" she said to Dr. Chandy. "If only we had it here at Vellore!"

"Yes," he agreed soberly.

Perhaps it was at that moment that Mary felt the stirrings of a new dream, persistent, audacious.

Her old friend Ammini Mathai, now Ammini Thomas, had recently returned to Vellore after a period of study under a Rockefeller Fellowship at Duke University in the United States.

"I met the most interesting man there," she reported to Mary at their first meeting. "He was in charge of Physical Medicine at Duke, a disabled person but, oh, so dynamic and capable! He walked with crutches."

Mary was only mildly interested. The United States and Duke University seemed very far away.

"One day I told him about you," continued Ammini. "Want to know what he said?"

"Of course," replied Mary politely.

"He wanted me to write you immediately and tell you to come to New York. It seems he was trained under a Doctor Rusk at New York University, a world leader in rehabilitation. He wanted me to be sure to have you write to him, so he could tell you firsthand about Dr. Rusk. 'Has your friend written yet?' he kept asking me." Ammini was regretful. "And I never even got around to telling you!"

"No matter," returned Mary. She smiled indulgently. "Can you imagine me going to New York!"

Ammini did not smile. "Yes. I believe I can."

Startled, Mary said no more then, but she did not forget the conversation. The idea it had planted sprouted with surprising vigor. Suddenly she knew she must talk again with Ammini.

"Do you remember the man you told me about?" she asked casually. "The one who wanted me to write to him? I thought I might send him a letter."

Ammini was overjoyed. They wrote the letter together, Ammini prefixing a complimentary introduction about Mary. Reading it, Mary winced with embarrassment. But protest did no good. Ammini was equally strong-minded, and the letter was sent.

Mary disliked any publicity about herself. She hated even to hear her name spoken in public. After Paul Brand had told her story at the Mission to Lepers' Annual Meeting, in May, 1958, some of the account had been printed, causing Mary acute embarrassment.

When I sit in my office [Brand had said] I can look through my window and see down the little path that leads from the main hospital to our leprosy clinic. I can see the leprosy patients that are gathered there waiting for their clinics, and as I look down I can see Dr. Mary Verghese coming down the road, busily wheeling her wheel chair, ready for her morning's work. But as I see her in the distance I love to look not so much at her, but through the other window where I can see deformed, crippled, paralyzed patients waiting for their examination and treatment. I love to see their faces as Mary comes around the corner. Before her coming I look at these boys—in their despondency, their despair, their apathy—and then I see Mary coming, still with the deep scar across her face where it was once cut open. As she comes round the corner, wheeling her chair without any assistance, I see a light come to the faces of these leprosy patients. They see somebody there who has come to life out of death, somebody who even now is only partially alive but who has dedicated all her life, strength, skill, love, all her compassion to their needs. They see somebody who is more paralyzed than they will ever be, more anaesthetic than they will ever be, somebody who has more disability than they will ever have, yet she has won through to a high degree of skill, and all of that skill she has put at the feet of the Master on behalf of the people who are suffering and who need her. . . .

Mary flushed and squirmed as she read this.

"But your story can help other people," protested Grace and others of her friends. "Just knowing that you have had faith and courage to conquer will give other disabled persons the same confidence. Can't you see?"

Mary could see. Very well, she agreed grudgingly. If it would help others, she would not argue. But she hoped people would understand that none of the credit was hers. Without the constant help of Another she could not have done it.

Though Dr. Brand returned from England in October, he was away again in November, this time to Japan and other centers of the Far East. The demands of Mary's work in the understaffed leprosy unit drove all thought of the letter to America from her mind. Never, it seemed to her, had she been so busy or able to accomplish so much. She rejoiced in the new facility of motion which made her additional labor possible.

The rigors of the operating room were lightened by the presence of Dr. Hugh Johnson, the American plastic surgeon, who assisted with many of the difficult cases. Never would she forget the look on his face when he first discovered, after watching her perform an operation, that she was a paraplegic—nor when she removed her mask and showed him her face. Almost at once he had proposed operating on her cheek, but somehow she could never find the time until. . . .

One day M. P. came to Mary's room bringing her daughter Gita, now grown into an adorable wide-eyed cherub of two. Greeting the child, Mary caught the look of fear as Gita gave a little cry and buried her face in her mother's sari. Quickly M. P. tried to divert both the child's and Mary's attention with a babble of monologue. But, though Gita seemed to recover quickly from her fright and was soon well enough acquainted to chatter happily to "Auntie-in-the-ricksha," Mary did not forget. She knew well enough what the look of fear signified. She had seen it on other children's faces in the wards and clinics, on the streets; even on her own nieces' and nephews'.

For Babi's twins, Kochuman and Mol, her unusual appearance had provoked less fear than curiosity.

"Does Mary *Kochamma* have legs?" one had asked the other in a whisper.

"She does," Kochuman had announced to his less aggressive but no less curious sister, after boldly lifting Mary's sari. "Aunt Mary does have legs, but she can't walk!"

The legs and the wheel chair Mary could do nothing about, but the scar. . . .

She was appraising her face one day in the mirror fastened to her bed when Ramani entered the room.

"Vanity!" the girl teased. "You're pretty, Mary. You don't have to worry about your looks."

"Pretty!" scoffed Mary. "With this scar?"

Ramani looked bewildered. "A scar? I hadn't even noticed."

Mary probed the girl's eyes for some sign of insincerity, then shook her head wonderingly. "I believe you really mean it."

Bending, Ramani kissed the disfigured cheek. "It's the truth," she said honestly. "Your friends simply don't notice it. You're always so full of smiles and radiance that we can't see anything but beauty."

In spite of this reassurance Mary was not satisfied. Her friends, perhaps, yes. But what about her patients? What about children like Gita, especially the ones who needed her services as a doctor? If others would enjoy her presence more with the scar made less prominent. . . .

She told Dr. Johnson she wanted the operation.

It was performed in January, 1959, with Paul Brand assisting. Knowing the difficulties attending her previous surgery, Dr. Brand insisted on taking every conceivable precaution.

"A doctor always expects complications when operating on another physician," agreed Dr. Johnson, half jokingly. "Doctors and nurses seem prone to them."

"We're not talking about an ordinary doctor," returned Paul Brand, unsmiling. "We're talking about Mary."

"I know. And we both know paraplegics are prone to have bleeding problems," Dr. Johnson said soberly.

Before the operation was over both doctors were faced with the problem of severe hemorrhaging.

"I'll think twice before I operate on a doctor again!" exclaimed Dr. Johnson when the ordeal was over. "That girl will want to shoot me. And I don't blame her if she does."

But even more memorable to Dr. Johnson than the complications of the operation was the fact that never in the weeks that followed did he receive from his patient one word of complaint, only kind words and smiles.

Mary's friends in the small prayer group, accustomed to meeting in her room in the Internes' Quarters, had decided to hold their next meeting in her hospital room. Then came the news of her serious condition.

"We had better change our plans," Grace told Mary when the day came.

"No," insisted Mary, still finding it difficult to speak. "I want you. I have so much to be thankful for."

"It wasn't worth it," exclaimed Grace, her eyes filling. "You knew there would probably be complications. Why did you run all that risk?"

But Grace knew the answer.

After a few weeks Mary began to see the results of the operation —though less in her mirror than in the faces of strangers. There was no longer that look of shock followed by the swiftly averted eyes, the note of pity in the voice. Children fingered her wheel chair curiously, stared wonderingly at the remaining scar, but were no longer frightened by its ugliness.

25

As the months passed, Mary put her new dream into words: *Lord, let other people in India have the same kind of opportunity You have given me. Let some proper institution be established, if possible here in Vellore, but somewhere. Please send someone to do it.*

Not until the letter came from Ammini's friend in America did it really occur to her that she herself might be the one.

> I have sent your letter to Dr. Howard Rusk [the American wrote]. He is much interested in you. He wants you to write to him directly. Before you can be considered for a scholarship in his Institute, he needs to know your medical history, how much you can do, and what your work is at the present time. Please write to him immediately.

As soon as possible Mary told Dr. Brand about the letter she had written.

"Dr. Rusk? I met him in Hong Kong last November," said Dr. Brand. "We had a most rewarding conversation. He asked me if we didn't want to start a rehabilitation center for paraplegics in Vellore."

Mary felt her heart beat faster. "What did you say?"

"I said, 'At the moment—no.' "

Her disappointment was tempered by his choice of words. *At the moment!*

"I told him about you," added Dr. Brand. "He was tremendously interested. If you really want this appointment at his institute in New York, by all means write him."

"You—you really think I could do it?" she whispered.

Paul Brand smiled whimsically, but his sensitive eyes were unsmiling. "Mary," he said, "I think that if you believe this is something God wants you to do, nothing on earth is going to stop you."

Because of her own implicit confidence in divine tutelage, Mary accepted the developments of the next few months with quiet elation but no surprise. In due time she was granted a fellowship by the World Rehabilitation Fund. Specifically, she was made a grantee of the Charles Poore Memorial Fellowship, established with contributions to the World Rehabilitation Fund by the IBM World Trade Corporation in memory of one of its employees who had become a quadriplegic while working in Saudi Arabia.

Mary felt that there was no selfish purpose in her going to New York. She had completed her own rehabilitation program in Australia. Her eyes were set on one goal: sufficient training to qualify her to come back to India and supervise a new Department of Physical Medicine and Rehabilitation. Though the normal period of training in New York was three years, she hoped, with her experience already acquired, to complete the course in much less time.

But of what use becoming a specialist in rehabilitation if when she returned to India there would be no adequate channel for dispensing her new knowledge and training? As soon as her appointment was confirmed, she discussed the problem with Dr. John Carman, Director of the Christian Medical College and Hospital, together with Dr. Brand and Dr. Chandy, whose departments would be most concerned. All agreed that some way must be found to open a Department of Rehabilitation and have it ready for Mary on her return.

By December 9, which was Dr. Ida's eighty-ninth birthday, Mary's preparations for her journey were nearly complete. It was with sadness as well as exultation that she left her room for Dr. Ida's birthday celebration in the hospital compound. As she wheeled her chair toward the figure half buried in garlands and draped in the shawl of gold with which the people of Vellore had honored their most beloved citizen now entering her ninetieth year, Dr. Ida did not rise and come to meet Mary, for she herself was sitting in a wheel chair. A year ago, just before her eighty-eighth birthday, she had fallen and broken her hip. Like Mary, she would never walk again.

They sat looking at each other, smiling, the old and the young, these two women who were so different yet so very much alike, because they shared the same dream and the same dedication; symbolic of two worlds swiftly and tumultuously flowing together to become one.

The blue eyes, still bright as the Kerala seas in sunlight, seemed already to be focused on limitless horizons.

"My dear," Dr. Ida greeted Mary, smiling and extending both hands, "you look so pretty today! I do hope you're feeling as well as you look."

She doesn't know me, thought Mary with a little pang.

But it didn't really matter. Their kinship was deeper than words or visual recognition. For they were made of the same heroic stuff, the dark-skinned girl and the white-haired woman who came from opposite ends of the earth.

This may be the last time I shall ever see her, Mary told herself as she wheeled away.

Her fortnight's holiday with her family after she left Vellore proved far from restful. There she learned that her travel application forms, which had been sent to BOAC in London, were outmoded. However, authorization had been given the Bombay office to accept or reject her new application. She filled out the new forms and sent them to Cousin Kunjannam in Bombay. Fortunately, Dr. Brand happened to be in Bombay attending a conference, and it was possible to secure his signature immediately. Kunjannam and her brother went to see the BOAC medical officer at the Bombay office in an attempt to secure his authorization.

"No," he said stubbornly. "A woman in a wheel chair, half paralyzed, and traveling alone? No OK unless I see her first."

Mary was in despair. Fly to Bombay simply to display herself? Very well, if she must.

"Wait," Kunjannam advised her by telephone. "We have another plan. We are going to radiophone the airline office in London."

Again the anxious waiting, as in the days before her trip to Australia! Once she was almost ready to cancel the trip. Better to wait, perhaps, until someone else from Vellore would be traveling to America and could accompany her. But she did not want to wait. It might be months before the opportunity came. She wanted to go *now*.

Six days before her date of departure she received the permission from London.

Drawing a long breath of relief, Mary awoke to the fact that it was almost Christmas. Liela and Shiela and Biela, George's three daughters, had already hung a big star of colored paper and bamboo from the front porch of their house. Kunjani, George's wife, was busy in the kitchen supervising the making of holiday foods. Mary's nostrils quivered. Her eyes danced with the sheen of sparklers furiously waved by her little nieces on Christmas Eve. She felt like a child again.

The mood of gaiety lasted through Christmas Day Then suddenly it faded. She was no child but a woman, a half-woman imprisoned in a wheel chair, leaving comfortable security to fly on a lonely journey to the far side of the earth.

On December 26 the family gathered at George's house to bid her God speed and, incidentally, to have their picture taken. Nearly all of them were there, ranged in three rows in front of the sturdy pillars of George's porch: the three brothers and three sisters with their wives and husbands and their children. Even Appan was there, in substance as well as spirit, his portrait propped on the empty center chair where he would once have sat, Amma and Aleyamma on either side. All but one of the sixteen grandchildren were there, most of them sitting cross-legged in front, from curly-topped Usha, John's youngest, to Omana, Thankamma's only daughter, now a sari-clad young woman in her teens. Mary sat in her wheel chair between Amma and Thankamma, her godchild Shiela at her feet, and wondered if they would ever be all together again.

On the twenty-seventh most of the family accompanied her to the Cochin airport, where the three young nephews, Verghese, Kochuman, and another "Babi," were so entranced by the sight of a burly boxing champion, wearing his garlands with the casual aplomb of an Olympic victor, that they almost forgot to say goodby. Amma, George, his wife Kunjani, and second sister Annamma flew with Mary to Bombay. There, after a few hours' rest, Mary was lifted aboard the plane for London. As it soared into the night with her, Mary felt a rush of panic. For almost the first time since her accident she was now utterly dependent on her own resources. No Sushila was with her this time to share the long hours of the flight, though Sushila, now studying in Britain, would be meeting her in London. For a moment, in the darkness of the plane, she felt as helpless as an unborn child waiting to be delivered into a strange and hostile world.

But a few minutes later she assured the inquiring stewardess that she needed nothing—that she was quite comfortable. And she was, she told herself. How stupid of her to have even thought that she was *alone!*

If I ascend up into heaven, thou art there. . . .

The dawn was long in coming, for the plane was moving west.

When it finally circled over London, it was only mid-afternoon, though already evening again in Bombay. Mary welcomed with relief the descent through a film of clouds. Then with a burst of silent gratitude, she saw the familiar faces of those who had come to meet her—Sushila; Annamma Verghese and her husband Dr. Mammen Cherian, who was now doing graduate work in London; her brother-in-law, Dr. Mathai, and others she had known at Vellore Miss Sharp, the efficient secretary of the British Friends of Vellore, was also there capably managing all the details of her entry. A tall dynamo of a man named Mr. Jefcoate (Jeff, everybody called him) soon had Mary and Sushila bundled into his small car and on the way to his home in Amersham. Too weary to see or think clearly, yet far too excited to relax, Mary caught glimpses of smoking chimney pots, narrow curving roads bordered with neatly clipped hedges, steeply sloping roofs; finally a white doorway in a small stucco house, two blue Dutch wooden shoes fastened to the wall beside it, and over it the word SABOTS in big bold letters. The door opened, revealing a smiling woman with hair the color of brightly polished copper.

"Welcome to Sabots," Phyllis Jefcoate greeted her gaily.

"I'll carry you upstairs," said Jeff, immediately putting the words into action.

Mary felt herself lifted, held securely.

"I've carried Gwenda Lewis up these same stairs many a time," Jeff reassured her cheerfully. "Don't worry, we can cope."

It was a favorite Jefcoate saying, Mary discovered. "We can cope" covered any exigency from meeting an airplane to promoting a Vellore benefit concert each spring in London's Royal Albert Hall.

Mary stayed in England two days. On the morning following her arrival she visited the Stoke-Mandeville Hospital, where she met Dr. Gutmann, the head of its paraplegic rehabilitation program, and the teacher of Dr. Bedbrook. He regarded her with amazement.

"They tell me you actually operate, Doctor, from your wheel chair!"

"Yes," said Mary almost impatiently, for she had not come here to talk about herself.

Dr. Gutmann refused to be diverted. "I've known paraplegics to do unbelievable things, but never that. I wonder if you're not the only paraplegic surgeon in the world."

Presently, to Mary's relief, the discussion turned to the Paralympics. Dr. Gutmann told Mary they were to be held in a foreign country for the first time in 1960, in Rome, directly after the Olympic Games. This year, 1959, for the first time women paraplegics had competed in the National Games, and at the International Games there had been many more entries than formerly, with more countries represented.

Sometime India will be one of them, Mary promised herself.

She left London at noon on December 30. This time it was sunset which was long in coming, and she and the sunset reached New York almost at the same time. Though it was a ten-hour trip, her first glimpse of the New York skyline was against a western sky ablaze with glory.

"But I don't want to spend time on rehabilitation for myself!" Mary regarded Dr. Howard Rusk with consternation. "I thought that was understood."

Dr. Rusk, the director of the Institute of Physical Medicine and Rehabilitation, seemed almost to fill the small room in which he and Mary were conversing. A giant of a man physically, he seemed to Mary to possess formidable energy. From the first she had the impression that he was an extremely busy man. As time went on she learned that he not only supervised his Institute of Physical Medicine and Rehabilitation with its cooperating service in Bellevue Hospital, but served on a dozen boards and commissions, local, national, and international, wrote numerous articles on his specialties, and followed a lecture schedule that took him across the country and far abroad. For the techniques which he had originated as wartime Chief of Convalescent Services, United States Air Force, and developed later through the rehabilitation programs of the New York University Medical Center, were improving the treatment of disabled persons throughout the world.

Dr. Rusk leaned back in his chair. Just now he seemed to have all the time in the world. "Let me tell you about one of our patients," he said with apparent irrelevance.

Mary listened, first with impatience, then with interest. The patient, a polio victim, had come to the institute as a quadriplegic of many years' standing. She could now move about with crutches and had about 75 per cent use of her hands. To achieve this, she had undergone twenty-six operations including four spinal fusions.

"It took us seven months to teach that girl a technique whereby she could manage a sidewalk curb," said Dr. Rusk. "We had to redevelop every muscle she had until finally she learned how to do it. The day she learned it she repeated it ten times in the morning, and twenty times in the afternoon. She repeated it fifty times the next day, which was Friday, and we discharged her. Monday morning she took a full time job on the Bellevue switchboard. She has been filling that job capably for eight years now, has never missed a day, never been late." He smiled. "Worth while, do you think?"

Mary's eyes glowed. "Oh, *yes!*"

"In one way or another, we all have our curbstones," said Dr. Rusk. "Things which impede us from living our lives to their full capacity."

The techniques employed by the institute, he explained, were both simple and practical. Incoming patients were tested for more than a hundred needs in daily living, such as: Can you brush your teeth? Can you comb your hair? Can you get from your bed to your wheel chair, from your wheel chair to a car? The daily program was then fitted to meet the patient's particular needs and geared to teach him maximum independence. The results achieved by the institute over thirteen years with 40,000 patients were not magic, as some people seemed to think. They were attained by hard work, imagination, and by the patient's desire. "If the patient wills it," was one of the rehabilitation axioms, "nothing is too tough."

"Don't worry about the expense," Dr. Rusk told Mary. "You will be considered a trainee right from the start. And during your own period of rehabilitation you will attend lectures and conferences also. In short, you will be your own first patient."

Mary was soon involved in her rehabilitation program. New and more efficient braces were ordered. She was provided with a new and better wheel chair. But the most valuable piece of new equipment was, amazingly, the most simple: a small plank fitted with a loop so it could be hung on her wheel chair. Valueless yet invaluable, this device bridged the abyss into a new world of self-sufficiency. With it Mary could transfer herself from her wheel chair into an automobile without assistance, and from an automobile back into her chair.

The Australian rehabilitation technique had emphasized pull-ups, with the use of bars. The method here was based on push-ups. There were hours of progressive exercises for strengthening the upper extremities, for the push-up system demanded excessive strength of the shoulder depressors and triceps. Also, an hour each day was spent in mat exercises, for general conditioning and improvement of balance. Much of Mary's time was devoted to training in Activities of Daily

Living, the institute's major emphasis. All of this Mary worked at intensely, even the renewed attempt at ambulation. For three months she persisted doggedly, obedient to the cheerful directions, manipulating her new braces like a captured animal dragging its trap.

"Fine, Doctor! Just once more across, shall we? Aren't you pleased with the progress we're making?"

No, Mary was not pleased. And she knew she was not making progress. The same spasticity that had interfered with her efforts to walk in Australia was a deterrent here also. The one test of value Mary applied to every step of her rehabilitation program was *function.* Hundreds of hours of arm-strengthening exercises, thousands of pushups? Yes. Small price to pay for new facility of motion and independence! Painstaking labor in Occupational Therapy inexpertly carving a leather pocketbook? Of course. Later, in India, she might need to supervise such work. But—hours of creeping, shuffling efforts merely that she might one day boast, "Look at me! I can walk!" *No* Doggedly, she struggled through three months of the program, then requested that she be permitted to start her residency immediately. The permission was granted.

As a Fellow of the Institute of Physical Medicine and Rehabilitation of the College of Medicine of New York University, Mary became one of the 268 doctors, nurses, and therapists from 59 different countries trained by the institute since its establishment in 1948. Training with Mary as recipients of scholarships from the World Rehabilitation Fund were 44 other Fellows representing almost as many countries.

In addition to the conferences and lectures which were a part of her training, Mary was soon doing full time work as a resident. The Rehabilitation Department at Bellevue consisted of two large wards, one male and one female, where patients needing a full program were admitted. In addition many out-patients came for therapy, as well as patients from other services, such as Neurology, who needed special training. Mary's work brought her in contact with all three groups. She participated in the evaluation conferences by which patients were admitted, following examinations by a medical doctor, a psychologist, a physiotherapist, an occupational therapist, a speech therapist, and a social worker. She assumed responsibility for certain patients in the wards and for some out-patients.

Except that Mary was given no night calls, she had the same schedule of patients as the other residents. In fact, her handicap created more personal than professional problems. Since she was unable to live in the main building with the other residents, the bathrooms being too small to accommodate her wheel chair, she was given a room in the Psychiatric Building. The problem then was · how to get to the main building through the basement, which contained two long ramps? Dr. Rusk solved it by providing an electric wheel chair.

At first Mary did not like the chair. Its noise attracted attention, making her conspicuous in one of the few places in the world where she could hope not to be conspicuous. But the ease and speed of the new conveyance were indisputable. It was like exchanging Kerala's old hand-drawn ricksha for the bicycle- or motor-driven ricksha of other parts of India. Soon Mary's sole quarrel with the motor chair was that she could not make it move fast enough.

Until the day it broke down with her! She was returning to her room along the basement ramp about seven o'clock one evening. Since all the basement employees went off duty at five, the area was now empty of traffic. Her chair whirred and rumbled through the dead spaces. Then—silence. It stopped short, as devoid of energy as her own limbs. There were no large wheels so that the chair could be pushed by hand up the long ramp that was still ahead. Mary considered her predicament. Few people used the basement crossing after five. She might remain here for hours—all night—before help came. Being Mary, she prayed . . . and waited. Ten minutes passed, fifteen, twenty. At the end of twenty-five minutes she heard the hollow echo of footsteps far in the distance She held her breath. It did not even occur to her to cry out. The sound grew louder, pounded through the emptiness like drum beats. Finally one of the doctors appeared.

"I wonder if you would be willing to give me a push," Mary said calmly. "I seem to be having chair trouble."

The price of independence was sometimes high indeed. When Mary moved into her room in the Psychiatric Building, she was completely alone for the first time since her accident over six years before. More exultant than fearful, she reveled in the new privacy. No more nurses, no more *ayahs*! With a telephone close to her bed, a large bath adjoining the room, a bed of convenient height, she was confident she could meet any emergency.

Too confident. One evening soon after her arrival in the room she had a sudden desire to study the geography of her new location. Did her windows face east toward the river, north toward the United Nations Building, or west toward downtown Manhattan? From her wheel chair it was impossible to tell. Wheeling to the bathroom window, she hoisted herself up. She caught a brief but dazzling glimpse of the city's lights. Then she was huddled on the floor, the chair slipping slowly but inexorably away behind her.

She stared after it helplessly, angry with herself, frustrated, more than a little frighened. What to do? What *could* she do? There was no one near enough to call. She was a resident in the building, not a patient. The telephone, a dozen feet distant, might have been as many miles away. Nobody would be coming near the room until the maid arrived next day. She would not be missed until she was due to go on duty at nine in the morning.

"Stupid!" she chided herself aloud. "Unless you can get yourself out of this you don't deserve to be trusted alone."

She determined that she would get herself out of it.

Satisfied that she had not hurt herself in the fall, she managed to drag herself across the room by a series of push-ups until she reached the wheel chair. No more than two feet above the floor, the seat seemed at first as unattainable as a mountain top. She removed the cushion, placed it on the floor beside her, and managed to hoist herself upon it. Hunching and sliding, she dragged herself to the side of the bathtub, reached in, and removed the seat. Good! It was just a few inches higher than the cushion. Somehow she managed to transfer herself to this new level. She then looked around for a higher plane to conquer. She found it in the form of a small table. From that she was able to transfer to the toilet seat, and from there, at last, to the wheel chair. The emotion she felt was more triumph than relief. As her friend Mr. Jefcoate would have said, she had "coped."

Mary had not been long in New York before she developed a hunger for sightseeing. Every time she went to the roof, the shining finger of the Empire State Building, tantalizingly near, beckoned her. On one of her days off she persuaded a nurse, Miss Jacob, to accompany her there. Another nurse and a boy patient, a quadriplegic, joined the party, and they went to the building in a taxi. By elevator they rose to the first observatory, then later to the second at the hundred and second floor. Guards lifted the two wheel chairs up the steps when necessary. Mary was able to push herself up and look out the windows, but her pleasure was somewhat spoiled because the young quadriplegic could not lift himself. She was almost ashamed to be blest with two strong arms in the presence of one paralyzed in both arms and legs.

"We'll lift you," the nurses said, but the boy refused to let them. "Girls shouldn't lift," he insisted stubbornly.

At last some male observers noticed his plight and hoisted him to their shoulders, not once but four times, giving him a view of the city from all angles.

They stayed at the top of the building until nine o'clock that evening, suspended between pale stars and burgeoning city lights.

But Mary already knew too much about the dark undercurrents of the city's life to be blinded by its glamour. New York's problems—sickness, poverty, tension, frustration—poured in a never-ending flood through the doors of Bellevue Hospital.

Mary kept comparing what she saw of America with her own India, and not always to the latter's disadvantage. She had always thought of the United States as a Christian country, yet spiritual health and religious faith did not appear to be among its strong points. To the bewildered Easterner garnering first impressions it seemed first of all a land of gadgets and gimmicks—and of garbage pails full of uneaten food. There might be two million leprosy victims in India, but there were five million alcoholics in the United States.

As a doctor concerned with the health problems of the two countries, Mary found the contrast between India and the United States a disturbing challenge. India, statistically, had one doctor for every 5000 of her population, one nurse for every 16,000; while the United States had one doctor for every 700, one nurse for every 350. India, had a hospital bed for every 4000 inhabitants, as compared with the one bed per one hundred considered adequate by Western countries. Americans were shocked to learn that one of their number died from tuberculosis every forty minutes, but in India one died from the disease every minute. The life span of the average American had passed the seventy mark. In India it had only recently gone above thirty.

In her own area of rehabilitation Mary was fiercely jealous of Western achievements. For in India there were very few government or non-government agencies to supply the disabled with care and equipment and vocational training, few societies for the handicapped. Although in Bombay there was the All-India Institute of Physical Medicine and Rehabilitation, and in New Delhi the All-India Institute of Medical Sciences had shown interest in starting an Institute, the amount of trained leadership was as yet negligible. Here at Bellevue she was part of a program that expended twenty-nine dollars per day on each patient. If in India one could have only two dollars a day, wonders could be accomplished. And in India no vocational centers had been established If a man was helpless, his wife would have to devote herself to his care, unable to work herself even if their children were starving.

One day Mary saw an impressive demonstration of what rehabilitation could lead to in the economic sphere. She visited Abilities, Inc , a Long Island manufacturing company founded by Henry Viscardi, Jr., to prove that the disabled could work as productively as the non-disabled. Viscardi himself, who had been born without normal legs and had learned to walk with artificial limbs only after he was twenty-seven years of age, was Mary's guide. His business, which had started in 1952 with five men who among them had only one usable leg and five arms, had grown to include nearly four hundred employees, all severely disabled, yet now engaged full time in highly skilled labor ranging from the manufacture of electronic components to the specialized packaging of materials. The physical plant had expanded from a small two-car garage to a large air-conditioned building with spacious work rooms, recreational facilities, and offices. Hank Viscardi stated his philosophy in terms that reminded Mary of Dr. Rusk's view:

"There are no 'disabled people,' " he said tersely, "only people. Everybody is disabled in some way or other."

Abilities, Inc., he explained, was competing successfully with other manufacturing plants of its size. All the equipment was standard industrial machinery with only minor modifications. All the employees worked a full forty-hour week and managed their own transportation, yet all were victims of such disabilities as polio, cerebral palsy, paraplegia, epilepsy, and visual and auditory defects.

In the eight years of the company's operation Viscardi's faith had been more than vindicated. The assets had increased from a borrowed $8,000 in 1952 to a gross business of $2 million in 1959. As a result of its safety record Abilities paid less than half the average premium of comparable organizations for its compensation insurance. The employees, all of whom were earning standard wages, averaged 1.0 days sick leave per 100 working days, as against the national average of 1.3, and their rate of absence for other personal reasons was one third of the national average.

Mary marveled as she inspected the rows of absorbed craftsmen, many of them in wheel chairs, operating complicated machines. She was introduced to a number: Art, stricken with polio at age two and a half, the first employee of the plant and now its vice-president and works manager; Murray, a World War II casualty, whose desk in the cost control department was a mobile stretcher, now a competent and well paid executive, but once a bitter, helpless, idle, state-supported liability; Alex, born without arms or legs, a newsboy for many years but now foreman of the packaging department, happily married since he came to work at Abilities and the father of a small daughter; Ellen, another polio victim, now the director of personnel.

"This isn't just a job," Ellen told Mary earnestly. "It's really a way of life."

But it was another employee, Ray, who struck the most responsive chord in Mary's being. She watched this young man, once a concert pianist, draw melodies from an electric organ, using a pair of steel hooks for the hands he no longer possessed.

If he had hands, thought Mary wonderingly, he might have been a very ordinary pianist. Never could he have stirred a person's soul like this. Yet when he lost them, like me he must have thought his world had ended.

The next thought came like a blinding flash: *Suppose she had not had her accident. She might have been just an ordinary gynecologist, and her country had many of them. Would she have cared enough, then, to devote herself to the disabled of India?*

One day Mary received a letter with a Kerala postmark, addressed in a hand she did not recognize. Opening it, she studied the signature. George Mathew, the quadriplegic at Vellore who had said so bitterly, "*Don't talk to me about God, you who have good strong arms and legs!*"

Eagerly she read the closely written pages:

I saw your story in a Malayalam newspaper. . . . So now you know what it means to be both alive and dead . . . have heard about some of the things you have done . . . thought you might like to know some of the things I am trying to do. . . .

Since returning to his home in Kayamkulam, Kerala, George had started a *sakhyam,* a social center for children, many of whom were handicapped like himself. At first, having no wheelchair, he had the children in his room and directed their activities while he lay in bed. Now, with a wheel chair, he could meet them out of doors, a good thing, for the original group of twenty had already grown to twice that number. After the schools and colleges closed in March, his student friends would come and help him. He was planning a big parade of children for Nehru's birthday, in November; also an excursion for poor children at Cape Comorin. He was trying to arrange for them to meet the governor of the state in Trivandrum. Of course he could not go himself, but that was unimportant.

Joyfully Mary read about his plans for raising money to build a vocational center for handicapped children and adults on land he himself owned. He needed 11,000 rupees for the building and 7,000 more for the children's section and open-air auditorium. Of course as yet it was only a dream. . . .

But what a dream! thought Mary exultantly.

From that day she resumed her work as a trainee with even greater vigor. She concentrated on one goal and one alone: rehabilitation. Dr. Franciszka Dworecka, one of the residents under whom she trained for a period, did not find her easy to work with. If Mary was told to do something and did not want to do it, she said nothing, simply did not do it. Advised to go to bed when she suffered a skin breakdown, she appeared at work as usual. Less and less interested in medical complications, she preferred to let the medical residents handle them. She gained the reputation among her colleagues of being stubborn.

"But heaven knows she needs to be!" Dr. Dworecka admitted. "And, after all, why shouldn't she be exclusively interested in rehabilitation? Did you ever see a true surgeon who was interested in anything but surgery? Let's be thankful for her sake that she has a stiff backbone, figuratively as well as literally."

26

Dr. Ida was dead!

"At first we couldn't believe it," wrote one of Mary's friends from Vellore in late May, 1960. "Of course we had always known it would happen, but now it had really come we were all stricken. The whole hospital seemed to stop moving. We were like a body from which the spirit has gone out. And then suddenly we seemed to become one, like a family. We knew we were all feeling the same thing, doctors, nurses, orderlies, the humblest probationers, even many of the patients. We were like brothers and sisters who have lost their mother."

Reading, Mary knew exactly what they meant. For she herself felt the same emotion—disbelief, emptiness, then sudden unity in grief with the organism of Christian healing that Dr. Ida had created and left behind her.

As she read on, she could see it all as it had happened half a world away: the car traveling silently through the darkness to Vellore from Hill Top, up in the mountains 400 miles away; the hands working all night to prepare the open carriage, making it lovely as a birthday chair with fresh flowers; the stricken townspeople, for Dr. Ida was as much a part of Vellore's life and tradition as its founder, Bommai Reddy, the builder of the 700-year-old-fort. More, for Bommai Reddy's monument was dead, while Dr. Ida's gave new life daily to a thousand human beings.

Now, to do her honor, they came in such crowds as only India could muster. For the public service they poured into the courtyard of the hospital, because there was no church or hall in the city that could even begin to hold them. They followed in a dense mass after the flower-decked carriage; lined the streets as the beloved figure, face visible to all after the Indian custom, made its last slow journey along the familiar road where so often it had rushed to their aid in pony cart, *jutka,* ancient Ford, modern ambulance, or on its own tireless, swift-moving feet.

They crowded through the gate and over the wall of the small foreign cemetery, filling every inch of ground space, even climbing trees, and almost causing a crisis until a persuasive voice over the loud speaker system helped clear a space for those who were to conduct the burial service. Then finally they filled her resting place to the brim with the flowers she had loved, that glorious abundance of beauty which was India's compensation for her season of drought and dearth and dust.

So vivid was the experience that Mary could almost smell the flowers, feel the blazing heat, taste the acrid dust. Yet her emotion was not one of sadness. Dr. Ida dead? Of course not. She had lived her ninety years to the tune of trumpet calls, and they had always sounded reveille, never taps. The last and clearest, for which she had long waited with faith and expectancy, even impatience, was no exception. For never had she been more alive. Her skilled hands and brisk feet were now multiplied by thousands, all dedicated to her sublime task of healing.

I can't be feet for her, thought Mary, but at least I'll try to be a good pair of hands.

Suddenly homesick for Vellore and familiar faces, she looked forward to the coming of Dr. Brand in August for the Eighth World Congress of the International Society for the Welfare of Cripples, to be held in New York. Of course she was going to attend its sessions herself. For it would be the first international congress on rehabilitation ever held in the Western Hemisphere and the largest such meeting yet held anywhere.

But how to get to the meeting place? Her dependence on friends to drive her or accompany her in a taxi to all the places she wanted to go in New York was a continuing embarrassment. Hospital workers were always too busy to leave. And she *would* not beg favors of the friends she had made outside the hospital. Transportation, it seemed, whether here or in India, was always going to be a major problem.

As the time of the August congress approached, Mary's determination crystallized. She would learn to travel alone. The day before the meeting she telephoned the United Nations headquarters. Yes, they assured her, they would be able to accommodate a visitor in a wheel chair.

Going down to the hospital's ambulance entrance, Mary asked one of the attendants to hail a taxi for her. The taxi driver was cooperative but skeptical.

"It's OK by me, lady, if you think you can manage it. But I don't see how—"

When Mary slid along the plank from her chair to the car seat, then quickly pulled her useless limbs after her, the driver whistled admiringly. Given a few brief instructions, he folded the chair and put it in the back of the cab. At the United Nations building he helped Mary out, then remained to watch with paternal interest while she wheeled herself up to the entrance. A guard lifted her up the one step into the building. She was welcomed graciously but without embarrassing effusiveness and given a personally conducted tour by one of the guides.

Mary returned to the hospital triumphant. The next evening she took a taxi to the Waldorf Astoria Hotel, the meeting place of the rehabilitation congress. Her second taxi driver was incurious about either her condition or achievement. He would have displayed, probably, the same impersonal efficiency if she had been a sack of potatoes.

She found Dr. Brand near the conference room. He greeted her with enthusiasm. "Mary! How did you get here? Who brought you?"

"Nobody," she replied with composure. "I came alone."

His first incredulity changed to amusement. "Trust you to find some way! Next thing you'll be telling me you're planning a trip to the top of the Empire State Building."

When she told him she had already been there, he laughed and then congratulated her.

In spite of the size of the assembly, Mary found that she felt perfectly at home. Many of the delegates and visitors were in wheel chairs. Further, a sari was no more conspicuous here than a tweed suit would be in one of the cities of India, for the delegates, representing sixty countries, wore a great variety of dress.

At one of the meetings Mary saw Dr. Brand receive the Lasker award, one of medicine's highest honors, for his outstanding achievements in leprosy rehabilitation. Thrilling to the implications of the act, she then heard the assembly vote to change the name of the

International Society for the Welfare of Cripples to the International Society for the Rehabilitation of the Disabled. Then Dr. Rusk addressed the delegates on the theme "Rehabilitation for Peace."

"Once you have justice, peace will come. Peace is like friendship; it cannot be sold or bought; it must be earned. If we could first have world justice, then we would have world peace.

"I believe this is the feeling of all people and especially of disabled people, those who represent the greatest minority group in the world today. Justice to them means the right to compete with their so-called normal brothers; the opportunity to be treated and trained to live the best lives they can with the abilities they have. They ask to be judged on their abilities, not on their disabilities. . . . Here is a great human tool more powerful even than the harnessed atom, because it brings new skills to produce, and new hope into the hearts of men.

"Much has been done, especially in the past decade, to develop rehabilitation programs. But many of the needs of the disabled throughout the world are still unmet. For example, it is estimated that there are twice as many working hands in the world disabled from Hansen's Disease alone than by all the other diseases and disabilities known to medicine, including polio, arthritis, injuries. . . ."

Mary felt a surge of relief, of exaltation. She was not alone in her long struggle. India, with her seemingly insoluble human problems, was not alone.

"We are all dedicated to one goal," Dr. Rusk concluded. "We are here today for one primary purpose—to learn—to take back from this week together new knowledge, new techniques, and a renewed spirit. We working in rehabilitation are truly blessed that in this world so technologically advanced yet spiritually retarded, we speak a common language."

As Mary continued her work at the institute and at Bellevue, such moments of exaltation sometimes seemed far apart. The weeks and months proceeded for the most part on an uneventful level. Days of ward duty, admissions, evaluation conferences, lectures; nights of loneliness, of compensating for the long hours of sitting by even longer hours of lying on face or side, of trying to cram three hours of study into one, because she could not read or write when lying on her face. Then the heat of New York in summer, and the constant discomfort of compensatory perspiration in a body unable to perspire below the waist.

"Ingrate!" she would admonish herself when tempted to indulge in self pity. "You ought to be ashamed. Think of all the paraplegics in India who have no fans in their rooms and no wheel chairs to sit in."

Not that the wheel chair was an unmixed blessing! The electric one proved to have too hard a cushion, and pressure sores developed, sending her to bed for three weeks. Even a change of the seat, did not entirely solve the difficulty. Constant vigilance and frequent changing of position were the only weapons with which to fight the ever present danger.

Constant vigilance!—watchword of the paraplegic. Day after day, week after week, year after year, for as long as one should live, the patient, exacting ritual: examining the body thoroughly for reddened areas, using a hand mirror for back, hips, heels, and elbows; bathing daily with warm water and soap, then rubbing lightly over paralyzed parts, applying powder when the skin was dry; using foam rubber pads to keep pressure off any part that showed signs of redness; making sure that no part was subjected to pressure for more than an hour; keeping the skin dry; treating every slightest abrasion as if it were a mortal wound. Monotonous, time consuming routines, but for the paraplegic, a matter of life or death!

Winter brought Mary increased responsibility in her work. It also brought her an unexpected and disturbing proposition. The woman who had written the biography of Dr. Ida wanted to write a book about her, Mary Verghese.

She shrank from the idea. Lay bare her inmost thoughts and desires, her pitiful weaknesses and frustrations, her most intimate and precious memories? It would be like exposing one's nerve tips to probing instruments. And what was more, what had she done that could possibly be worth writing about? No, no, *no!* Every fiber of her spirit rebelled at the thought.

But the friends to whom she mentioned the proposition thought otherwise. Grace Koshi, Helen North, Annamma Cherian—all wrote their enthusiastic approval.

"You must do it," they said. "Just think of how your experience might help others to conquer their handicaps as you have done."

But I have done nothing! Mary told herself. *It is God's grace and power that have done it all.*

Then she could almost hear her friends replying: "Do you not want others to know what God has done for you?"

Oh—yes! But to parade my little thoughts and acts as if I thought they were important!

"And this dream you have of helping the disabled of India—do you not want as many people as possible to know about it?"

Yes, yes—but—

Even Dr. Brand, returning to America in January to give a lecture before a medical association, did not discourage the idea. In his way as retiring as Mary, he also was shrinking from the glare of publicity, feeling startled, humble, a little guilty because his lecture, involving plane travel between India and America, was costing the sponsors at least $100 a minute.

After prayer and soul-searching, Mary agreed to let her story be written.

"It worries me," she wrote the author, "when I think of the publicity part of it. But I do not have the courage to say no when people tell me that this may help some others with disabilities like mine. Some of my friends may hesitate to tell you about my weak moments. It will be a mistake if you paint a picture of continuous victory. That will be far from truth. It is the story of God's abundant grace working in a very ordinary human being in spite of and through her many weaknesses and failures."

Presently a tape recorder was placed in her room, and Mary set herself to answer the author's long list of written questions. Some were difficult and involved, some embarrassingly personal. Others seemed foolish and unimportant. Who in the world would be interested in knowing what sort of house she had lived in as a child, what games she had played, what her brothers had quarreled about, what foods they had eaten! But she tried to answer honestly, her scientific mind probing patiently for details. At first she held the microphone awkwardly, feeling as shy as if in a stranger's presence, but gradually it became a friendly companion, accompanying her into well-loved and familiar places.

"This is Mary, remembering her early life back in Cochin, South India, now a part of the state of Kerala. I was born on a small island called Vypeen, just off the coast in the Arabian Sea. It is a thickly populated island, with about four hundred and eighty thousand people. We lived in a little village called Cherai. . . ."

27

She lived in three worlds that spring and summer of 1961, and there were times when New York seemed the least tangible of the three. Certainly the East River, less than a block away, was no more substantial than the remembered backwaters of Kerala, now swollen by the June monsoon and rampaging over coconut plots and rice fields.

"Never have we seen such floods," wrote third sister Thankamma from Cherai. "Seventeen families have had to leave their huts in the vicinity and seek shelter here in the house with us. At night our floors look like the sidewalks of Bombay, so covered with white-shrouded mounds that we can hardly pick our way around. And it keeps Amma busy all day trying to plan what to feed them."

The changes taking place in distant Vellore seemed far closer to Mary than the raising of steel girders for a new building two blocks west on 34th Street.

"The development of the Physical Medicine and Rehabilitation Department," reported Dr. Carman, "has become an important 1961 project. Dr. Brand has stimulated a great deal of interest in many parts of the world in the leprosy rehabilitation work. Gifts have already come from Switzerland, Sweden, and the United States. We trust these will provide facilities to set up an international training center for surgeons, physiotherapists, and others to aid in the worldwide campaign for rehabilitation and treatment of leprosy patients and in the more general application of the principles of rehabilitation for all our patients."

The ground floor of the new building would be the Physiotherapy

Department. The second floor would contain the leprosy surgery ward and facilities for the rehabilitation of leprosy patients. In the new program at Vellore they hoped to treat all disabilities, whether caused by accidents, congenital deformities, or disease. It would be an ambitious program, the first of its kind in all India.

The emphasis, at least at first, would be more on medical than on vocational rehabilitation, though for Mary there were hopeful signs that the Indian government might soon interest itself in the latter field. Rajkumari Amrit Kaur, the former Minister of Health, had visited the institute on her last trip to New York and was encouraging the establishment of a similar training institution in New Delhi. The Indian Minister of Education had written to Mary asking if she knew of any place in India where training was being given for the Paralympics. In December, also, the Ministry of Education would be sponsoring the first All-India Seminar on the education and employment of the physically handicapped.

One of her greatest problems in adapting western rehabilitation techniques to India, Mary knew, would be in the area of appliances. In a country whose per capita annual income was sixty dollars, the people she would be treating could not afford the price of braces, artificial limbs, and wheel chairs. The institute's "Horizon House"—a model home functionally designed for the physically disabled with low push-button appliances and sanitary fixtures—would be an absurdity for a nation whose average family had yet to secure a smokeless clay stove and a bore-hole latrine.

Mary finally saw that she must learn not only the functions of orthopedic appliances but their construction as well. For they must somehow be manufactured in India and of the most inexpensive materials possible. She spent hours studying the various self-help devices, many of them handmade, simple, and ingenious. She pored over designs and blueprints of braces, wheel chairs, artificial limbs.

Slowly she developed the knowledge and skills necessary for a medical supervisor in rehabilitation, in order that she might head the new department at Vellore. She learned the functions and techniques of staff members who would be working with her: the physiotherapist who would be responsible for training disabled bodies in muscle strengthening, ambulation, and activities of daily living; the occupational therapist who would improve bodily function by skills, then help the patient adjust to his new vocational life, either helping him to return to his previous occupation if possible, or if not, to explore other occupations; the social worker who would act as a liaison between the patient and his family and discover agencies for financial assistance and employment.

In July 1961 Mary moved into new living quarters in the institute itself. This involved more adjustments, for the door of the bathroom adjoining the resident's room was too narrow to admit a wheel chair.

"Never mind," Mary soothed her distraught advisers.

Rather than cause more inconvenience to others, she would use the common bathroom on the floor. She would manage.

But they would not hear of it. Off came the bathroom door, together with its frame. On went a curtain. The increased comfort of her new quarters was a blessing. Besides air conditioning, she now had a drive-in shower, into which she could wheel herself, transfer to a chair, and bask in hot sweet cleanliness or refreshing coolness.

In her new lodging Mary became increasingly self-sufficient. A small electric refrigerator which she intended to take back with her to India, together with a hot plate, provided breakfasts or other meals when she preferred not to go below to the cafeteria, and even produced an occasional hot curry, far tastier than that served her in the Indian restaurant she once visited on 34th Street. She had found its fare disappointingly bland, its currys and chutney prepared for Western rather than Eastern palates. Although Jennie, a garrulous and motherly cleaning woman, took pleasure in running errands for her, Mary required surprisingly little assistance. She did all her own washing and ironing, spreading a pad over her desk as a base for the latter. Fortunately, the new saris of synthetic materials which she wore at work dried quickly and needed no ironing. But her lovely South Indian silks must be worn for others on special occasions. She wore them proudly, and without adornment. Not since the accident had she worn a single piece of jewelry.

Occasionally Mary's worlds of India and America overlapped, as when she picked up the microphone of the tape recorder and exchanged the distant din of New York traffic for the rustle of coconut palms, or when a visitor from Vellore took time to travel down to 400 East 34th Street.

Dr. Carol Jameson, calling on Mary as she passed through New York on her way home to retirement, was impressed with the new assurance and poise of her former pupil. Mary entertained her in the garden of the institute. As they sat there talking in the sunny enclosed space, a young American doctor came rushing up.

"Pardon, Doctor Verghese," he said respectfully to Mary, who happened to be the senior doctor in charge. "My train is due in ten minutes and my relief hasn't arrived. Would it be all right if I went along and left you to cover?"

"Surely," replied Mary. "Go ahead."

She had come a long way, reflected Dr. Jameson, since that day of the accident on the road to Gudiyattam. Farther by wheel chair than by airplane!

As Mary considered the practical problems that would face her when she returned to Vellore, she foresaw that learning to drive her own automobile was a necessity. She made arrangements with a driving school which specialized in teaching the handicapped to use hand-controlled cars, and started her lessons.

"I suppose you want to go outside the city," the instructor, used to training paraplegics, said at their first meeting. "You'll find it easier for your first lessons."

"No," said Mary with decision. "It would take too long."

Not being a resident of New York, she was ineligible for the free services of the state Division of Rehabilitation, and since she must bear the entire expense of the training herself, she wanted to get the full benefit of her two-hour lessons.

The instructor gave her a startled look. Then he grinned. "OK. But I hope you know what New York traffic is like."

Mary soon found out. He took her downtown, giving instructions as they traveled, then turned over the controls to her. The steering was done with the right hand; the other controls—brake, accelerator—were operated with the left.

It was a nerve wracking two hours. Mary had always found it difficult to concentrate on more than one thing at once. Now she had to think of everything. Buttons, levers, up motions, down motions, right turns, left turns. . . . If she watched the traffic, she lost the gas control, and vice versa. Her arms ached with the tension of synchronizing the multiple demands of eyes, brain, and the voice of the man at her side. A tendon operation, she told herself, would be child's play beside all this.

After three months of weekly lessons, followed by two months of delay during which she had no lessons, the day came for her test.

When Mary caught sight of the licensing official who was to take her out, her heart sank. He was unsmiling, taciturn.

The test was held on an uptown street. Mary tried to remember all the confusing procedures, unfamiliar now after two months' lack of practice: starter, brake, gas control, reverse. She knew she had been slow to learn, but once a technique was mastered, it was hers forever. Please—let him call for the right things!

"Stop," ordered the officer.

She drew up beside another car parked by a curb.

"Park."

Carefully Mary eyed the short space behind the car on her right. Backing was one of the skills she had mastered. She acquitted herself well, but her satisfaction was short-lived.

"Make a U-turn," said the officer.

In failing to make the turn, Mary knew she had failed the test. But she had been prepared for this outcome. It meant only that she must have more lessons, more practice, then try again.

In December she flew, alone as usual, to Maine for two weeks of rest and interviews with her biographer; more interviews than rest, for she was bombarded with questions during nearly all her waking hours.

In the author's house there were the usual difficulties to be overcome · a bathroom door too narrow, a bedroom too small, a mattress too high. The door was sacrificed along with precious privacy. The bed was jammed against the wall to make room for the wheel chair, the mattress exchanged for another. But these were mere incidentals. Three things Mary was to remember vividly about her vacation in Maine: nights of silence so startling after the city's din that at first she could not sleep; pure white snow on evergreens; roads and countryside amazingly empty of people.

Back in New York, Mary entered on the most strenuous six months of her professional career: preparation for the comprehensive examinations to be held in June, which, if passed, would make her an accredited specialist in her field, qualified to head the new department at Vellore. Though three years of residency training were ordinarily required of a candidate for these examinations, given each year by the American Board of Physical Medicine and Rehabilitation, Mary, as she had hoped, received credit for her training in India and was therefore eligible to sit for the examinations in June, 1962.

Mary used every available moment outside her full schedule of hospital duties for her studies. She spent hours in the library. In the evening hours when she was obliged to lie down in order to compensate for the long periods in her wheel chair, she took the heavy volumes, briefs, lecture notes, theses, and other materials to bed with her, for the range of knowledge covered by the examinations would be wide. She would be expected to answer any question that might be asked in the areas of neurology, orthopedics, arthritis, and physical medicine.

Study was only one of her many hurdles in reaching the goal. In January, 1962, she was hospitalized for ten days with fever, and again in March. It meant precious time lost, but she endured the setbacks, as always, with patience. Then she redoubled her efforts to make up for the lost time.

There were occasional lighter moments, as when the President of the United States came to visit his father, who was receiving rehabilitation treatment at the institute and living in its Horizon Home.

Early one May evening, long before the President's arrival, the institute's entrance area was preempted by guards and Secret Service men. The reception room and corridor were lined with staff and patients, Mary among them, her wheel chair shoved inconspicuously into a corner not far from the elevators.

Dr. Rusk greeted the President outside. As they walked in through the reception room and hall, the President shook hands with or spoke to each person along his line of transit. Mary was not one of these. Seeing him turn toward the door leading to Horizon Home, she felt a little pang of regret. It would have been pleasant to say she had shaken hands with the President of the United States of America.

Turning at the door, Mr. Kennedy smiled and nodded at the rest of the assembled group. His eyes lighted on Mary, lingered with interest on her Indian face and sari. Suddenly he turned back, crossed to Mary's chair, and took her hand.

28

A week before the examinations were to be given in Chicago Mary came down again with fever. For once she found it difficult to maintain her serenity. Dr. Brand and his colleagues were expecting her to return to Vellore in the fall. The ground floor of the new rehabilitation building there was already opened. The Physiotherapy School had been started and already had five pupils. They were depending on her to assume the post of supervisor as soon as possible. She simply had to go to Chicago.

The fever subsided just in time. Mary flew to Chicago alone on Wednesday, June 27, a day ahead of the eleven other doctors who were going from the Institute. She went early so that she might have a day of rest before the examinations. At the New York and Chicago airports there were new ramps, and Mary could be wheeled instead of carried on and off the big jet plane, another step to independence.

Blessed FAMILY again, its protection reaching out across the seas! Mary had distant cousins in Chicago. One of them met her at the airport and drove her to the apartment of still another cousin, George, a construction engineer, and his wife Shiela, who was a medical technician.

"Our bathroom door is only 22 inches wide," they had written anxiously. Mary had solved this problem in advance by borrowing a child's wheel chair for her trip. It worked so well that she decided to order one for her own to use on the trip back to India, sending her larger one through Church World Service to become the property of the Vellore hospital. The Chicago apartment presented only one other difficulty. The guest bed was so low she could not transfer from it to the wheel chair. But that was easily solved. George and Shiela gave her their own bed. She rested on Thursday, unable to enjoy even the good Indian food with the day of reckoning approaching. Never in her life, she felt, had so much depended on her waking with a clear mind and steady judgment.

On Friday George drove her to the Veterans' Research Hospital, where she was one of a hundred candidates taking the examinations —and the only one in a wheel chair.

The examinations consisted of 350 multiple-choice and matching questions. Mary found the factual questions easiest to answer. Some dealing with the philosophy of rehabilitation and vocational counseling left her feeling uncertain. Suppose her opinions on these more controversial matters did not agree with those of her examiners? The examination format gave her no opportunity to give her reasons for many of her conclusions.

Even for the able-bodied candidates it was an exhausting day. When Mary left the building at six in the evening she felt drained of energy. All she could do now was wait. Even praying would not help.

The pleasure of her following two weeks of vacation in Canada with several friends of Vellore was at first impaired by worry over the outcome of the exams. Knowing that word would be received unofficially at the institute within a few days, Mary had asked one of her fellow candidates to let her hear it as soon as possible. Arriving in Montreal on Monday to be the guest of Ewart and Connie Everson, and expecting her news within two or three days, Mary became increasingly uneasy. Finally, sure that she had not passed and that her friends were reluctant to tell her, she telephoned the institute in New York. Yes, she was told, the results of the examinations had been received. Yes, Dr. Mary Verghese had passed.

The relief was overwhelming The grass of her hosts' lawn, sloping down to the Ottawa River, was suddenly the brightest emerald, the water a celestial blue. She relaxed into complete and carefree enjoyment.

While Mary was in Canada the newspapers were headlining the doctors' strike against the medicare legislation recently passed in Saskatchewan. A reporter, interviewing Mary, asked her opinion of the doctors' behavior. She hesitated only a moment before speaking her mind. "I don't know anything about your politics in Saskatchewan," she said, "but I do not think any doctor should refuse to treat a human being in need. I myself could not refuse anyone treatment.

Perhaps because I have been a patient myself, I can't help feeling deeply about this."

Driving from Montreal to Toronto, and then beyond, with Mrs. Kay Smith, once a nurse at Vellore, Mary came to the scenic high spot of her visit to Canada: Niagara Falls. She gazed at the thundering flood with all the incredulous rapture of an American traveler finally face to face with the Taj Mahal.

Returning to the institute in New York, Mary found that most of her thought was now directed to the modest structure that was rising out of a bamboo staging at Vellore. "We have been granted a five months' supply of cement and steel," Dr. Carman reported to her when he and his wife, Naomi, came on furlough to New York. "That means we can go ahead and finish the Rehabilitation Building without delay. It was up to the top of the windows when we saw it last."

One day the institute's recreation committee arranged for a three-hour boat tour of New York harbor. Mary and a large group of the institute's staff and patients and their families were aboard the boat as it passed close to the Statue of Liberty—so close, in fact, that Mary, sitting with the wheel chair patients on the deck, had to twist her neck to see the uplifted torch.

No wonder Americans are proud of such a glorious symbol! she thought. But it was only a symbol, an ideal, she reminded herself, looking around at the fifty wheel chairs, not a reality. For liberty meant not only justice but opportunity for every human being, and no people on earth had yet attained it.

She enjoyed another exciting moment a few days later when her big purchase, an automobile, was delivered at the institute. A small standard model, its bright color—turquoise—would make it look quite at home among the flamboyant blues and greens of South India. Her fingers itched to get at the controls, for already it seemed a part of her, an extension of her arms, life and movement for her lifeless, motionless feet. But because of the pressure of her work she had been unable to continue her driving lessons. She would have to wait until she got home before she applied for her driver's license.

The problem of the import license for her car had already been solved. Church World Service had assumed responsibility, and less than a week after its delivery at the institute the car was on its way to Madras, where Mr. Savarirayan, the hospital manager, would arrange for driving it to Vellore. Mary could hardly wait to follow it.

But she still had one task to perform in New York. Her biographer came down from Maine and together they went over every sentence of her story until finally Mary half-shook, half-nodded her head in that peculiar Indian manner that to an American looks like "no" but really means "yes." The story was as near the truth as they could make it.

"I have decided what I want to do with my share of the royalties," Mary said quietly. "It's going to buy appliances—crutches, braces, pulleys, maybe even wheel chairs—for those of my patients who can't afford them. I shall call it my 'loaves and fishes fund,' because, even though it is small, in the Master's hands it may keep growing."

The Vellore authorities expected to fly Mary back to India first class, but she insisted that tourist class would be quite comfortable enough. The money saved, she suggested, could be used for more important needs. Besides, she would be making the trip in stages, which would make it easier, flying first to London to study British rehabilitation work for several weeks, then on to Bombay, then to Cochin for a reunion with her family. Then, too, if present plans held, after she had finished two years' experience at Vellore, she would have to return to the United States—another expensive flight—to take her final oral exams before the American Board of Physical Medicine and Rehabilitation.

Departure day came at last. She said goodby to her many institute friends. She passed through the silently opening outer doors, their electric-eye mechanism a commonplace now instead of an act of magic She slid along her precious board into the waiting car, drove to the airport, was carried without leaving her chair into the huge plane.

"Are you all right?" asked the stewardess when she was comfortably seated. "Is there anything more we can do for you?"

"Quite all right," replied Mary, smiling. "Don't worry, please. I am able to do all that is necessary for myself."

The doors were closed, the seat belts fastened. The great plane began to move clumsily toward the runway, like a bird out of its proper element . . . or like a human being intended to run on swift limbs but doomed to lumber on wheels. It came to a stop, shuddered as if in mortal agony, then with a roar burst its bonds, mounted upward into freedom. Mary felt a kindred surge of triumph. She saw far below a huge city shrunk to incredible smallness, a blue expanse dotted with toy ships, then nothing but sunlight and clouds and infinite skies. She closed her eyes in wondering gratitude.

I asked for feet, she thought humbly, *and I have been given wings!*

ABOUT THE AUTHOR

Dorothy Clarke Wilson, the wife of a Methodist minister, lives in Orono, Maine. Her writing career, which began when her first poem, written when she was ten, appeared in the children's section of a local newspaper, has seen the publication of six novels, five of them with Biblical backgrounds, many religious plays, and innumerable stories and articles published in religious periodicals.

Take My Hands is her fourth book on an Indian subject. In 1949 the Board of Missions of the Methodist Church sent Mrs. Wilson to India to gather material for a novel dealing with its missions there. *House of Earth,* a story of village life, was one result; another was a journal of her six months' stay in India. Her continuing interest in the country and its people prompted her to undertake a biography of Dr. Ida Scudder, the founder of the Vellore Christian Medical College and Hospital, and in 1957 Mrs. Wilson returned to India, established herself at Vellore, and from there traveled widely to gather first-hand material for her book *Dr. Ida.* Her background knowledge of South India and of the institutions at Vellore proved of great value when she undertook this biography of Dr. Verghese, whose personal story she explored in detail during the years 1961–1962 when Dr. Mary was studying in New York City.

CPSIA information can be obtained
at www.ICGtesting.com
Printed in the USA
BVHW050152210522
637236BV00022B/136

9 780343 286743